ANIMATED BY UNCERTAINTY

T0355503

AFRICAN PERSPECTIVES
Kelly Askew and Anne Pitcher
Series Editors

Animated by Uncertainty: Rugby and the
Performance of History in South Africa
Joshua D. Rubin

African Performance Arts and Political Acts
Naomi André, Yolanda Covington-Ward, and Jendele Hungbo, Editors

There Used to Be Order:
Life on the Copperbelt after the Privatisation of the
Zambia Consolidated Copper
Patience Mususa

Filtering Histories: The Photographic Bureaucracy
in Mozambique, 1960 to Recent Times,
by Drew A. Thompson

Aso Ebi: *Dress, Fashion, Visual Culture, and*
Urban Cosmopolitanism in West Africa,
by Okechukwu Nwafor

Unsettled History: Making South African Public Pasts,
by Leslie Witz, Gary Minkley, and Ciraj Rassool

Seven Plays of Koffi Kwahulé: In and Out of Africa,
translated by Chantal Bilodeau and Judith G. Miller
edited with Introductions by Judith G. Miller

The Rise of the African Novel:
Politics of Language, Identity, and Ownership,
by Mukoma Wa Ngugi

Black Cultural Life in South Africa:
Reception, Apartheid, and Ethics,
by Lily Saint

A complete list of titles in the series can be found at www.press.umich.edu

Animated by Uncertainty

*Rugby and the Performance
of History in South Africa*

Joshua D. Rubin

University of Michigan Press
Ann Arbor

For questions or permissions, please contact um.press.perms@umich.edu

Published in the United States of America by the
University of Michigan Press
Printed and bound by CPI Group (UK) Ltd, Croydon, CR0 4YY
First published September 2021

A CIP catalog record for this book is available from the British Library.

Library of Congress Cataloging-in-Publication Data

Names: Rubin, Joshua D., author.
Title: Animated by uncertainty : rugby and the performance of history in South Africa /
 Joshua D. Rubin.
Description: Ann Arbor : University of Michigan Press, 2021. | Series: African
 perspectives | Includes bibliographical references and index. |
Identifiers: LCCN 2021015872 (print) | LCCN 2021015873 (ebook) | ISBN 9780472075003
 (hardcover) | ISBN 9780472055005 (paperback) | ISBN 9780472129393 (ebook)
Subjects: LCSH: Rugby football—Political aspects—South Africa. | Sports—Political
 aspects—South Africa. | South Africa—Politics and government. | South Africa—
 History. | BISAC: SOCIAL SCIENCE / Ethnic Studies / African Studies
Classification: LCC GV945.9.S6 R82 2021 (print) | LCC GV945.9.S6 (ebook) |
 DDC 796.3330968—dc23
LC record available at https://lccn.loc.gov/2021015872
LC ebook record available at https://lccn.loc.gov/2021015873

Publication of this volume has been partially funded by the African Studies Center,
University of Michigan.

Cover illustration: Rugby player puppet cartoon from *Die Suid-Afrikaan* (Winter 1986).
Courtesy of Hermann Giliomee.

CONTENTS

Digital materials related to this title can be found on the Fulcrum platform via the following citable URL: https://doi.org/10.3998/mpub.10217204

ACKNOWLEDGMENTS

Thinking happens in places and moments in time. As I glance over this book, I am thrown back into specific locations—a conference room at the University of Pretoria, a friend's dinner table in Portland, Maine, a sitting room in North Andover, Massachusetts, a campus coffee shop at Yale. In some of those locations, writing could hardly have felt lonelier or sadder or more frustrating. I am reminded of a swing space in a labyrinth of an apartment in New Jersey, where I cut a disjointed chapter into ribbons and taped it back together in the hopes that I could convince it to work itself into some sort of meaningful structure. I remember the wedding of a close friend in Pennsylvania several years later, at which—in the very late evening—I cried on the shoulder of a second close friend because that very same chapter was *still* out of joint. As other writers who are reading this book might appreciate, I was inconsolable not just because I was so frustrated with my own writing but also because I was tired of being unable to find the words to explain exactly what I was frustrated about.

Some of the locations where this project took shape were institutions of higher learning. I owe a tremendous debt of gratitude to Yale University, and its dissertation and pre-dissertation research grants; Stellenbosch University and Pretoria University, with their stimulating seminars and colloquia; and Bates College, for its longstanding support of me and my research as well as its commitments to faculty collegiality and interdisciplinarity. Pieces of this project have been shared at Bates, at Yale's Ethnography and Social Theory Colloquium and African Studies Brownbag Series, at the American Anthropological Association's annual conference, and the North Eastern Workshop on Southern Africa. In each of these venues, it benefited tremendously from feedback from thoughtful peers. A few of those scholars, like Peter Alegi and Derek Catsam, improved my thinking with their sports-centered expertise, but most challenged and encouraged me from points of view more super-ficially distant from my research. Those conversations were always valuable because they pushed me to think creatively about my research and its broad-est possible significances.

Thinking happens with people. Even when the practice of writing is at its loneliest and most isolating, I find that I have a chorus of voices in my head. At present, the ones foremost in my mind belong to the editorial team with which I have been fortunate to work at University of Michigan Press. Kelly Askew and Anne Pitcher have been model series editors from my first conversations with them—supportive at every turn, generous, open-minded, cognizant of the anxieties and challenges facing a first-time author. Ellen Bauerle, Kevin Rennells, and Flannery Wise have been endlessly tolerant of my questions and incredibly accommodating. I am grateful to them for their professionalism. I am also grateful to the editorial guidance I received from Anne Allison and Charles Piot on the selection of this book that was pub-lished previously in *Cultural Anthropology* while the journal was under their stewardship, as well as Andrew Offenburger's editorial feedback on the piece that was published in *Safundi*. I am also grateful to Susan Brownell and Niko Besnier for their readings of this project when it was not yet clear to me what it would become. I very much appreciate their patience, and advice, during that uncertain time.

While at Yale, I had the immense privilege to study under an array of scholars who were unfailingly open with their time and willing to discuss topics and regions quite distant from their own areas of expertise. I thank Kalyanakrishnan Sivaramakrishnan, Eric Harms, Douglas Rogers, Jonathan Gilmore, and James C. Scott for their courses, their open doors, and the intel-lectual homes they built around me during my time on campus. I owe a tre-mendous debt of gratitude to William W. Kelly, not only for his mentorship but also for the rigorous, yet patient, style of thought he always practices. Kamari Maxine Clarke presented theory, and especially Critical Theory, in ways that I had never previously imagined; Mike McGovern slammed politics and aesthetics together so forcefully and so compellingly that I haven't been able to separate them since; and Jafari Allen introduced me to fearless and grounded poetic thought that inspires me to this day. Dan Magaziner was my intellectual saving grace, arriving at Yale just when he was most needed. As a mentor, a friend, and a source of scholarly inspiration, his value to me and this project is incalculable. Reading again over this list of names, it is clear to me that this project would have been impossible without the texts these supportive scholars shared with me and the scholarly conversations into which they guided me.

The guidance I have received from peers on this project, from almost the first moment of its conception, has been extremely valuable as well. I consider myself lucky to have arrived at Yale when I did, surrounded by cohorts of students eager to learn together and develop together as young academics. Though I met many such people, Dana Graef, Annie Claus, Nathaniel Smith, Sarah Ousterhoudt, Vikramaditya Thakur, Atreyee Majumder, Adrienne Cohen, David Kneas, Sarah LeBaron von Baeyer, Anne Stefanie Aronsson, Isaac Gagne, Jun Zhang, Jamie Miller, Matthew Keaney, and Ryan Sayre stick firmly in my mind as peers who shaped dramatically the course of this project. At other institutions, in South Africa and across the United States, Jeffrey Paller, Nicholas Rush Smith, Nick Valvo, Nina Hagel, Britt E. Halvorson, Yuka Suzuki, Chet Fransch, Fraser McNeill, Jason Sumich, Hermann Giliomee, Isak Niehaus, Eric Worby, Albert Grundlingh, and Marizanne Grundlingh have also proven vital interlocutors. I would be remiss if I did not address Erik Mueggler and Ruth Behar here as well, though speaking of them as peers feels wrong to me given the vitally important roles they played in my anthropological education. Whether they know it or not, their voices have influenced this project at every stage—not just during and after, but also in the formative years well before it was a project.

Peers at Bates have been no less valuable. Senior colleagues in Anthropology, like Val Carnegie, Elizabeth Eames, Steve Kemper, Danny Danforth, and Áslaug Ásgiersdóttir have been endlessly supportive since the moment I stepped onto campus. Colleagues in American Studies and Africana, like Kristen Barnett, Myron Beasley, Mary Rice-DeFosse, Dale Chapman, Anelise Shrout, Sue Houchins, Andrew Baker, Marcelle Medford, Cassandra Shepard, Patrik Otim, Baltasar Fra-Molinero, Charles Nero, Therí Pickens, and Jacqueline Lyon have helped me in countless casual conversations and program committee meetings to improve as a scholar and to develop and refine my critical voice. Though book projects end without ever truly being finished, as Kamari Maxine Clarke might say, the feedback and support I have received from these scholars have brought this project much closer to its appropriate finish than I ever could have gotten it alone. Elsewhere on campus, I have been fortunate to become friends with and learn from Christina Bell, Christine Murray, Pete Schlax, Paul Schofield, Ethan Miller, Lisa Maurizio, Caroline Shaw, Ben Moodie, Su Langdon, Melinda Plastas, Eden Osucha, Asha Tamirisa, Raj Saha, Alissa Maraj Grahame, Franes Eanes, Stephanie Pridgeon, Senem Aslan, Tiffany Salter, Jason Scheideman, Rebecca Herzig, Steve Engel, and Erica Rand. These colleagues have offered the rarest of things in academia—relationships that are equal parts intellectual nourishment and care (in extremely challenging times no less). For this, and so much else, I am thankful. I am also thankful for the legions of incredible students I have had the privilege of teaching at Bates. Their perspectives and provocations have enriched my thinking in countless ways.

Thinking is an embodied practice, and I am thankful for all those people (many of whom, alas, I cannot name here) who opened their homes and lives to me in South Africa—in Kylemore, Pretoria, across the Western Cape, and beyond. Special thanks are due to Piet and Anne-Marie Muller and their incredible family for making Clydesdale into a place where research opportunities were always close at hand but never so close that I felt suffocated. Thanks are also due to Annie Antonites and Xander Antonites. I consider my inability to decide where to put the two of you in these acknowledgments to be a sign of just how much I have asked of you over the years, and how much you were willing to give. Xander deserves special recognition for translation assistance, which he could have withheld but—in keeping with his character—provided freely (even enthusiastically) instead. Last thanks in this regard are due to Kathleen Lorne McDougall, whose friendship during the most isolating and most disorienting periods of my fieldwork means so much to me even now. I count myself extremely fortunate to have had someone with her brilliance to think with when the core themes of this project were fragile and just beginning to come into view.

My final thanks are reserved for those who know just deeply the practices of thinking and writing have buried this project in me. I have thought about this project for nearly 15 years, start to finish, and Susanna Fioratta and Mike Degani have accompanied me through every phase of that journey. Your advice, your off-hand remarks, your attention to argumentation, your suggested word choices, and your enthusiasm for my ideas on days when I couldn't find that enthusiasm for myself are evident throughout this book. To Radhika Govindrajan, Jayadev Athreya, and David Walker, I owe a gratitude so deep that I struggle to express it. You three have made me a better thinker and a better social actor. Learning, growing, and caring together has been an honor. Matthew Trenary and Karl Seibert have provided breaths of fresh, witty, irreverent air whenever I've found myself needing them most. Thank you both for your silly wisdom. To my extended family—my aunts, uncles, and cousins with whom I am so close—I thank you for your gentle love and your firm, consistent, support. To my parents, Gretta Spier and Jonathan Rubin, I owe all the thanks in the world. I love and respect you both so much. I will never be able to find the words to thank you, Melissa and Izzie, for all that you have meant to me during the crafting of this book. I plan to live my gratitude, and my love for you, in every moment I have.

Introduction

I first conducted fieldwork for this project in 2008, the year before the film *Invictus* was released. Based on the book *Playing the Enemy* by John Carlin (2008), *Invictus* begins its story in 1994, just after Nelson Mandela became South Africa's first democratically elected president. Although Mandela's election announced the end of formal racial segregation, known as apartheid, in South Africa, the film approaches the political transformations of the moment from within a somewhat unexpected direction, South Africa's triumph in the 1995 Rugby World Cup.

Directed by Clint Eastwood and starring Morgan Freeman (as Mandela) and Matt Damon (as François Pienaar, captain of South Africa's national rugby team, the Springboks), the film seeks to convince us that the 1995 tournament was of tremendous social and political significance. South Africa hosted the World Cup not long after Mandela's election, and the film shows that rugby was a meaningful touchstone for conflict, tension, and unification during that turbulent and uncertain period of transition. At the beginning of the film, rugby is linked explicitly with the country's segregationist history. A white coach demonstrates his anxieties about the future of the country when he tells his players, on the day of Mandela's release from prison, that they must remember that day because "this is the day our country went to the dogs." A black woman patiently explains to a white woman why a young black boy won't accept a Springbok rugby jersey from their charity. While the white woman believes that the boy is lucky to receive such a warm and durable garment, the black woman tells her that he will be beaten up if he wears it. "Because for them [i.e., the boy and his peers]," she says, "the Springboks still represent apartheid" (Eastwood 2009). However deeply embedded in South Africa's rugby these political antagonisms might appear, Mandela and Pienaar work together over the course of the film to transform rugby into a device for facilitating national unity. When the Springboks finally win the World Cup, South Africans of all backgrounds celebrate wildly together. Mandela's plan, it seems, has been successful. Rugby, a sport once closely associated with racial segregation, became the very thing to inaugurate South Africa's post-segregationist era.

My thoughts about that big-budget Hollywood movie have evolved alongside my research. When I first heard of the film, I was struck immediately by the similarities between its project and my own. My research concerned the contemporary significance of rugby in South Africa, and the 1995 World Cup was undoubtedly an important moment in the country's rugby history. Many of my informants—particularly those who were older (not surprisingly), but also those who were white—had fond feelings about 1995 that they eagerly shared with me. One who recalled a jet flying low over the field (a scene replicated in the film) remembered—perhaps anachronistically—worrying momentarily about a terrorist attack. She said that once that fear had passed, the game and the celebration that followed it were incredibly exhilarating. A man who mentioned Mandela's decision to walk on the field and acknowledge the crowd remarked that a post-apartheid South Africa had not felt truly possible to him until that moment. A third person contrasted the spirit of the 1995 victory to the spirit of the Rugby World Cup of 2007, which South Africa also won. On that second occasion, he said, there were no celebrations of national unification. Sporting success had become, in the interim, a bittersweet reminder of promise lost.

Rugby is indeed deeply interwoven with South African politics and social relations. At various moments, the sport has served as an athletic manifestation of British colonialism and a site of struggle between British South Africans and their white Dutch- and French-descended Afrikaner counterparts (Allen 2003). It has been a vehicle for producing and promulgating white nationalism (Grundlingh 1994; Nauright 1996; Niehaus 2014) as well as a tool for contesting race-based inequality and exclusion. During apartheid, rugby was an important discursive and practical locus for international opposition. Anti-apartheid activists protested matches and agitated for the cancellation of tours. They couched their critiques in a slogan that explicitly connected sports in general and rugby in particular to the political conditions in which they were played: there could be, they said, "no normal sport in an abnormal society"—that is, no apolitical sport nor, in apartheid's later years, a strategically desegregated one in a white supremacist South Africa (cf. Booth 2003; Davies 1986; Jacobs 2010; Lapchick 1979). The 1995 Rugby World Cup appears to be the international and domestic realization of that slogan. Since South Africa had set itself on the path of "normalizing" its society, the country could finally make a legitimate case to normalize its sport as well. Given that the Rugby World Cup drew much of its significance from those deeper currents of history, it seemed likely to me that *Invictus* would need to do justice to that complicated context if it intended to tell a compelling story.

Once the movie finally arrived at my local theater, I found that it fell short of my (admittedly high) expectations. For one thing, the on-camera depictions of rugby felt palpably odd. Having played rugby for over a decade, my body had apparently acquired its own, felt understanding of how players move on a field. I was viscerally aware of the choreography that lay behind the actions of the players on the screen; even when I accounted for the changes in the speed of play over the years, the players seemed to move a fraction slower and a bit more deliberately than my body expected. The rugby scenes had failed to capture the contact and the unpredictable liveness of actual play, and I felt a strong desire to drag the players forward in time, out of their planned movements and into the full immediacy of the game as I had experienced it. That relatively minor aesthetic critique would become a central piece of this book's argument.

At the time, though, my stronger objection to the film was reserved for the claims it made about the importance of the World Cup itself. Like many of the critics who analyzed *Invictus* after its release, I was troubled by the straightforward narrative of national unification that the film presented. At the end of the movie, Nelson Mandela strides onto the field, just as my friends remembered. His public presence appears to confirm the relevance of rugby—and all that rugby had come to represent in South Africa—to the country's post-apartheid era. That relevance is ratified in the film not only by the Springboks' victory in the World Cup final but also by the actions of a black child that the camera follows during the final match. Having spent most of the game inching tentatively in the direction of a pair of white police officers, so that he might better hear the details of the match on their radio, the child finally throws caution to the winds and celebrates the victory with them. Outside the stadium, Mandela's chauffeur-driven car picks its way through a euphoric and multiracial crowd. Mandela smiles to himself and puts on a pair of sunglasses, and the curtain drops. Hardly a more triumphant conclusion could be imagined.

Because the conclusion of the film was so triumphant and so without compromise or qualification, it was hard not to think that the film and its creators believed (or wanted their audiences to believe) that the Rugby World Cup put a real and definitive end to South Africa's long struggle with white supremacy. All that the country required, *Invictus* seems to suggest, was the democratic election of Nelson Mandela and a series of compelling victories in world rugby's most important tournament. Stated outright, that thesis seems patently ridiculous. Apartheid was no momentary blip in the country's history. The "apartheid era" ostensibly spans the years between 1948 and the early 1990s, but it traces its administrative and theoretical roots to the colonization of southern Africa by the British and the Dutch (cf. Chidester 1996; Comaroff and Comaroff 1991; Elbourne 2002; Mamdani 1996). Called "separate development" by its proponents, apartheid was a collection of laws and state policies that delineated rights and social resources according to imposed conceptions of racial and cultural difference. The scope of those policies was extremely broad. The state sought to regulate everything from land tenure and places of residence to education and jobs, from the terms of acceptable sexual and domestic partnerships to participation in sports teams and other leisure activities. Persons placed in the racial categories of "Coloured," "African," and "Indian" were permitted access to "White" spaces only in highly regulated ways (cf. Beningfield 2006; Cock 1989), and because all of the regulations were premised on inflexible and fallacious conceptions of race, they were dangerous and arbitrary as well as unequal (Breckenridge 2005; Posel 2001). Apartheid policies, in all their violence and arbitrariness, were enforced by a security apparatus that imprisoned, disappeared, banned, and murdered with impunity (Feldman 2002; Ellis 1998). The election of Nelson Mandela may have confirmed the unraveling of the official policies of apartheid, following years of international and domestic opposition, but several centuries of violence, terror, and formal and informal practices of racial inequality could never be wished away. That *Invictus* seemed to suggest otherwise struck me, as it undoubtedly struck many people, as ignorant of the working of history at best and willfully obscurantist at worst.

As I explained to anyone who asked my opinion of the film, Mandela's election was only the beginning of a long, painful, and ongoing process of social transformation and historical reckoning. Indeed, in the wake of that election, South Africa organized a truth and reconciliation commission motivated by the twin goals of calling the crimes of apartheid into view and clearing a public space for South Africans to seek and offer forgiveness to each other. The precise details of that commission's findings are beyond the scope of this book, but the commission is nevertheless relevant here insofar as it demonstrated (in both its articulations and its absences) the breadth and depth of the damage that apartheid had done to the resident populations of South Africa (cf. Bozzoli 1998; Chipkin 2007; Feldman 2002; Mamdani 2002; Wilson 2000).

Social scientists have documented the contemporary traces of this damage in meticulous detail. Post-apartheid South Africa plays host to a range of new social formations, including, among other things, increased fluidity and creativity in the articulation of identities (Nuttall 2009), a greater attention to indigenous rights (Robins 2008, 56–57), the post-apartheid state's commitment to economic liberalization (Chance 2015a; Hart 2008), and an expanding African elite (Nattrass and Seekings 2005). Apartheid-era social relations and structures continue to inform the shapes those social formations take. In 2002, for example, Shula Marks traced South Africa's HIV/AIDS crisis to its roots in the "unequal pattern of industrialisation and urbanisation" that was enforced by the apartheid state (17–18). The possibility that the pattern might contribute to a public health catastrophe, she adds, was recognized as early as the 1950s. Prepaid electrical meters, which von Schnitzler has argued serve now as a mechanism to produce virtuous citizens in the post-apartheid era, found their footing in South Africa as an element of the apartheid state's attempt to "delink questions of payment and infrastructure from larger claims to citizenship" (2013, 681)—that is, to deliver social services without providing the rights that those services might imply. Ironically, writes von Schnitzler, such apartheid-era initiatives have now made South Africa "a 'global' leader in prepayment technologies" (690n19). Even Johannesburg, a city with a vibrancy and energy that exceeds the sum of its histories, testifies to the racial logic of its past (Mbembe 2008a, 59). The scene of the child's celebration with police officers within the narrative of *Invictus* has been rendered especially disconcerting by the deaths of striking miners at the hands of police in the country's North West Province in 2012 (cf. Kynoch 2016). That notably bloody occasion of violence, as well as the violence of the South African Police Service more generally (Smith 2017), may not be identical to the violence perpetrated by the apartheid state, but the more recent violence nevertheless bears a symbolic familiarity to police actions of the past (Chance 2015a, 865). Neither Mandela's election nor South Africa's rugby triumph could possibly have been sufficient to put the crimes of apartheid and colonialism to rest.

Apartheid-era racial terminology has not disappeared either. Scholars and activists have noted how the continued use of a term like *coloured* risks reinscribing the violent enforcement of its connotations that was a hallmark of apartheid policy and practice, affirming, in doing so, the erasure of the lived fluidity of social identities; nevertheless, the term retains social significance (Petrus and Isaacs-Martin 2012). "Coloured" remains an administratively and popularly legible identity, in that it appears on the South African census and is used as a meaningful marker of identity in everyday interactions (Seekings 2008, 6). As a result, as Mohamed Adhikari (2005) and others have highlighted, that identity also serves as a readily available means for persons who claim a mixed-race ancestry—whether linking themselves to "Malay" slaves from Southeast Asia, indigenous Khoi and San communities, or mixed white-black unions—to locate themselves in South Africa's social and political landscape (Williams and Stroud 2015). Despite the pernicious history of the term *coloured*, as well as the many possible valences of mixed-race identity and the different positionalities it can conceal (Fransch 2010), many of my research collaborators appreciated the term and used it to describe themselves. Because of the pernicious history of the term, though, many others rejected it but found themselves represented as coloured by others in any case. The alternative term I encountered most frequently was *black*—used to gesture back to solidarities between members of the designated "Coloured" population and those of South Africa's African groups that developed around the anti-apartheid struggle and Black Consciousness movement (Magaziner 2010, 142). Even that term is not unproblematic, though, given that its use can efface how the apartheid state positioned African and "Coloured" persons with respect to an explicit racial hierarchy, which located a "Coloured" identity between whiteness and blackness and distributed resources, power, and political voice accordingly (Hammett 2010, 249; Erasmus 2001, 13; Farred 2000, 4–8). Indeed, for that reason, some South Africans self-identifying as coloured have embraced the term to differentiate themselves from people of African backgrounds.

To account for those contrasting preferences, histories, and politics, I have opted, in the present project, to mark "black," "coloured," and "African" as three often-overlapping (but also meaningfully distinct) political identities. Doing so, I feel, has allowed me to attend more precisely to the politics of a particular research collaborator's identity, given that the use of a specific term will recognize the collaborator's preference while still acknowledging the history and politics that weight the categories differently and shape their meanings relative to each other. Within this text, I have decided to describe those identities collectively as "underrepresented" and "marginalized." (I also occasionally use the term *nonwhite* to indicate situations where a person's or group's lack of whiteness is thought specifically to be at issue, as a consequence of apartheid ideology.) Importantly, I do not intend the terms *underrepresented* or *marginalized* to refer exclusively or even primarily to the racial makeup of the most highly competitive rugby teams in the country. Though, as the South African state has often noted, those demographics do matter for a variety of reasons, I endeavor to show in this book that the racial demographics of influential professional or representative teams should not and indeed cannot be taken as independent of the racial demographics of other powerful groups such as coaching staffs and the administrative bodies of top teams and elite high schools. Those groups remain predominantly white, with people of other racial backgrounds largely absent (at least, at the time of my fieldwork) from their upper echelons.

With the lingering significance of South African history framed in this way, it is probably unsurprising to discover that rugby's place in South Africa's momentous transformation is not nearly as clear as it appears in *Invictus*. The film's assumption that rugby is a sport of paramount symbolic and social importance in South Africa is open to question, given the popularity of football and the deep political history of that sport in the country (Alegi 2004, 2002; Bolsmann 2010, 2012; Jacobs 2010; Worby 2009). *Invictus* also overlooks the extent to which the sport of rugby emerged from and was unavoidably enmeshed in the racial schema and political economy of apartheid. If apartheid ideology constructed racial categories on the basis of social identities as well as phenotypic qualities, rugby was there to be a marker of a "Coloured" identity, football a marker of an "African" one (Posel 2001, 61). If apartheid distributed resources inequitably on the basis of those racial categories, Richard Lapchick observed of sports subsidies in 1979 that "the 4.4 million whites [in South Africa] received 180 times more per capita expenditures than the 18.6 million blacks" in 1977 (159). The consequences of those and numerous other practices and policies dramatically shaped the dimensions of South Africa's rugby during apartheid and continue to do so today. Indeed, the three sites in which I conducted the majority of my research for this book demonstrate how political South Africa's rugby is and how deeply it is indebted to history.

For 8 of my 17 months of fieldwork, I conducted research in one of the most well-known rugby-playing high schools in the country. During apartheid, that school, like most of the highly successful rugby schools in South

Africa, was categorized as a "Model C"—that is, a "whites only"—institution, and many of the country's legendary white players either graduated from that school or sent their children there. Today, rugby is so popular at the school that, in any given year, upwards of one-third of its 1,200 students play the sport competitively (with, it must be said, various degrees of seriousness and commitment). My fieldwork for that portion of this project consisted of investing myself in the sporting lives of the people who populated the school. I spent long hours in the teacher's lounge and the office of its sports administrators. I interviewed some teachers who coached rugby in their spare time and some who hated the sport and wanted nothing to do with it. In casual conversations and formal interviews, I spoke with administrators about the future of high school rugby in South Africa and the specter of steroid use. I asked them questions that, though deceptively simple on the surface, often proved extremely difficult to answer: Why do parents let their boys play rugby if the boys are so likely to get hurt? Does rugby teach players anything about life? If rugby does teach players something, exactly how and where do they learn that something? Could cricket or football teach those same things? With such questions, I sought to identify not just the reasons why the administrators cared about rugby but also why rugby itself was worth caring about. The answers I received appear throughout this book, and they reveal much about the roles that Model C schools currently play in South African rugby's political landscape and have played in the past.

I watched the tail end of one rugby season and participated in the preparations for a second. I traveled with the school's teams to several away matches, attended numerous practices and training sessions, and chatted with students on and off the rugby field, in the stands, and during lunch periods. In an effort to get to know as many players as I possibly could, I designed a simple survey that featured questions about favorite players and teams, reasons for playing rugby, injury histories, and rugby aspirations. The survey also asked players about their first rugby memories. I gave the survey to 88 players, whose answers to the questions were invariably insightful and amusing. All the players smiled as they recounted how they ran off the field to eat a sandwich during a game, how they scored accidentally for the other team or tackled their own teammate, or how cold their feet had been when they played rugby barefoot in the winter. On one miserable occasion, I even practiced with the school's best players and immediately discovered how much stronger and more confident in their rugby actions those 17-year-old South Africans were than I had ever been in mine.

Given the importance of rugby at that particular high school, the skill and confidence of the very best players was easily explained. High school rugby in South Africa is divided into four age-groups (under 14, under 15, under 16, and under 18 years old), and the school where I conducted my research featured enough players to host six or even seven teams for each age-group. The teams ranged from highly competitive (the A and B teams) to casual (the E, F, and G teams), and most of the boys who managed to play consistently for the school's top team were recognized as the most talented and/or committed rugby players in the school. Some had been earmarked for the A team while they were still playing in the under-16 age-group, and a few of the very best under-18 players during my fieldwork were already involved in contract negotiations with South Africa's professional teams.

I conducted eight months of additional research with one such professional team, the Blue Bulls. Based in the capital city of Pretoria, that team is one of the most historically successful in the country. The Bulls organization has teams that participate in a number of tournaments throughout the year. During the time of my fieldwork, their most experienced and mostly older, "senior" players participated in two tournaments: Super Rugby, a tournament that long featured professional teams from South Africa (as well as teams from New Zealand, Australia, Japan, and Argentina); and the Currie Cup, a domestic tournament of South Africa's professional teams. Their less experienced and younger, "junior" players competed in a junior version of the Currie Cup. The Bulls also played matches in several additional leagues and tournaments, calling on players from the senior and junior teams along the way. I interviewed the coaches, managers, and trainers of the Bulls' senior teams, but I spent the vast majority of my day-to-day fieldwork with the junior players and their coaches. The Bulls field two junior teams, one for players less than 19 years of age and one for players who are not yet 21, and those players come to the Bulls straight from high school. None of the high school players I knew happened to have signed contracts with the Bulls in the year of my research, but I did follow students of their graduating class as they climbed one rung higher in South Africa's rugby hierarchy.

In some respects, my research with the Bulls resembled that which I conducted at the high school. I spent almost every weekday at the team's facilities, attending practices and gym sessions. On Saturdays, I sometimes traveled with the teams to road games. I interviewed coaches, trainers, and administrators, and I chatted regularly and casually with players. In other respects, though, my research was transformed by the conditions in which I conducted it. The demands that professional teams place on their players are much greater than the expectations of even the best high school teams, and my involvement in rugby-specific activities increased with the Bulls as well. While I attended one (and, so far as I know, the only) film session with the high school's A team, I usually attended one or two film sessions each week with the Bulls. Whereas the high school team practiced a few times each week and trained together in the gym a few times more, the Bulls' players practiced twice every day and went to the gym once between practice sessions. I attended almost all of those workouts and practices, shuttling back and forth between groups of players and peppering coaches with questions when it seemed appropriate to do so.

When I was not watching, listening, and asking questions, I was put to work. The Bulls' junior teams had a pair of extremely capable team managers and, for much of my research, an equally capable equipment manager, all three of whom were able to find menial tasks to keep me occupied. On game days, I unpacked energy drinks, helped the managers check the headsets the coaches wore during games, posted motivational slogans on locker-room walls, and laid out the appropriate jersey at each player's designated space. After each game, I collected damp towels and sweaty jerseys and picked up all the tape and wrapping materials that the players had peeled from their bodies. During one match, the team doctor recruited me to help her stitch a player's eyelid shut. There was a sensory and material richness to many of these tasks, and I pay special attention to the significance of that richness in chapter 3 of this book. On practice days, I fetched the odd forgotten tackle pad or bag of balls, filled water bottles with ice and water, counted and sorted jerseys, and tidied up storerooms. The relationships I was able to develop as a result of those odd jobs far outweighed my actual contributions. Between the various sessions and when my work was finished, I was permitted to follow the coaches and trainers to the café adjacent to the field and bother them with additional questions about team strategy, coaching style, and their own rugby experiences. I was also allowed to attend a number of staff meetings and was therefore able to listen to coaches, trainers, and medical personnel debate all manner of team policy, player injuries and performance, and match expectations.

Taken together, my two research sites are broadly emblematic of the path to professional success that most accomplished players in South Africa presently follow. A player will work his way through the rosters and age-groups of an elite high school, make a name for himself with scouts and all-star team selectors at big (and often televised) high school matches or rugby festivals, then sign a junior contract with a professional team and move to a new city to start his career. From there, a tiny subset of junior players goes on to play for larger senior contracts with top professional teams in South Africa. Others relocate to professional teams in Europe or the UK, sign smaller semiprofessional contracts with second-tier professional teams in South Africa, play for a university or a local club, stay with rugby as agents or scouts or managers, or quit the game entirely. Players will occasionally bounce from second-tier teams to top ones or from Europe back to South Africa, but the flow of players moving in those directions is far narrower than the opposite flow, which heads away from the centers of South African rugby, the pinnacle of which is the Springboks, and toward its various peripheries. This conception of player movement represents South African rugby as something of a centrifuge, which draws talented players inevitably inward and upward and sends less talented players down and out. Most of my informants at the high school and with the Bulls would likely agree with that representation, perhaps with the qualifications that undeserving players are occasionally overvalued and that talented players sometimes fall through the cracks.

For others in South Africa, the structures of player identification and development seem quite evidently premised on history, the legacies of apartheid ideology, and contemporary inequalities. That was the case for many of the residents of my third and final field site, Kylemore, a village geographically close to the elite school described above but socially and economically distant from it. Many of the residents of Kylemore, who self-identified for the most part as coloured or black, served as cheap labor in white-owned businesses and homes during apartheid (Lucas 2006, 173–74; van der Heijden 2014, 159), and some continue to do so today. I lived in Kylemore for a month and interviewed current and former players about their experiences with rugby in South Africa. If South African rugby operates as a centrifuge, it appeared to many in Kylemore to be one that was designed to center white players and push others down and out, irrespective of their talents or commitment to the sport. Schools like the one at which I conducted my research, for example, are among the most expensive in the country. Their high cost is no coincidence. In response to the post-apartheid state's efforts to democratize and desegregate the country's educational system, such schools protected their exclusivity (and their resources) by raising their tuitions. While they now purport to exclude students on the basis of class or ability rather than race, the historically unequal distribution of wealth in South Africa ensures that those schools continue to educate students who are predominantly white

(Besteman 2008; Brook 1996; Nkomo, Mkwanazi-Twala, and Carrim 1995; Sharp 1998).

Some expensive schools offer athletic scholarships, and parents try to secure those scholarships for their children by contacting schools directly or working through well-connected community coaches. The stakes, especially at the high school level, can be extremely high: players who manage to get rugby scholarships are able to access tremendous rugby resources and educations that their families would otherwise be unable to afford. Players who emerge from the crowd of interested candidates are generally exceptional, with talents so undeniable that scholarships are readily attainable for them. For the vast majority of eligible players, those scholarships and the schools offering them are largely out of reach.[1] Given that situation, when those schools generate their next class of top players—honed by competition with their classmates and tested against their rivals at other elite schools—almost all of the members of that class will be white.[2]

Underrepresented players who attend elite schools and manage to secure professional contracts for themselves encounter additional obstacles. Rugby became a professional sport in 1995, just after the World Cup in South Africa and exactly 100 years after its ball-in-hand sibling, rugby league. That process of professionalization was instituted by the International Rugby Football Board and therefore had to do more with the allocation of television revenue than with the end of apartheid. While professionalization has carried all sorts of unexpected implications for international rugby—to name just a few, player strikes, the consolidation and elimination of teams, the transformation of the rugby season into a year-round event, the increasing specialization of roles, and a tremendous increase in the average weight and height of premier players (Chandler and Nauright 1999; G. Ryan 2008)—the interaction between democratization in South African life and professionalization in the country's rugby has produced notably South African consequences as well (cf. Grundlingh 2008). Much as elite South African high schools were able to protect their race/class exclusivity by raising their school fees, elite rugby teams (particularly those that represented South Africa's provinces) were able to use professionalization as a means to maintain a measure of control over their selection of players. In a political and social climate in which rugby training (and other markers of professionalism) was itself not equally distributed, the Bulls' allegedly apolitical preference for fitter, stronger, "better-prepared" recruits meant that white players were more easily and more often coded as qualified to play at the highest levels.

Together, structural limitations, compromises, and tacit preferences have produced a circuit of exclusion that, independent of explicit bigotry and prejudice, ultimately serves to reproduce elite South African rugby as a predominantly white sport. The post-apartheid government, for its part, has attempted to implement its own transformations of rugby. Government officials have made public statements about the players selected for the Springboks, and ministers have threatened to pressure the South African Rugby Union (SARU) into more accurately representing the racial demographics of the nation, by insisting that the Springboks meet specific racial distribution goals in their team (Grundlingh 2008). In 2016, Fikile Mbalula (then minister of sport and recreation) announced that SARU had failed to meet its own goals for racial transformation and, as a result, would be forbidden to host major international events. Mbalula's successor, Thembelani Nxesi, lifted the ban in 2017, but he did so with a warning that the ban could be reinstituted if transformation efforts did not continue to move in a satisfactory direction. The state has also exerted significant pressure on SARU to replace or supplement the Springbok emblem, which officials interpret as having close symbolic associations with the apartheid state (Booth 1999). Despite such efforts, rugby's historical significance has proven difficult to shed. Official histories continue to foreground the "glory days" of segregated rugby (Ansell 2010; Booley 1998; Odendaal 1995), and the post-apartheid and professional eras have only reconfirmed the connection between predominantly white schools, predominantly white professional teams, and the predominantly white-run businesses that invest in those teams.[3]

In contrast to the legislated violence of apartheid, the implicit obstacles in contemporary South Africa that sanction the whiteness of "elite" rugby can be relatively easy to overlook. To people, such as those who lived in Kylemore, who encounter impediments time and again and find themselves continually pushed to rugby's peripheries, the obstacles are often impossible to ignore. While administrators at premier rugby-playing schools might tout the number of underrepresented players they are able to recruit with athletic scholarships, many of those players told me that they felt separated from their peers on the basis of race, class, and sometimes language. Some players reported that they only seemed welcome at their school when they performed on the sporting field. While professional administrators insist that they select the best available players and give them the best possible resources to make sure they succeed, some players and their families suspect privately that white players are paid more than their nonwhite peers, because (as one man put it) "they [team administrators] think that black players can live on less." Those experiences and anxieties, taken together, indicate a through line of race/class politics that extends from colonialism and apartheid directly into the "new" South Africa.

Two moments in my fieldwork brought the contemporary inequalities into notably stark relief. The first occurred at a rugby tournament at the University of Fort Hare in October 2010. In honor of Heritage Day, a holiday celebrating South Africa's cultural traditions, the university was playing host to some of the oldest and most venerable of the country's traditionally black clubs. I had met the president of Young Ideas, one of the teams participating in the tournament, at another rugby event a few weeks prior. He generously invited me to attend and watch his team play.

Amateur rugby festivals and tournaments in South Africa share a common rhythm. Over the course of multiday events, teams will play several matches (often shortened) to make the trip worthwhile. Larger events will offer games in quick succession, to accommodate the needs of all. The stands are generally crowded, because players have little else to do in their downtime but tend to their bruises and watch others play, and tournament fields are surrounded by food and equipment vendors eager to cater to teams and their supporters. Sometimes music is played in the brief pauses between the matches, to keep the spectators entertained. Children often take to the field during the breaks, to play a free-form and two-hand-touch version of the game, appropriately called "touch." In those respects, the Heritage Tournament was like most others. Enterprising students from Fort Hare had purchased sacks of sausages and lamb chops to grill and sell at the edge of the field, and the president of Young Ideas (who was also a representative from one of South Africa's dealers of sporting goods) sold equipment and jerseys out of his sponsored car. The music was house—a brand of fast-paced electronic club music—and the DJ wove his rhythms together with the flow of the games.

Between two of the matches, a group of young boys were busy playing "touch." They used a plastic water bottle as their ball, and the game wandered all over the field, with little regard for its boundaries. As I watched the boys, I noticed that they were not just playing. They were pacing their play in time to the music, using it to develop their rugby and dance moves simultaneously. That fluidity between rugby and dance was compelling in itself, and I began to record a video of their performance with my camera. As I did so, the DJ decided to intervene in the music with a personal touch. He mixed into the song a fragment of Martin Luther King Jr.'s "I Have a Dream" speech. For nearly a minute, before the next match began, the boys danced and played, the music pulsed, and Dr. King expressed his syncopated hopes for a day when the "sons of former slaves and the sons of former slave owners will be able to sit down together at a table of brotherhood."

The next large-scale rugby event I attended occurred almost exactly six months later. The head of scouting for the Bulls was kind enough to allow me to accompany him on a drive from Pretoria to Johannesburg, to study high school prospects at three rugby festivals that schools in the city host concurrently for the Easter holiday. Because the Easter Festivals invite participation by teams from across South Africa (and sometimes from Zimbabwe), the events serve as important focal points of South African rugby's sprawling network of players, parents, coaches, and sponsors. Given that many top players attend the prestigious festivals, scouts are provided with a moment of rare opportunity as well. Hundreds of hours of travel time can be condensed into a single day's worth of continuous observation and analysis. Food and apparel were for sale, and little boys kicked around a ball and chased each other aimlessly between the matches, as at Fort Hare. The similarity prompted me to document the moment. There was a nondescript Top 40 song playing over the stadium's speakers when, to my surprise, a booming voice broke in over the music. Rather than the voice of Martin Luther King Jr., it was a digitally modified female voice, encouraging the crowd to give serious consideration to opening a retirement account with First National Bank, the festival's official sponsor.

The auditory distinction cracked open the similarities between the two events and exposed the differences that the similarities concealed. Although players came to the Easter Festivals from a variety of different backgrounds, some of their schools undoubtedly more exclusive and expensive than others, the soundtrack commented implicitly on the opulence of the festival as a whole. Some of the teams that attended the Easter Festivals had traveled hundreds of kilometers to get to Johannesburg, by plane or luxury bus. At least one of the hosting schools offered room and board to visiting teams when they arrived. Some schools opted to send their players to hotels anyway, so they could get more rest and perform at their best. First National Bank evidently supposed that the parents of such players would be interested and able to allocate resources for their retirements.

The voice of Martin Luther King Jr., in contrast, spoke explicitly to those who could recognize it and knew his famous speech. The presence of his voice also commented implicitly about the inequality and history of activism within which the historically black teams of the Heritage Tournament were situated. That situation stemmed, most immediately, from the location of the tournament itself. Originally a mission school, a significant number of the most influential political leaders from South Africa and southern Africa passed through the University of Fort Hare, including not only Nelson Mandela and Robert Sobukwe but Robert Mugabe, Joshua Nkomo, and Julius Nyerere as well. Teams attending that tournament, in contrast to most of those at the Easter Festivals, drove great distances in rented minibuses. Young Ideas owed their drivers about R4,000 (between $400 and $500) for their 1,900-kilometer round-trip transport from Cape Town to Fort Hare, and one of the drivers refused to take the players home until he was paid. After a long debate in isiXhosa, the team decided that half of the players would be taken home while the rest would stay at Fort Hare, until the unhappy driver received his payment, via Western Union, from those who had already returned. While they were participating in the tournament, the players of Young Ideas stayed together in a common room in the basement of a house belonging to a friend of the team. At the conclusion of the Heritage Tournament, a representative of SARU gave a speech emphasizing the political importance of the tournament and the need for a more concerted effort to transform the sport—that is, to bring more black players into the country's professional teams. To the best of my recollection, the speeches I heard at the Easter Festivals foregrounded no such aspirations.

The two recorded voices also gesture toward quite distinct stories about the relationship between South African rugby and history. I visited all three Easter Festivals that weekend, and all of them framed history in terms of the reputations (historically derived) of the teams invited to participate. That framing elevated the importance of the festivals but also bracketed both the politics of South African history writ large and the ways that this history had shaped the distribution of power and wealth in the country in the present. It allowed each festival to seamlessly and unproblematically unify economic and sporting concerns for the fans in the crowd. The Heritage Tournament also emphasized the historically derived reputations of its teams, but because it emphasized black teams in particular and placed the tournament at Fort Hare, it located the history of those teams within South African history as a whole. Therefore, the tournament was informed by politics from the very start and unquestionably *in* history. As the voice of Martin Luther King Jr. demonstrated, to participate in the Heritage Tournament was to tie rugby to South Africa's past and present and potentially to its future. It is thus not surprising that the tournament was also an occasion for the discussion of work still to be done in the reformation of South Africa's rugby.

The contrasting narratives about South African life that are told through rugby go a long way toward explaining the mixed emotion that so many South Africans feel about the 1995 Rugby World Cup as well. For many white South Africans, Mandela's presence on the field signaled the continuing social relevance, in the post-apartheid era, of the Springboks and the white masculinity that the team had historically represented. That event therefore provided white South Africans (especially men) with a stable cultural position in which to ground their post-apartheid identities and critique the changes instituted by the country's democratically elected government. By 2007, as implicated by my previously mentioned informant who saw the 2007 World Cup victory as a pale shadow of the win in 1995, many white South Africans considered the excitement and promise of the post-apartheid era betrayed by the failures of the post-apartheid state (cf. Mbembe 2008b). That reading of rugby's post-apartheid significance is reflected in the dominant critical interpretation of *Invictus*, which takes the film as telling a profoundly white and conservative story—of Mandela and the state accommodating rugby and putting a definitive end to the sport and its political history. That reading of rugby's significance also explains why many white South Africans view state interventions into rugby as needless meddling and political grandstanding. They interpret such interventions as threats to the integrity of an august and (now, after apartheid and the advent of professionalism) firmly apolitical social institution. Although that interpretive approach positions fans so that they are likely to see nonwhite players as "political" selections (as the consequences of state pressure rather than merit), the selection of white players is, of course, no less a product of politics. The apparent desirability of white players and their availability for selection are outgrowths of systematic social advantages.

For many of the self-identifying African, black, and coloured South Africans that I met in my fieldwork for this study, the era of promise had never truly begun. The 1995 World Cup could have marked the last gasp of segregation and inequality, but when the tournament ended, South African rugby was left unchanged. Sustained by the same institutions as in the past and inseparable from them except by means of large-scale social transformations that have not (as yet) occurred, rugby teams continue to evince South Africa's apartheid and colonial history. Because they are notably aware of the lingering significance of the past, which appears to saturate the sport's conditions of possibility and manifests itself in performances on the country's rugby fields, players and coaches of marginalized racial identities often wonder if rugby can ever shed the burdens of its history. Can rugby's elite teams ever represent a democratic South Africa? Or might rugby's ties to the past have rendered those teams irredeemably problematic?

Faced with such questions, a critical reader could perhaps be pardoned for observing that many of rugby's problems of politics and inequality would be rendered irrelevant if South Africans simply stopped playing the sport altogether. From that perspective, the narrative shortcomings of *Invictus* take on a somewhat different appearance. Rather than depicting a sanitized and simplified narrative of South African politics, one that ended before the real work of transformation could begin, the final sequence of *Invictus* now looks more like a provocative political statement. Perhaps the curtain *should have* dropped on South Africa's rugby history at the precise moment that it descended in the film. This introduction has so far endeavored to show just how much social and political work rugby had done by the time Mandela celebrated South Africa's victory in 1995. Rugby had served the colonial and apartheid regimes, the struggle against those regimes, and Nelson Mandela and his insurgent organization turned political party, the African National Congress. It had cleared the symbolic space for South Africans to conceptualize a democratic present. Perhaps rugby is no longer a relevant feature of South African life. Perhaps a new sport, a post-apartheid sport, should have replaced rugby in the scene. Because all South Africans would find themselves equally distant from that new sport, its significance in the country might escape the burdens of inequality and history. Its meanings could be built from scratch and would be equally accessible to all people, irrespective of their place within historically and politically constituted conceptions of race, gender, class, and sexual identity.

Of course, such an abrupt transition would be impossible to implement. Even if there is no essential reason why South Africans must play rugby— making it theoretically possible for them to stop playing it if they chose to do so—such a strict prohibition could never be realized in practice. The sport (curiously enough) feels both too important and too innocuous to warrant such drastic action. Equally implausible is the idea that a new sport might break definitively with the past. No sporting activity, not even one with no prior history in South Africa, could ever take root on the country's playing fields without tapping into deep wells of local meaning and politics. If practices such as sport refuse to go quietly into the night, their refusal must be attributed in large part to the interpretive frameworks that make them feel important and meaningful. In the case of South Africa, those frameworks are inextricably bound to apartheid, colonialism, and the struggles against both.

If those interpretive frameworks continue to lend significance to rugby's post-apartheid manifestations, then this alternative reading of *Invictus* becomes yet more interesting to consider. From the vantage point of the film, which would wish those frameworks away in favor of a perfectly unified South Africa, the frameworks' continuing salience becomes both empirically undeniable and analytically significant. When high school rugby administrators (and some professional coaches) fear that greedy parents and scouts are "selling players' souls" and turning them into "slaves," *Invictus* insists we recognize that those administrators are refurbishing language from South Africa's colonial history, repeating (almost verbatim) phrases that were used to describe the payment of amateur players in England more than a century ago. When predominantly white crowds shout "Beaaaaaaaast!" as Tendai Mtawarira, a black player, carries the ball or tackles an opponent, *Invictus* demonstrates that spectators are tapping into colonial-era logics of race. The apartheid state amplified and stabilized those logics even as it transformed them. When Martin Luther King Jr.'s voice booms out over the Heritage Tournament at, of all places, the University of Fort Hare, *Invictus* reminds us helpfully that South Africa's struggle against white supremacy really ought to have been put to rest in 1994. In light of the naivete of *Invictus*, the fact that such a proposition is unthinkable becomes all the more obvious and painful. Such a reading of *Invictus* is, then, resolutely subaltern. It leaves open the possibility of a total reimagining of South Africa's rugby and a dismantling of its dominant historical significances. In doing so, it resists the widely circulated and commonly accepted (white) narrative of an apolitical post-apartheid rugby.

Such a reading also transforms rugby into a testament to the incompleteness of the country's broader post-apartheid project. For a South Africa that struggles to define its contemporary moment in terms that exceed the structuring violence of the past, rugby poses pressing questions—about the political salience of South Africa's history in the present; about race, wealth, and masculinity; and even about the import of such apparently frivolous activities as sport. If rugby cannot be abandoned, neither can South African history. If rugby cannot be redeemed, what place can it hold in South Africa's future? In the present moment, the unfilmed postscript of *Invictus*, rugby stands against the post-apartheid state and nation as a "splinter in the eye" (Adorno 1978, 50). Neither redeemed nor abandoned, it calls attention insistently to the ways that history weighs down South Africa in its third post-apartheid decade, as well as to how, despite frequent attempts to shed that weight by means of memorialization, reform, reconciliation, and violence, that history continues to shape the ways that South Africans interact with one another.

UNCERTAINTY AND THE POLITICS OF *RUGBY'S* SOUTH AFRICA

While many institutions and forms of material culture carry legacies of South Africa's past into the present (cf. Coombes 2003), rugby's capacity to serve as a sociopolitical "magnifying glass" (Adorno 1978, 50) is amplified by its characteristics as a sport. In this book, I argue that sports do not merely reflect existing political conditions but can also intervene in and actively reshape them. In that respect, sports behave quite a bit like artistic forms. There is little debate that different types of artistic production lend themselves to different kinds of narrative. Theater, ballet, painting, and film versions of the story of Romeo and Juliet, for instance, all tell the same tale, but in ways specific to each medium. A painting might render the play as a tableau. That work would make a singular intervention in the plot of the play and signal that intervention in its content, form, and any supporting text (Danto 1981, 117–18; Berger 2008, 82). A film would depict the play in quite a different way. As Susan Buck-Morss (1994) has argued, it would shape how audiences perceive the narrative by means of, for example, its use of space, its construction out of multiple takes and angles, and its existence as an enclosed work of art. These brief examples are sufficient to demonstrate that while the story of Romeo and Juliet is never determined by its representation in any artistic form, it is inextricably bound to and modified by the forms we use to share it.

Furthermore, artistic forms reshape the narratives they contain in the liveness of performance. One might assume that a painting is less "alive" than a jazz set, because the painting locks its moment of creation in the past, whereas jazz brings that creation into the immediacy of the present. But theorists of performance, such as Rebecca Schneider (2011), caution us against drawing stark distinctions—politically or even empirically—between ephemeral performances and the permanence of the archive. Doing so, Schneider argues, risks concealing the mutuality and codependence of these apparently contrasting forms of representation. The archive, for example, needs to be performed as permanent, in that its producer(s) and viewers/interpreters must be actively excluded from the significance of the archive if it is going to stand alone, for itself. That performed permanence therefore favors certain interpretive readings over others, particularly those that can dictate which interpretations appear to be transparent and unchanging. Performances do not stand alone in their ephemerality but build on and contribute to archives of affect, materiality, and meaning. Seen in this way, no jazz set is so fresh and novel that it is unmoored from past sets, and no works of art are ever so "finished" as to efface the open processes of creation that produced them (Fabian 1996, 261–22; Meintjes 2003) or to foreclose new significance when they are displayed in new interpretive contexts (Askew 2002; Coplan 2008; Turino 2000; White 2008). Performance and other theorists thus seek to identify the features of artistic works that come to life in performative moments, the reasons why performances are thought to succeed or fail, and (in many cases) the historical and political significance that those performative moments engender (cf. Feld 1988; Kapferer 1986; Keil 1995; Schieffelin 1985).

Like Shore (1994), this book considers sports in terms of that vibrant set of conversations. Rugby too, it argues, possesses features that allow it to shape the stories that South Africans can use it to tell. Those features include not only the sport's formal rules (which set rugby apart from other sporting activities) but the spatial and temporal limits to that form. Such limits, which establish that a rugby game should last for little more than 80 minutes and unfold only within a narrowly delimited geographical space, "frame" the match and make it possible for the sport to generate its contextual meanings.[4] Within that temporal and spatial frame, a moment of contact becomes interpretable as a tackle. Outside that frame, that contact reads as a different sort of violence altogether.[5] Rugby also has its own qualities of performance, including the unpredictable escalation of one moment of action on another, the fragile boundary between playfulness and aggression, and the physical implications of players running into each other at high speeds.

Those qualities of performance, unfolding within rugby's formal conventions, give the sport the capacity to shape the actions of the athletes that compete within it and, this book argues, to enter ultimately into existing political conversations with its own voice. Most explicitly during the liveness of play, when teams and players are working at cross-purposes and producing interactions that nobody could predict, rugby demonstrates that it possesses a kind of autonomy[6] as a social form. Human actors are asked to respond to its expectations and to account for the material forms and affective forces it sets into motion. In such moments, rugby becomes a "Thing" that "looks back" (Ingold 2010, 4; W. Mitchell 2005, 156; cf. J. Bennett 2010, 2) or, perhaps more fittingly, part of a broader category of what Kathleen Stewart has called "complex *uncertain* objects" (emphasis added), which "fascinate because they literally hit us or exert a pull on us" (2007, 4). In chapter 6 of this book, I show that rugby's living unity of formal presentation and performance even acquired a distinctly South African name. In 1981, in response to the advent of televised sports, rugby administrators termed it the sport's *beeld*, or "image."

Thinking of rugby and its players in such terms requires a measure of what Jane Bennett has called "methodological naiveté" (2010, 17), insofar as it asks that we overlook what sports in general (and rugby in particular) seem to show so clearly: the assertive agency of the bodies that participate in them.[7] Rugby players, we might initially suppose, struggle with one another, with the ball, and within the conditions of the sport, in the interest of completing goals of various scales. They want to win the moment, in order to win a sequence of play, in order to win the match. The successful completion of those goals demonstrates the capacity of players to assert their creative capacity in relation to and over others.

While that interpretation of sport may provide persuasive explanations for the outcomes of play—for example, why one player tackled another or one team defeated another—it is less useful for describing the significance of the process of play itself. No athletes are quite so skilled as to be able to achieve their goals with absolute certainty (i.e., to act definitively on the field and to pay no heed whatsoever to their opposition, the material weakness and exhaustion of their own bodies, a given strategy, or the conditions of play). Athletes who threaten even to approach that threshold of definitive action— such as Tiger Woods at his best (Starn 2011, 15) or Joe DiMaggio during his famous hitting streak (Gould 2003, 187)—are venerated for their talents. Such exceptional cases demonstrate, in both their scarcity and the way that they are celebrated, that players' decisions on the sporting field are ultimately bound to the conditions in which they occur. They are reactive rather than active, responding not merely to the actions of other participants but also to the sports they play.

An approach grounded in theories of performance resonates with strands of theory that appear in other anthropological studies of sport. Those works have demonstrated that acting bodies are less authoritative (even agentive) than they might initially appear.[8] Studies inspired by Pierre Bourdieu (2007) and Marcel Mauss (1979)—such as those by Brownell (1995), Wacquant (2007, 2004, 1995), and Downey (2010, 2005)—emphasize that the lived self is produced, in no small measure (and perhaps even entirely), by the social practices in which it participates. In that formulation, sporting activities and other manifestations of local "body cultures" (Brownell 1995, 8) shape their practitioners as much as their practitioners shape them. Theories that build on the work of Michel Foucault similarly situate the body within a sociopolitical field that disciplines, shapes, and cultivates it (Markula and Pringle 2006; Pringle 2009; Pronger 2002). The acting body contributes to the production of that field, performatively and discursively, but it plainly does not author anything in it. As Foucault himself has argued (1998), authorship is just as much a product of a preexisting discursive space as any other social phenomenon. Anthropological works, then, offer both explicit and implicit challenges to the dominant social image of actor-driven sport, insofar as they insist on deconstructing and ultimately decentering the actor and its representations. The present book participates in that broader process of decentering, though by different means. Rather than deconstructing rugby players, the book seeks to deconstruct rugby. Rather than decentering that actor by looking outward, with a wider social lens, the book decenters it by first looking inward, toward the moment of performance and that moment's unpredictability.

That approach helps to explain my visceral reaction to the depiction of rugby that I found in *Invictus*. Rugby in South Africa, like rugby in every country, unfolds in bursts of action. It inhabits each particular instant of the match before passing into oblivion, and players and their bodies react to that instant in the contingency of the moment. The terms of any given moment are determined not by the players but by the contingency of the moment before it, the moment before that, and so on. That unfolding contingency is, of course, the source of much of the excitement and energy of any sporting event. Nobody involved in the event—not the players, the coaches, the trainers, or the fans—can predict what its narrative will be until the event comes to a close. In *Invictus*, though, the bodies of players moved where their choreographer had planned them to go. No choreographer could fully coordinate every aspect of the movement of bodies on the field, but those little unplanned movements appeared to my eyes as a residual kind of uncertainty. The broader trajectory of the movements was missing the spontaneity and the violence that the immediacy of rugby brings, and it therefore registered in my eyes as a step too slow and a beat too late.

Rugby coaches and players in South Africa possessed their own deep understanding of the unpredictability of rugby. They struggled with it constantly, theorizing it during strategy sessions, training for it in their practices, and debating it in their post-match film sessions. They discussed it casually over coffee. Far from seeing the sport as an activity that they controlled, the experts treated rugby as a capricious social entity that manipulated their strategies and set bodies into motion in unforeseeable (and often harmful) ways. The title of this book is drawn from that perspective. Rugby, with its indeterminate futures, animates its players.

The conception of rugby animating its players finds a concise allegorical expression in "Rastelli erzählt . . . ," a story Walter Benjamin shared with the children of Berlin on his short-lived radio program. Mehlman (1993, 9) provides a concise synopsis of the plot.

> It is the tale of an idiosyncratic juggler, whose genius consists in his unprecedented manipulation of a single ball. "Those who had seen the master at work had the impression that he was playing with a live accomplice—alternately docile and recalcitrant, tender and mocking, obliging and faltering—rather than with a lifeless object" [Benjamin 1972, 778]. In point of fact, the "master's" secret, or fraud, is that his ball is, or at least contains, a living being. His accomplice is a dwarf, who is secretly hidden inside the ball, and is able to activate it through a complex system of internal springs. The tale recounts the juggler's greatest (and riskiest) performance. Before a notoriously capricious sultan, a cruel despot, he gives the performance of his life. It is only upon leaving the theater, that he is handed—late—the following sealed message from the dwarf: "Dear master, don't be angry with me. Today, you will not be able to appear before the sultan. I am ill and cannot leave my bed" [780].

Mehlman's interest in this story lies in the delicate balance of falsehood and truth on which the final revelation relies. The master, a successful fraud, is himself defrauded in the process of his own greatest success. For the purposes of the present book, the physical absence of the "dwarf" in the performance before the despot is the point of emphasis. The juggler's mastery emerges from his control over the single ball and, in particular, his apparent capacity to make the ball behave as though it were alive. That talent is fraudulent because the ball is actually alive, insofar as it possesses within itself a living body that manipulates the ball on the master's behalf. His genius mastery over the ball is nothing but a kind of spiritualist parlor trick. What appears to be a living ball is, ultimately, an expression of human collaboration. That the "dwarf" is not merely necessary to the performance but concealed within the ball further underlines such a reading. As was the case with so many actual automatons (Abnet 2020, 48–49), the magical ball only appears to live because it has, at its heart, a living being.

When the "dwarf" is absent, though, we discover a new reality. The ball itself is a living accomplice in the act. It, not the "dwarf," is docile, recalcitrant, tender and mocking, obliging and faltering. Although we might be inclined to assume, in the spirit of many a sporting film and commercial, that the ball's behavior proves the master's "true" talent—that he possessed the skill to manipulate the ball and lacked only the self-confidence necessary to put his skill to use—that reading overlooks that the ball behaved as a living thing in previous performances because it really had been imbued with life. Unlike in the case of magical basketball shoes, a living being (the "dwarf," not the juggler) brought the ball to life. What we learn in the story's final twist is not so much that the fraudulent juggler possessed a true talent but that the ball possessed true life. Only once the human actor is removed from the scene do we discover the excess life the ball contains, above and beyond that acting person, his springs, and the charade as a whole.[9] We could carry this line of reasoning forward even more and argue that rather than two people animating the ball, it animated the juggler and his co-conspirator all along. After all, the lifelike behavior of the ball turned the juggler into a master and brought him before the capricious sultan in the first place.

Coaches may view rugby's capacity to animate players as a technical challenge to be navigated and sometimes overcome, but Benjamin's allegory helps to locate that challenge within a broader social and political context. Specifically, because it implies that the living ball is capable of making the juggler's reputation, it asks that we remember that the technical perspective is a kind of animation in its own right—not identical to the actual play of rugby, but certainly not independent of it—because coaches are using that perspective as a means to respond to the "life" of the sport. Seen in that way, rugby's broad historical and political significance becomes clearer. The sport's "life" actually extends outward, far beyond the field of play, to the strategies that coaches develop, their previous experiences as players and coaches, the drills they design for players in practices that serve those strategies, their justifications for the utility of those drills (moral as well as practical justifications, as I show in chapter 3), the interpretations they generate of players as they go through those drills, and so on. Thus, when I show (in chapter 1) that the strategies coaches adopt in the face of rugby are informed at a fundamental level by South African history, politics, and social relations, this book understands rugby itself to be pulling those influences into view. Accidental references to

19th-century worries about the dangers of professional sports (as considered in chapter 2) and interpretations of players that mobilize contextually specific conceptions of race, class, and gender (which appear throughout this book) can be understood in similar ways. So can injuries—material residues, with long-term implications in some cases, of rugby's capacity to act back on those who play it.

None of this is to suggest that rugby acts on every person in exactly the same way. One's social position shapes what rugby mobilizes. New players who have little experience with rugby will feel their bodies moved in ways that experienced players, practiced in the habitus of rugby's performative expectations, do not. An experienced player's body, though, is still moved. It can, for example, be injured, and experienced players will feel their injuries differently than a coach does. They will be inclined to treat that injury differently too. While it would certainly be a mistake, then, to remove human actors entirely from the play of rugby,[10] this book shifts them off the center of the stage, in the interest of seeing more clearly everything else about South Africa's history and politics that rugby gathers up when it calls on people to move.

If persons can be pulled by rugby differently, and have different embodied encounters with it as a result of where each person is located with respect to politics and history, the significance that rugby carries could never be monolithic or transparent to all.[11] With that caveat in mind, the relationship between rugby and history that this book analyzes is not one readily documented in a chronological lineage of names, dates, and key events. Such a lineage, though subjectively constructed and inevitably incomplete, would risk concealing its very incompleteness, the very differences that exist between one person's relationship to rugby and another's, behind a sheen of matter-of-fact objectivity and transparency. Like any narrative, lineages have their sutures and erasures, as even a cursory reading of the dominant chronology of South Africa's rugby history shows. The best-known players and teams—those whose accomplishments have been most diligently recorded and who appear(ed) in the Easter Festivals—are known not because they are the best but because they are white. By contrast, the most important nonwhite rugby players in South African history are remembered mostly in traces and fragments—in framed photographs in people's homes, in stories told at social gatherings, or in trophy inscriptions in team clubhouses.

A chronological approach, with its implied delineations between past, present, and future, would also present an inaccurate picture of the liveness of history. As the Heritage Tournament demonstrated quite clearly, a linear movement from a "colonial era," through an "apartheid and anti-apartheid era" to "the 1995 Rugby World Cup," and a "post-apartheid era" confuses a utopian project of historical transcendence for an analytical project of historical narrativization. In its confusion, that movement becomes a process of ideological erasure, in that it locks historical moments into their discrete eras and, in doing so, overlooks the multifarious ways that the past manifests in and shapes the present (Seremetakis 1994, 7). The 1995 Rugby World Cup is not just an event that ended in 1995 with a Springbok triumph, as a chronology of South African rugby would have it. It also entails how the games are discussed, felt, and remembered—as a momentary blip in a long and slow process of social transformation (as it appears to many black players and fans of rugby), a marker of national unity against which the "failures" of post-apartheid South Africa can be measured or the inauguration of a new apolitical era of sport (as it appears to many white fans and players), and a missed opportunity for the abandonment of rugby and the racist politics with which it was associated (as it appears in *Invictus*).

Those interpretations are manifestations of existing social identities as constituted by history and politics, but they also reinscribe (and sometimes transform) those identities as they are experienced and shared. If rugby animates the people who surround it, it also animates their understandings of their identities and the identities of others. For instance, as I show in chapters 3 and 4, masculinity is not (just) an identity that makes rugby meaningful. Rugby is a way for masculinity to be understood; masculinity gets made and remade in the performance of rugby. The same is true for race, as apartheid ideology crudely demonstrated. Rugby was not (just) something that "Coloured" persons did. Rugby was something that made people "Coloured." To be pulled into rugby's orbit now, in the post-apartheid era, is to have one's identity partially constituted through the sport, its performative qualities, and its historical meanings.

This book is particularly concerned with South African history as it is lived in the present. In keeping with rugby's capacity to act, to throw persons into unexpected situations, the lived experience of history often emerges unexpectedly, in traces or hints or momentary tableaus. This book is built around such instances, and I—like Seremetakis (1994; 2019, 118), Stewart (2007, 6), and Taussig (1993, 24–25), as well as Benjamin (1968) and Bloch (1996) before them—try to hold on to those particular instances, in the interest of looking from them outward and backward (and perhaps forward too).

Methodologically, my exploration involves considering the processes through which an apparently meaningful fragment or trace of experiential history comes to appear through rugby, then using those processes as a means to link that instance of history with others that I encountered elsewhere in my research. As an interpretive exercise, this project involves considering how historical processes and instances work together to generate meaningful performances of history—identifying, in other words, the conditions of possibility that bring a fragment into being and make it meaningful—and examining how those performances speak to particular understandings of South Africa and its broader patterns of violence, economic and racial inequality, white supremacy, and anti-colonial and anti-apartheid resistance.

As my third reading of *Invictus* emphasizes, rugby is not inherently or inevitably meaningful. Its meanings in South Africa, as elsewhere, are products of particular (and never definitively stable or fully articulated) instantiations of history, social relations, and politics. They are also products of the formal demands that the sport places on its players, demands that are historical, social, and political too. When I frame rugby as a "performance of history," I do so in an attempt both to turn attention to the layers of historical and political sediment that rugby agitates in South Africa and to make it possible to analyze the significance of that sediment today, in contemporary South African life, without losing sight of the performative practice that lies at the heart of the matter: rugby itself.

CHAPTER SUMMARIES

Argumentatively speaking, this study's approach to rugby's historical significance does not lend itself well to a narrative structure that unfolds chapter by chapter, progressing from the origins of the sport in the 19th century to its current manifestations in South Africa. Nor is it particularly well suited to an account that treats each chapter as a discrete, self-contained study. Rather than adopting either approach, the chapters of this book are constructed (sometimes explicitly and sometimes not) around moments when rugby calls history and politics into view. Each chapter possesses its own argument, but the historical processes and social relations from which the arguments draw are so deeply interwoven with each other that the people and themes that appear in one chapter can also be found in others.

Chapter 1 affirms that South African rugby counts for more than the sum of its histories. Drawing inspiration from the writings of Claude Lévi-Strauss and Franz Boas, as well as from the aesthetic theory of Theodor Adorno, that chapter demonstrates that rugby contains an inherent dimension of unpredictability that allows it to recombine and challenge the symbols and sentiments assigned to it. Rugby players, coaches, and teams regard uncertainty as a problem to be solved, and they conceptualize and work through rugby's layering of unpredictable instant atop unpredictable instant in socially and historically specific ways.

Teams in the Bulls organization, chapter 1 shows, use violence and physical contact to dominate the game to the best of their abilities. They tend to favor large, imposing players and teach them a small set of coordinated actions that are reliable, if unspectacular, guarantors of success. Drawing from interviews and the observations I collected during training sessions, games, film sessions, and executive meetings, I argue that the roots of that stylistic preference are buried in the country's violent past. Many of the coaches who espouse that style served in South Africa's military, police, and correctional services during apartheid and are therefore intimately familiar with tactics that aim to limit, control, and destroy unpredictability. With their stylistic approach to rugby, those coaches demonstrate the relevance of South Africa's history to the country's post-apartheid present.

Chapter 2 continues this book's exploration of professionalism and post-apartheid politics. In the years since 1995, when rugby union became an explicitly professional sport, players, teams, and coaches in South Africa have debated among themselves about the costs and benefits of professionalization. High school headmasters complain that professional rugby is ruining the sport, and scouts and professional administrators retort that those headmasters are viewing rugby through a myopic lens. Chapter 2 refuses to adjudicate the dispute. Instead, it analyzes how, when, by whom, and in response to whom the contrasting positions are mobilized. Elaborating on Adorno's work on art and political commitment as well as Arthur Danto's 50-year exploration of the aesthetic implications of Andy Warhol's *Brillo Box*, the chapter considers how debates about rugby's autonomy are framed and what those framings foreclose.

To advocate that rugby should be viewed like any other job, as some professionals do, is to overlook that rugby does operate autonomously, insofar as players and teams must construct worlds for themselves in which tackles are tackles and scores have value. To believe that rugby should be fully independent from matters of everyday life, as amateurs often do, is to treat autonomy as an inevitability, which is plainly not the case. Autonomy, as a way of understanding sporting and artistic forms, has a history of its own. It rose to prominence in the 19th century and developed largely in response to the expansion of industrial capitalism and the emergence of a white European middle class. Far from drawing a definitive separation between sports and matters of everyday life, the category of autonomy carries within itself a legacy of exclusion based on race, class, and, as I show in chapter 3, gender (Walsh and Giulianotti 2001, 64).[12] Chapter 2 moves back and forth between past and present framings of autonomy and, in doing so, shows how amateurs and professionals in South Africa mobilize history, as well as histories of exclusion, as they try to justify and implement their respective positions.

Chapter 3 continues the previous chapter's investigation of the politics of rugby's autonomy, by focusing on one particular point of tension: players and their bodies. Rugby allows players to collide with one another at high speed, provided that they do so during the duration of a given match, on the space of the match's dedicated field, and within the limits established by the rules. When those conditions are met, collisions register as "tackles," which differ from identical off-field collisions in much the same way as Gregory Bateson (1972, 182) argued that "nips" differ from "bites": the former, while resembling the latter, is made "fictional" by means of a "play frame" that participants continually perform into being. Chapter 3 uses rugby injuries to contribute additional complexity to Bateson's analysis. Because players carry injuries with them when they leave the field, players and the materiality of their bodies demonstrate how rugby's "play frame" overlaps with everyday life.

As I show in chapter 3, attention to the materiality of play opens up a new space for thinking about the ideological dimensions of South African rugby specifically. Because rugby presents itself as play with "nips" rather than "bites," for example, it is comparatively easy for nonparticipants (coaches in particular) to overlook the violence of the sport's collisions and dismiss the reality of resulting injuries.[13] Interpretations of injuries are made yet more complicated by the theory of gender that emerges from rugby's autonomy. If rugby insists that its players react to changing circumstances, to uncertainty, and to each other, it also invites the possibility of a player who can truly and definitively act while playing the game. That ideal player would be able to truly "impose his will" on situation and opponent alike. Unsurprisingly, coaches attach much value to players who can most closely embody that subject position. That said, the modifier "ideal" and the pronoun "his" have not been idly chosen. As theorists like Seyla Benhabib and Judith Butler have clearly demonstrated, the autonomous subject does not and indeed cannot exist. Rugby players may not articulate their perspectives in those philosophical terms, but some still draw on the spirit of gendered critiques of autonomy in debates with their coaches. In doing so, players also question the assumptions about masculine performance that their coaches often deploy.

Chapter 4 elaborates on the theory of gender and sport that emerges from chapter 3. It examines the ideological connections between rugby and a collection of violent practices of discipline and social education that I encountered in the school in which I worked. In a country in which whiteness (particularly white masculinity) is not quite the privileged and protected category it once was, rugby provides a canvas that adults and boys can use to explore the implications of apartheid's demise. Invested adults who watch young men respond spontaneously to the violent and ever-changing conditions of play judge them according to their ability to live up to the masculine standards of past generations. Far from being a space for unencumbered play, then, rugby and its concomitant openness allows for the careful policing (cf. Lake 2009) of male students, their bodies, and their motives.

Rugby's structural conditions may permit such interpretations to emerge from its moments of action, but the sport also refuses to compromise when those interpretations are called into question. When boys use performance-enhancing supplements (both legal and illegal varieties) and aspire to professional careers in rugby, those strategies sabotage the disciplinary potential of rugby in the eyes of many adults. Unlike other forms of sporting ill-discipline, though, supplements and professional aspirations are perfectly consistent with rugby's conditions of uncertainty, immediacy, and violence. Players use supplements to perform at a higher level and to adhere more precisely to rugby's demands. The congruence means that when adults look to rugby to tell them about those particular flaws in the masculinity of young men, the sport remains resolutely silent.

Chapter 5 emerges primarily from interviews and observations that occurred during my fieldwork in Kylemore. The chapter uses "imaginative resistance"—a term that seeks to describe how a person might refuse, consciously or not, to participate in a fictional world because the person finds the morals of that world to be repugnant—as a means to explain how rugby became a key vehicle for political participation in the 1970s and 1980s. Communities like Kylemore broke politically along rugby lines: playing for the nonracial South African Rugby Union signaled a commitment to the struggle against apartheid, and playing for the state-affiliated South African Rugby Football Federation indicated collaboration. As I discovered during the life history interviews I conducted with former players, the line was so starkly drawn that athletes of contrasting ideological sentiments used to harass each other in the streets and fight each other at community events.

Although the distinction came to revolve around one particularly fraught question ("Are you a SARU player/person/family/town or a Federation one?"), I complicate its presumed dichotomy by describing some of the winding paths players took to one or the other side of that political divide. In doing so, I suggest that we can only understand the practical ambiguities of the SARU/Federation question once we have investigated how those organizations chose to deal with the gap between rugby and everyday life. While Federation players tended to treat rugby as an autonomous social activity, SARU players effaced any boundary between sport and the politics of the world that surrounded it; they refused to "play normal sport in an abnormal society." Despite their different responses to the gap, both SARU and the Federation called attention to the politics of rugby in ways that neither the formal settlement of the SARU/Federation question nor the end of apartheid has adequately resolved. To this day, a resident's decision to publicly support South Africa's national team is a meaningful expression of local political commitments and family ties.

Chapter 6 explores rugby and nationalist symbolism. Much of the popular and scholarly debate about rugby in the post-apartheid era has hinged on the lingering salience of the symbols of apartheid. Particular attention has been devoted to "Die Stem" (the apartheid-era national anthem), the apartheid-era flag, and the political significance of the Springbok emblem (Booth 1998, 1999; Nauright 1996). While chapter 6 does not dismiss the legitimacy of examining the historical significance of those symbols, it endeavors to add complexity to the existing set of conversations. It observes that state projects in and academic critiques of South Africa's rugby tend to overlook the political history of South Africa's rugby styles. If the movements of rugby players are reactive rather than active and occur within a conceptually delineated frame, then theorists of rugby's politics must acknowledge that the sport carries as much information in its styles of play and formal qualities as in the bodies that appear to enact its performances.

That perspective, I argue, has profound consequences for how we think about the relationship between sport and nationalism more generally. The post-apartheid state can influence which bodies appear on South African fields and can replace the apartheid national anthem and flag, but those efforts will not sufficiently transform the national team's "image." Apartheid lingers on, as a kind of ghostly presence (cf. Worby and Ally 2013), in the ways that South Africa's leading rugby institutions choose to respond to the sport's uncertainty. For the country's rugby, the politics of style in South Africa might well be as pressing an issue as the politics of representation. If post-apartheid South Africa cannot follow the lead of *Invictus* and abandon rugby entirely, then, how should its rugby performances look? Implicit in that question is a second one, prompted by several earlier chapters in this book: If apartheid South Africa answered uncertainty by crushing it out, how will the post-apartheid nation respond?

The three central themes of this book are the liveness of play, the politics of autonomy, and rugby as a performance of history. The book's conclusion draws those themes together around a single recent event. Fifteen years after the 1995 Rugby World Cup, South Africa hosted the FIFA World Cup. For rugby fans in Pretoria, that tournament in 2010 was significant not only for its own reasons but because FIFA had reserved the Bulls' home stadium for tournament use. The stadium was therefore unavailable to the Bulls, despite the fact that the team had earned the right to host a home semifinal and final of a prestigious rugby tournament. Unable to play their matches on their "true" home field, the team decided to play them at Orlando Stadium, in the nearby Johannesburg township of Soweto. As a result of that compromise, Bulls rugby (including its stylistic associations with the apartheid state) was transported wholesale into a hotbed of anti-apartheid activism.

I trace the discourses that unfolded around the 2010 matches, from the perspectives of players, coaches, and journalists. While the Bulls' trips to Soweto were most commonly figured as profoundly exciting moments of racial integration, they were also described as "unbelievable" and "unreal." In the conclusion, I argue that the "unreality" of the matches can be traced not only to the onetime intervention of FIFA, which made the Orlando Stadium matches politically viable in a way that they otherwise would not have been, but also to the sheer mass of Bulls fans and scaffolding of the matches on the part of the Bulls organization, which transformed the Soweto matches into a celebration of racial integration that unfolded, seemingly effortlessly, on white terms. When Bulls administrators, players, and fans looked at the "unreal" sight of thousands of predominantly white team supporters traveling to Soweto, to socialize en masse with township residents and to watch the Bulls dominate uncertainty on the field, they found in it a performance of history. They saw themselves as following in Nelson Mandela's footsteps, insofar as they believed themselves to be using the matches as an occasion for political reconciliation. But they also caught fleeting glimpses of settler colonialism, police violence, and their own historical relation to both. Even within that decidedly "unreal" event, rugby called South African history into view.

CHAPTER 1

Making Art from Uncertainty
Magic and Its Politics in South African Rugby

In 1986, historian Herman Giliomee and rugby player Tommy Bedford published an essay in *Die Suid-Afrikaan* exploring the ideological similarities between South Africa's predominant rugby style and the political style of the ruling National Party. Writing during the country's so-called state of emergency, the seeming fact that the apartheid state responded to South Africa's international isolation with increasingly conservative positions troubled the authors. Could the same, they wondered, be said about the nation's rugby? "In South Africa," they decided, "the whole approach is: there is a crisis; we cannot waste any chances, [we must] be disciplined, [and] follow the authority figure. This is how we operate our politics, this is how we play our rugby" (Giliomee and Bedford 1986, 56).

Although they offered their answer tongue in cheek, it did claim an explicit connection between the performance of rugby and the performance of politics in apartheid South Africa. In that claim, the authors were hardly alone. A number of scholars have noted that while the sport of rugby may have arrived in southern Africa as a British colonial practice, it quickly became a preferred (even privileged) avenue of expression for the white, male, Afrikaner identity characteristic of the apartheid regime. As chapters throughout this book will demonstrate, multiple social institutions produced and confirmed that association, including the country's segregated educational system, as well as its military, police, and correctional services and the Dutch Reformed Church (Coetzee 1988; Grundlingh 1994; Holdstock 1990; Morrell 2001c; Niehaus 2014). If many state-sanctioned rugby teams in South Africa adhered to the mandate to "follow the authority figure," the young men who played on those teams encountered that approach both on and off the field.

The preceding passage from Giliomee and Bedford includes a second connection—arguably more provocative than the first—between rugby and politics. On both sides of the authors' formulation, the condition demanding conservative response is "crisis." For the apartheid regime in the 1980s, the sociopolitical crisis was clear: the state faced opposition, violent and nonviolent, from groups both within South Africa and beyond its borders. The call to make South Africa "ungovernable," issued by the African National Congress in 1984, was meant to produce precisely that condition. The source of rugby's crisis, in contrast, goes unarticulated. What produced rugby's crisis situation? What new analytical possibilities emerge if we explore the crisis that rugby seemed to entail?

With such questions in mind, this chapter argues that rugby's crisis emerges not from any particular moment of play or opponent on the field but from conditions inherent to the sport itself. The actual performance of rugby, as participants well know, is marked less by certainty and deliberative action than by unpredictability and spontaneous responses to rapidly changing circumstances.[1] Players, coaches, and teams must negotiate that unpredictability if they wish to participate at all, and those negotiations grant the sport the capacity to influence the world around it, by shaping possibilities and entering into existing political conversations with its own voice. With that dialectic in mind, I draw inspiration from the writings of Claude Lévi-Strauss and Franz Boas, as well as from Theodor Adorno's reconsideration of Walter Benjamin's notion of artistic aura, and propose that we can describe rugby's inherent crisis by framing it in terms of art and aura.

If rugby elevates unpredictability as a defining structural principle, unpredictability can likewise be reframed as the sport's unique aesthetic problem, with which all parties involved must contend. By opening that small space of uncertainty, I suggest, we can gain insight not only into the political salience of rugby in apartheid and post-apartheid South Africa but also into how we might theorize sports in relation to other forms of creative expression. In particular, such a perspective shows that rugby's layering of unpredictable instant atop unpredictable instant produces not only occasions for violence and injury in South Africa but moments of magic thick with political significance as well.

MAGIC, AURA, AND THE LIMITS OF THE BULLS' *MAAK VAS* STYLE

Nominally representing the city of Pretoria and northern Gauteng Province in South Africa's professional rugby geography, the Bulls have gained a reputation for playing what is termed, in Afrikaans, *maak vas* (perhaps best translated as "secure," implying both safety and tightness). That sort of rugby is premised on a strategy of efficient organization and physical dominance, and the coaches have composed strategic sequences of action, called patterns, to guide their teams. All Bulls players are expected to learn those coordinated actions, which are designed to be equally useful on all parts of the field. Within a given pattern, the player holding the ball can choose between two or three preconceived options, but the strategy discourages breaking from the pattern and trying something completely new. Coaches deem such off-the-cuff actions problematic, because the team will struggle to organize itself into a functional whole if its members operate independently. Plus, as one particular coach added, a prepared action is inherently superior to a spontaneous reaction because prepared actions allow players to anticipate the future movements of their teammates. A player with knowledge in hand can act more decisively than one who must recognize and accommodate a teammate's independent decisions. In response to the spontaneous, unprecedented situations that rugby continually offers up, Bulls players respond with safe, predictable actions.

In addition, when a team chooses to run tightly controlled patterns, novelty becomes damaging. Teammates do not expect spontaneity from each other, so something that surprises the opposition also surprises one's teammates, perhaps even more. As a result, once an organization has embraced patterns and dominance, it effectively forecloses all other styles of play. *Maak vas* perpetuates itself.

That commitment to patterns manifests in every Bulls practice necessarily, because the strategy requires the team to run its patterns as perfectly as possible. Players spend the majority of their field sessions performing a very small range of tasks over and over. They practice their patterns repeatedly, running into teammates holding cushioned bags, so that they can identify and eliminate errors in form. Such repetitive action, coupled with the recruitment of players considered well prepared (physically and mentally) for that particular strategy, seeks to school players in coordination. It is no coincidence that the words Bulls players and management use most regularly to describe their style include *dominant*, *precise*, and *structured*. One coach told me bluntly that the Bulls attempted to "control everything," that "people know it's coming but it's how we execute that makes the difference. With the Bulls we dictate. If our opponents try to play [a free-flowing] game, we kill it and bring it back to our style." Another coach, who spent much of his rugby career as a Bulls player, refers to his players as *masjiene*, or machines.

The description of players as machines may be more significant than the coach intended. The Bulls management feels confident that its strategy, properly executed, will reliably produce identical results, not only at the level of the final result, but in every discrete action on the field. The same sequence of patterns, run on different fields against different opponents in different weather conditions, should look and unfold identically. In effect, the players are expected to train and perform mechanically, with the hope of someday becoming (literally) automatic.

Though spontaneous actions may seem like problematic thorns in the hooves of the Bulls, professional rugby matches have become so tightly contested that spontaneity can prove vital to success. Teams play more matches now than they did in the past, and most are televised and immediately dissolved into statistics, allowing teams to analyze each other for their tendencies. If the Bulls introduce any sort of innovation, all their future opponents will have recognized and prepared for it within a matter of days, quickly negating its advantage. In that competitive environment, the tiniest errors grow in significance, because unexpected opportunities arise in the moments after an error is made. Recalling a situation in which an opposing player made a mistake, one Bulls coach reported that "suddenly the whole field was open." The surprising creation of possibility out of nothingness makes uncertain moments crucial. In response to such open situations, the Bulls coaches have concocted a special strategy that (temporarily) permits their players to make their own spontaneous decisions. They call the strategy "magic."

The articulation of that term by a team that wants to produce *masjiene* is significant. It indicates that even if the Bulls do everything perfectly and control the game entirely, a window of possibility inevitably remains. The right player with the right skills, in the right situation and equipped with every additional qualifier, can still mobilize a moment of rugby to build something incredible and improbable. As Alfred Gell's work suggests, this notion of magic is hardly unique to a particular South African rugby team. Considering gardening as a technical activity, Gell (1992, 57) writes, "The idea of magic as an accompaniment to uncertainty does not mean that it is opposed to knowledge, i.e. that where there is knowledge there is no uncertainty, and hence no magic. On the contrary, what is uncertain is not the world but the knowledge we have about it. One way or another, [the garden] is going to turn out as it turns out; our problem is that we don't yet know how that will be." Rugby will likewise "turn out," and the Bulls find magic only in the precise instant when that turning out escapes their grip.[2]

When the Bulls acknowledge magic in such moments, they give a name to the same element of rugby that Giliomee and Bedford termed a "crisis." Recognizing magic is how they respond to rugby's inherent uncertainty—its capacity to act on them, to shape them, and to disrupt their plans.[3] In those respects, magic shares a fundamental similarity with Theodor Adorno's definition of artistic aura. Unlike Walter Benjamin (2003, 253), who found aura in an artwork's unique physical existence and in its singular movement through history, Adorno (1997, 33) argued that aura emerges during the process of the artwork's making, when it first forces its viewer to distinguish between itself and the seeing of it (see also Buck-Morss 1977, 154). In a Western European artistic tradition, that point is when an artwork begins to take shape as a monad distinct from its creator. Artworks may be human-made objects, but they are also, as noted by Fredric Jameson (2007, 204), uniquely blind to the world. They are blind, he writes, "both because we see [them as objects] and because [they] cannot look back at us, or indeed out at any empirical reality." As such, they stand in defiance to our gaze (cf. Buck-Morss 1989, 194; Taussig 1993, 265n9), demanding a measure of autonomy as social and historical productions. We can feel something of that defiance in singular pieces of material art (e.g., paintings and sculpture), but it is perhaps even more apparent in works re-created from a template (e.g., a theatrical script or a score), because we can watch as aura transforms such templates into something discrete and new in every performance.

Such transformation is what Adorno referenced when he wrote that "artworks have the immanent character of being an act" (1997, 79). Howard Becker put the situation even more clearly: "Similar artworks also have differences: no two play performances are alike, and they may have different characters as a result"; "ignoring the changes does not mean that they do not persist" (1984, 302). Paintings and dramatic performances are united in their ability to exhibit themselves with the suddenness of an act—that is, with the suddenness of their coming into existence—whether that act appears in a congealed form (as in a painting) or in an apparently immediate one (as in drama). For Adorno (2007b, 41), openness and contingency of objectification protects a live Beethoven symphony from appropriation (cf. Bernstein 2001, 115). Once the openness of artistic production can be repeated over and over mechanically, however, artworks "become vulgarized" (Adorno 2007b, 40). Mechanical reproduction destroys the artwork's aura; the act loses its immediacy.

Given the similarity between Adorno's conception of aura and the Bulls' notion of magic, it is no surprise that Adorno's pessimistic reading of mechanical reproduction captures well the political dimensions of the Bulls' post-match video sessions. In such sessions, coaches reproach players who deviated from an expected sequence of play. A coach will often play the footage of an error through to the end and then show it again, pausing just before the spontaneous decision was made. The freezing of time is designed to reproduce the feeling of possibility in the instant of its emergence, and the player is expected to justify his actions to his coach and teammates. Generally, the player will have no ready response (because he and everyone else recognized his impulsive choice as a mistake moments after he made it), and he will sit back in his chair, chastened. With the aid of increasingly precise video technology, coaches can both police mistakes and splice successful sequences of play into new, fantasy performances that offer glimpses of a fully realized *maak vas* script.

UNCERTAINTY AND THE POLITICAL HISTORY OF STYLE

While it might be tempting to analyze the Bulls' post-match video sessions and response to magic in terms of rugby's increasing professionalization, Giliomee and Bedford's observations invite a more nuanced argument. Rugby union only became an officially professional sport in 1995, but the Bulls have played some variation of *maak vas* strategy since the early 1960s. Then known as the Northern Transvaal Rugby Union (NTRU), the team drew its players on an invitation-only basis from the strongest amateur clubs in and around Pretoria. Until the early 1990s, three of the most influential clubs in the region were the army, the police, and the correctional services. Given that the apartheid state required a massive police, military, and prison system to keep its policies afloat, one would expect the strength of those teams during that period. They not only provided the NTRU with many of its most famous players but also shaped its response to the sport's uncertainty.

With the 1967 institution of two years of mandatory military service for white males over the age of 18, then after the declaration of a state of emergency in 1985, potential players flooded those clubs. Young white men from around the country went to Pretoria for training, and those talented at rugby often received preferential treatment from their superiors. As more than one former soldier-cum-player told me, the most skilled rugby players in the army were never sent to South Africa's border for active duty, and few players left base at all. According to one often-repeated story from the 1970s, a veteran player approached the coach of the NTRU, a police brigadier general named Buurman van Zyl, to tell him that he planned to retire from rugby. When the player finished his story, van Zyl responded, "Do you want the long grass or the short grass?" The player took his meaning: Did he want the long grass of serious military service, combating an unknown insurgent threat in Angola or South West Africa (Namibia), or the short grass of the rugby field? He chose the short grass and continued to play. As that example shows, not only was rugby exchangeable, in some ways, with military service, but the sport was used as leverage to keep players in certain regions of the country. Pretoria, home to the Afrikaans-medium University of Pretoria, as well as of the headquarters of the army and the police, emerged as the epicenter of that logic.[4]

As institutions, the police, the correctional services, and the army could not tolerate uncertainty or spontaneity. In terms of both geography and individual bodies, apartheid ideology coded spaces of uncertainty and fluidity as dangerous zones of crisis. Order-keeping institutions had the express purpose of controlling such spaces and limiting the actions possible within them. If we momentarily ignore whether such spaces could ever be controlled or limited in practice, not to mention how the institutions of order actually operated (cf. Ashforth 1990; Breckenridge 2005; Cock 1991; Cock and Nathan 1989), we can see that the ideological relation to uncertainty governed the manner in which the institutions' clubs—and, by extension, the NTRU—encountered uncertainty on the rugby field. Sporting spaces, like social ones, required control and stabilization through dominant force.

Described in such terms, *maak vas* rugby has received a detailed theoretical explication elsewhere. In *Primitive Art* (2010, 10–11), Franz Boas posits that anthropologists might consider technical mastery, rather than formal "sophistication," a universal index of artistic accomplishment, and he argues that mastery lies in the artist's ability to execute an abstract, mental model in a particular, material work of art. Consider the similarity between his notion of the artist and that of the authority figure described at the beginning of the present chapter: the authority figure, a coach-artist, seeks to impose his mastery on the production of rugby by controlling the resources on which the sport depends, disciplining his performers and shaping their production toward an ideal *maak vas* performance. Boas further theorizes that ideal forms—be they perfect lines, geometric patterns, or figurative works—did not stem from inherent racial capabilities, as evolutionists generally supposed, but instead derived from a group's specific cultural history and the habits of movement and dexterity in which that history inhered (148). We might say the same about why the Bulls privilege *maak vas*. The team's social history provides many of its players and coaches with an apparently logical response to the problem of rugby's magic.

Technique may be culturally and historically situated for Boas, but masterful artistic production is only desirable because the uncertainty of that process allows raw artistic materials to resist their own perfect objectification. Boas writes, "The work is laid out in the mind of the maker before he begins and is a direct realization of the mental image. In the process of carrying out such a plan technical difficulties may arise that compel him to alter his intentions. Such instances can easily be discovered in the finished product and are highly instructive, because they throw a strong light upon the mental processes of the workman" (2010, 156). That striking quotation may indicate the place of uncertainty in Boas's theory of art, but it also contains an even more important point: namely, it suggests that theorists of art may find it rewarding to study the space between an ideal form and its material realization, because artists leave behind traces of human creativity as they negotiate between their preferred mental images, the uncertainty of artistic production, and the raw materials on which they work. Like imprints made in clay, we can use those traces to reconstruct the minds that produced them. As I show later in the present chapter, *maak vas* rugby can be analyzed in a similar way.

Before doing so, however, we must reckon with the ideal *maak vas* script. If we consider *maak vas* in terms of technical mastery, it becomes apparent that there is something persuasive, comforting, and perhaps even beautiful about the Bulls at play. When everything goes by design, when the team overwhelms its opponent and makes no mistakes, the performance can unfold so smoothly that it appears preordained. Such a performance manages to represent, if just for a few moments, the utopian dream of dominating uncertainty—the possibility of complete human control over a fundamentally unpredictable world. That aesthetic is so influential among the Bulls staff and players that the team has a second strategic response for the most chaotic and unpredictable of situations: a plan called "default." That strategy, in direct opposition to magic, targets uncertainty and destroys it, transforming the openness of possibility into the safest and least complex of the Bulls' strategies. In doing so, it trusts in the promise of *maak vas* even in rugby's most desperate moments.

Opting for default in the face of rugby's inherent uncertainty may reinforce the Bulls' particular ideal form, but the inevitable gap between ideal and execution raises an important question: What should we make of magic? Not only does a complete commitment to *maak vas* render magic difficult to rehearse, but the very existence of magic seems to belie the Bulls aesthetic as well. Specifically, naming magic appears tantamount to admitting both that uncertainty is actually inherent to rugby—rather than a stylistic gesture that can be added or subtracted—and that players can never truly become *masjiene*. Each action by each player continually produces a new unpredictable situation, demanding another novel response, and no amount of discipline and precision can bring *maak vas* to permanent fruition. More damning still is the fact that if the Bulls tried to squeeze uncertainty from rugby's live performance once and for all, they would alter the sport's fundamental character. In effect, rugby would then perform its own magical flourish and escape, transforming itself into an entirely different sort of activity. Bulls matches would look like video sessions performed live, with players of both teams carefully synchronizing and tempering their actions to ensure that the Bulls' patterns unfolded exactly as planned. With that consequence in mind, why does magic exist? Why is default not the only response for all eventualities? Why recognize a condition that, for ideological purposes, might better remain unnamed?

Though magic might appear problematic because it hints that the performance of *maak vas* entails its own failure, Boas's reflections on the limits of technique help us appreciate the ways that the South African state turned rugby's uncertainty to its advantage. First, if we consider magic from the perspective of the institutions that built the NTRU's rugby, it becomes clear that rugby's inherent uncertainty made the sport into a subtle barometer of a player's ability to follow commands and perform under stressful conditions. He would encounter a barrage of uncertainty and violence during each practice and match, and coaches would identify and discourage any irresponsible and spontaneous actions. Adorno noticed that dimension of sport as well, writing that apparently "free" sporting moments are examples "not [of] play but [of] ritual in which the subjected celebrate their subjection. They parody freedom in their readiness for service, a service which the individual forcibly exacts from his own body for a second time" (2007c, 89). In the interstices of order, in moments of magical possibility, a commitment to order could be demonstrated most definitively. As future chapters in the present study will show, that dimension of rugby's performance had and still has profound utility in South Africa.

Second, because each decisive action on the field produces new uncertainty, every moment became an opportunity for the apartheid state to perform and thereby renew the spectacle of its own authority. If state power is itself never stable or certain, one can see why the continual subduing of uncertainty would have some value, by continually realizing the apartheid state's particular and particularly brutal "state effect" (T. Mitchell 1991). If rugby could be depended on to reliably offer up small doses of uncertainty, the team from the Northern Transvaal would systematically crush it out.[5] Several other ethnographers of the apartheid state have recognized its dependence on the dialectic of certainty and uncertainty as well, albeit in other respects. Deborah Posel (2001) and Leo Kuper (1954), for example, observe that apartheid's capriciousness of racial categorization—its inconsistencies and its subjectivity, more than its immoral bureaucratic rationality—produced its mystique. Stephen Ellis's (1998, 275) account of the rise and fragmentation of the state's so-called Third Force demonstrates that dialectic on two distinct levels: first in the relative silence in which the Third Force conducted the state's dirtiest work; second, in the discursive "cultivation of ambiguity" that allowed senior apartheid officials to convey illicit orders to their underlings without explicitly implicating themselves in the process. Taussig (1992, 16), who recognized a similar phenomenon during Colombia's state of emergency, carries the same line of analysis further still. He argues that states do not simply use uncertainty but need and produce it for themselves. Intimate relationships with uncertainty, he suggests, give state terror its particularly "sinister quality." If that holds true and if extrajudicial uncertainty sustains the authority of any state, it comes as no surprise that the apartheid regime's policemen, soldiers, and prison guards were supplied with a strategy that played with the boundaries of discipline and order.

RESPONDING TO RUGBY'S "MYSTERIOUS CHARACTER": MAGIC AND CREATIVITY IN THE LIVENESS OF PLAY

Claude Lévi-Strauss, however, has shown us that the seed of magic that *maak vas* requires is fecund enough for us to grow alternative aesthetics. For him, technique marked only the beginning of art's significance. Responding directly to an essay by Boas about the aesthetic significance of split representation, Lévi-Strauss (1967, 255) observes that objects and their masterful embellishment often take shape simultaneously. A vivid example of that phenomenon, he argues, comes in the patterning of facial tattoos in the Maori tradition. The tattoo is, of course, tailored to the shape of the face and the experiences and family history of the person tattooed, but Lévi-Strauss recognized that the face is conceptually tailored to the tattoo as well. The face, he writes, is "predestined" to be tattooed because it realizes its social existence only through tattooing (256). That element of contingency, he suggests elsewhere, obtains in any object's decoration. A wood carving, for example, takes shape as a result of "the size or shape of the piece of wood the sculptor lays hands on, in the direction and quality of its grain, in the imperfections of his tools, in the resistance which his materials or project offer to the work in the course of its accomplishment, in the unforeseeable incidents arising during work" (Lévi-Strauss 1966, 27).

Such contingency (resulting not just from the limitations of human technical ability but also from the intersection of the human, raw materials, and the productive situation) proves vital to Lévi-Strauss's supposition that art is situated between scientific and mythological thought. He demonstrates that supposition by means of his famous analogy of the Engineer and the Bricoleur. In *The Savage Mind*, Lévi-Strauss characterizes the Engineer as a figure representing a mode of scientific thought that uses cognitive structures to produce events in the manner of an experiment. That mode resembles Boas's conception of art: an artist has an ideal form in mind, locates the proper tools and raw materials, develops the necessary skills, and attempts to realize that form in a piece of recalcitrant material. For his theorization of art, however, Lévi-Strauss (1966, 22) places the artist between the Engineer and the Bricoleur, who cobbles together structures from an experienced series of contingent and particular events.[6] That placement marks a crucial shift, because it allows the artist to draw on the Engineer's mastery and deliberation, as well as on the Bricoleur's willingness to engage the sensible world in a series of open encounters. For Lévi-Strauss, that tension and synthesis makes artworks cognitively potent, capable of expressing mythological thought in a semi-deliberate fashion (25). Art, then, is contingent not only because of the materials used but because it is only possible to know what one has been making when one finally finishes it, having traversed the process of artistic creation.

In other words, Lévi-Strauss's critique of Boas suggests that precisely the gap between ideal and material, abstract and particular, distinguishes art from other human endeavors. That distinction is why Boas finds such a rich vein of analytical possibility in the attempts of artists to rescue their projects of technical mastery: the magic of artistic creation, for Lévi-Strauss, lies in exactly those "imprints in clay." Danie,[7] a man who coached rugby in the Western Cape (a provincial hotbed of liberal opposition during apartheid), approached the sport in just that way. He called magic rugby's "mysterious character," and he argued that magic gave rugby the capacity to resist the implementation of an outside structure by a coach. Using a logic that mirrored a liberal formulation of self-actualization, Danie argued that an imposed structure becomes a barrier between the player and his or her abilities; the player will want to perform some action only to be consciously restrained by responsibility within the team. Danie diverged from that formulation, though, in his willingness to embrace the notion that the player's actions were necessarily contextual, a product of both the actions of the players around them and the demands of the game's own uncertainty. Rugby, Danie reminded me, requires spontaneous decisions. Time and space take shape simultaneously on the field, and the time it takes a player to recall and implement a set structure can result in lost space and missed opportunity. Danie had therefore decided that, in a moment of play, an intuitive move might (for all its spontaneity) be more effective than one a coach had imposed.

To teach his teams to react spontaneously in an unforeseeable moment in an unforeseeable future, Danie envisioned a square, one meter in size, surrounding each of his players. Describing what a player could do within that space—a space of "magic," we could call it—as the player's "skill set," the coach saw it as his responsibility to both expand the set of available skills and improve each facet. Rather than focusing on repetition to perfection as the Bulls' sessions generally do, Danie's practices emphasized creativity and inventiveness. That emphasis became most clearly articulated in one particular exercise, in which two offensive players responded to each other's instinctual reactions as they confronted a single defender. Rather than encouraging the offensive players to decide in advance which pattern to use to catch the defender unawares, Danie told them to answer to each other's improvised decisions. During the exercise, he urged players to employ whatever little individual tricks or feints they liked. If they wished to try something new, he asked them to do so—even if the effort resulted in failure. Danie advocated no overarching structure and taught neither offensive nor defensive patterns. Instead, he recognized and embraced the uncertainty of the game's inherent conditions, its magic.

Training players to build their performances from a series of open encounters may have satisfied Danie, but the Bulls coaches outright dismissed his strategy. Rejecting it as "not winning rugby," they observed that his approach seemed to increase both possibility and risk. In an environment with already small margins of error, they argued, coaches had to mobilize all available physiological, statistical, and economic resources to stack the deck in their favor. Danie, by contrast, questioned whether the metaphorical deck could ever be stacked. What other coaches saw as his strange unwillingness to control his players—that is, to impose on them an ideal aesthetic form—amounted, in his mind, to a recognition of the true state of things: no control was to be had in the first place. All Danie could do was prepare himself and his players to recognize magical moments and turn them to their advantage.

While the Bulls management tends to believe that the only way to ensure success is to preempt uncertainty with coordinated actions, Danie's perspective is notable because it accepts failure as a real—perhaps unavoidable—possibility. As a result, Danie and the players who share his mindset seem to regard spontaneous acts on the rugby field as situated, creative acts. Two young black players expressed that perspective clearly as they watched a particularly inventive and open match on television. After pronouncing excitedly how much he was enjoying the game, one explained that he liked the style because it "gives the players the freedom to do what they want." Just as he was enunciating the word *freedom*, his friend sat up on the couch and pounded a fist against his chest. "Freedom of speech, yo!" he quipped, interrupting his teammate's statement. In maneuvering from freedom in rugby to freedom of speech, the player in question did more than riff on his friend's word choice. More likely, his statement marked an earnest (and spontaneous) sentiment: he considered rugby a form of self-expression. Such a connection is possible only if one reimagines actions on the field as spontaneous reactions emerging from the body, emanating from (and producing) the author's embodied conception of self. Rather than trying to eliminate uncertainty, such creative logic depends on it. It conceives of sporting performance as contingent, uncertain, and dependent on context, rather than stable, structured, and abstract. In that conception, the athlete is an artist, not a master technician.

ANTI-APARTHEID RUGBY AND STRUGGLES OVER STYLE

Like the strategy adopted by the Bulls, the perspective based on creative logic bears the weight of social relations and history. Although Danie told me that he preferred his coaching style because it corresponded to the nature of rugby itself, many of the players and coaches who approach rugby in a similar way were once affiliated (or knew their fathers and uncles to be affiliated) with nonwhite leagues under apartheid. The politics of those leagues are articulated in detail in this book's fifth chapter. Here, it suffices to observe that teams in those leagues often played on run-down fields, in front of large and politically conscious crowds. Describing the situation in one region of the country, Abdurahman Booley writes, "After matches, players (leaving their rivalry behind on the field) would sit with administrators to strategise ways of overcoming the oppressive regime, particularly after the banning of people's organisations. In this way an easy transition was made from the sporting arena of the playing field into the political arena of the struggle against apartheid" (1998, 206). As Booley's statement suggests, anti-apartheid protests often transformed rugby participation into an unavoidably political act.

One coach's experience captured that transformation well. He told me that when he arrived for the first time at his boarding school in the Eastern Cape, all the senior boys asked him and the other new students if they supported the South African Rugby Union (SARU, the anti-apartheid rugby body) or "the Federation" (the South African Rugby Football Federation, a rugby organization sanctioned by the apartheid regime). If a new boy came from a Federation area, his peers labeled him a capitulator and intimidated him out of the boarding facility, forcing him to find housing elsewhere. More important than which group dominated that particular school is the fact that sides had to be taken at all. In such an environment, political neutrality was made impossible. To come into such a school and to play rugby meant that one had no choice but to locate oneself and the sport within a wider sociopolitical context, which that coach felt acutely. As he explained it, he had been a SARU boy by circumstance rather than choice. He had grown up in a SARU-dominated area and had no prior exposure to Federation teams or players. Only when he arrived at his boarding school and was, in his words, "sorted out" did he became politically aware. As he admitted, that awareness (and whatever conscious sense of "resistance" may have accompanied it) contained a strong coercive element. His family lived far from the Eastern Cape, and his parents could only afford to pay his school and hostel fees. Had he been forced out of the dormitory and made to seek housing in town, the price would have been too much for them to pay.

The aesthetic shape of that participation was no less of a concern. One of my informants presented that phenomenon to me in terms of a binary distinction. First there was the village club that affiliated itself with the apartheid regime. It practiced what he derisively called *stampkar* (bumper car) rugby, another term associated with *maak vas*. He told me that the team was unimaginative and conservative and relied on structure and violent domination to compete. Its players, he explained, "were *boere boeties* [little brothers to the Afrikaners]! They did what the whites did!" In opposition to the *stampkar* style stood the style adopted by the informant's team. It not only played a free and open style, taking risks and using the strengths of individual players to its advantage, but saw doing so as politically significant. The rugby field offered a stage on which the men on the team could perform their freedom.

Whether players became aware of the politics of rugby's magic by choice or coercion, parents have handed their perspectives down to their children. As a result, many young players of underrepresented and marginalized backgrounds recognize, in ways that few white South African players can, the extent to which the patterns they run, the tactical options imposed on them, and the manner in which they are coached draw their inspiration from the political logic of apartheid. Those legacies, furthermore, chafe most in moments of extreme uncertainty on the field, when a player feels that an organization's response to magic forbids him from expressing himself creatively.

It is not surprising, then, that players who feel strongly about their rights to self-expression and ones who are drawn (whether by professionalism or upbringing) toward *maak vas* often antagonize each other at the level of style. One young player who self-identified as coloured told me that his primary school taught him an open and expansive style of play that "clashed" with that of his white teammates several years later. What started as a difference in aesthetic preference grew, during each uncertain moment and game, into a full-blown conflict, as teammates continually operated at cross-purposes. Players inclined toward creativity took chances their more dominance-oriented teammates thought unwise and selfish, and dominance-oriented players ignored teammates' calls to pass and played it safe. The young player recounted what became of these tensions.

One guy just started yelling at us, all the coloureds. Then the coaches just walked away and told the captain to sort this out, and we came together and talked. Our captain is coloured, and this white guy, he says to my captain, "I don't want to be a part of this team." So I said to him, "Well you don't have to be a part of this team, just F-off," you know? And then he starts to cry, and then [another white player], he wants to hit our captain, and so there was a big fight.

Without a theory that accounts for rugby's uncertainty and the social conditions of its production, one might dismiss that incident as a conflict between South African racial stereotypes. Indeed, many at the player's school remembered it as such, describing the groups of players either as selfish thugs or as conservative racists, depending on their politics. Of course, such dismissal does little more than naturalize race in the bodies that rugby puts into motion. Such a conflict could similarly be blamed on the way that rugby's physical violence "raises emotions" or on the excessive emphasis that South African society places on rugby performance. Those explanations prove nearly as unsatisfactory, because they overlook that both physical violence and rugby's popularity result from the uncertainty the sport offers for display. Recognizing rugby's autonomy and its capacity to influence the historical and social sentiments that enter into and emerge from it clarifies how rugby's own conditions shaped that historically and politically overburdened conflict and the local conceptions of race with which it was associated, eventually drawing them into the present.

CONCLUSION

While people often assume that sports contain little in the way of true political possibility, conflicting responses to rugby's uncertainty suggest that if rugby cannot necessarily depict the content of political possibility, it can perhaps represent its form—its openness and deep contingency. The next moment in a rugby match and a moment five minutes to come are entirely unknowable and cannot be determined until the instant prior to their realization; each player, coach, and spectator must address the open possibilities using whatever social, historical, and economic resources they have at their disposal. Though it would be uncritical to claim that such representations of political possibility can bring us closer to a truly open political moment than can any other form of representation, rugby may well offer a different and often-overlooked lens through which to analyze how South Africans represent, debate, struggle over, and manipulate those magical moments as they come into existence.

The Bulls and players schooled in their tradition try to overcome that "crisis" situation and use it to demonstrate their capacity to shape the world to reflect an ideal image. Sometimes, for a few intoxicating moments, they are successful. On such occasions, the Bulls seem to be a step ahead of time itself, authoring events and controlling their own destiny. More often, though, the Bulls' patterns fall short of that ideal script. Rugby's magic intervenes, with physics inviting all manner of injuries and with small miscues doubling themselves again and again, until even the semblance of structure has collapsed. In such magical moments, the Bulls' coaches and players find that they have to contend with what Ian Hacking has called "the ancient and vestigial" presence of chance in the world (1990, 10). The Bulls may disavow that sort of chance when they turn to default, but history suggests that they willingly acknowledge it, in magic, when it is politically expedient to do so.

That residue of chance undergirds both the Bulls' magic and Adorno's aura, because both magic and aura constitute attempts to name (and thereby represent) the world's inherent uncertainty. For Hacking and the Bulls, that uncertainty makes for the deep contingency that becomes quantitatively knowable when human action seeks to control or eliminate it. The quality that, in Benjamin's formulation, first made itself known in religious ritual is precisely that which, in Adorno's work, exceeds the artist's plans during the making of art. That underlying similarity supports Hacking's suggestion that deep contingency found "its most subtle and many-layered expression" (1990, 10) in an artistic work, Stéphane Mallarmé's poem "Un coup de dés" ("A Throw of the Dice").

Mallarmé's answer to chance, notes Hacking (1990, 10), is not to try to tame it but to "transcend" it. We could describe Danie's coaching strategy as transcendence as well. Rather than acknowledging rugby's magic only in the moments when he has nowhere else to turn, Danie builds his team around it. He reasons that if rugby is nothing but a series of open encounters that enjoin urgent responses, his players must learn to react quicker, smarter, and more confidently. Though it might appear, at first glance, that Danie has simply replaced *maak vas* with a theory of performance that is built on players acting as isolated individuals, his emphasis on the openness of rugby itself indicates that he demands allegiance not to the player's own self (never mind to Danie as coach or to a final result) but to rugby and its inherent conditions. In that sense, his aesthetic theory is far more dogmatic than the one the Bulls employ. Neither he nor rugby are willing to compromise. The dogmatism of that strategy provides yet another reason why it resonated so widely among those players who sought to challenge and undermine the apartheid state. Not only does that aesthetic allow players to play with creativity, inventiveness, and a kind of freedom, but it also disdains the compromises that sustained that brutal regime. For Danie, there is no last-minute retreat to the safety of default. There is only magic, and the acute absence of any default form renders the politics of South Africa's historically dominant aesthetic uncomfortably transparent. Danie's aesthetic theory thus aligns particularly well with Adorno's own. As he writes in his essay on art and political commitment: "It is not the office of art to spotlight alternatives, but to resist *by its form alone* the course of the world, which permanently puts a pistol to men's heads" (2007a, 180; emphasis added).

CHAPTER 2

Sons and Commodities

Work, Play, and the Politics of Autonomy at the Margins of Professional Rugby

I once trailed behind a professional scout as he led a visiting high school rugby team on a tour of the Bulls' facilities. The touring school was one of South Africa's premier amateur programs, and the scout wanted to convince the players that any who decided to sign with his team would be well looked after. The boys seemed unimpressed, however. When the scout showed the team his state-of-the-art gym, dining, and training facilities, the players quietly compared them (unfavorably) to other professional setups they had encountered. To make matters worse for the scout, the visiting team's head coach had a dual appointment with one of the Bulls' main professional rivals and had no reason to encourage his most talented players to sign anywhere but with that rival. If the scout felt any sense of optimism when he distributed free hats to the players, on the grounds that he was "going to take every opportunity [he could find] to make you a Blue Bull," his remark when he gave the coach's parting gift ("You can use it for gardening clothes or something") suggested that he was somewhat less confident in his salesmanship.

The tour soon turned away from team partisanship and toward the realities of professional rugby. While the scout had tried to sell the players on the opulence of the Bulls life, the Bulls' youth coach offered a more sobering introduction to the life of a professional player: "We practice three times a day, five days a week. You're up for gym at 7 in the morning, you do speed and agility training at 11, and we run on the field as a team at 4 in the afternoon." He characterized rugby as a tough career for which being part of the Bulls would prepare them like nothing else: "The two-year foundation a Bulls junior contract gives you is unbelievable, but if you don't make it by the end of that process, you must have a backup plan. Don't stop your schoolwork. Rugby is a hard road. Don't be dumb." The coach concluded his lecture with a final cautionary tale. A former player of his had recently been tasked with giving a motivational speech to his teammates on South Africa's national team. Unsure of what to tell them, the player ultimately decided to remind his teammates about their days of school rugby. The coach reported, "He told me that guys began to cry just remembering how it felt to play in those kinds of games. In the professional era, money and fame have taken precedence. You don't play for your school anymore. Remember that feeling. At the junior professional level, we play just to play." The following speaker, a professional player and graduate of the school on tour, echoed the coach's sentiment: "I will never forget playing for our school. Those days will remain with me always. It's hard to keep up traditions in the professional era, but we do our best. We have Bible studies before training to bond the group together. All the things you learned in school are here. The Bulls will teach you to be a better man, a better father to your kid, a better husband to your wife. Wherever you choose to go, choose a place that will allow you to develop as a man and a player."

Together, the preceding remarks amounted to one of the more straight-forward descriptions of a career in professional rugby that I encountered during my fieldwork. From my perspective, too, they were not without legitimacy. The sport appears to have grown increasingly professionalized since its formal professionalization in 1995. Not only are young players starting to organize their lives around the prospect of professional rugby careers, but teams are busy drawing on new technologies to expand, develop, and rationalize their pool of available talent. Coaches who were once teachers or police officers or soldiers are now contracted members of companies and use video cameras and coding software to develop elaborate statistical profiles of their eligible players. Scouts and agents, two of South African rugby's subsidiary industries that have recently become ubiquitous, seek out high school players and attempt to win their signatures during rugby festivals that unfold, seemingly all season, on fields across the country. When the young players eventually sign professional contracts, they are thrust into webs of discipline, quantification, and drudgery for which no coach's warning could truly prepare them. The distinction between amateur high school rugby and professional rugby in South Africa could hardly appear more stark.

As we look closer at the aforementioned coach's warning, though, the line between amateur and professional rugby begins to blur. Contradictions emerge. The claim that professional rugby involves simply "playing to play," for example, is an odd one, given that "playing for the sake of play alone" is a phrase long associated with an amateur faith in the autotelic nature of sport. And what, furthermore, do we make of the facts that the coach of the visiting high school team is himself also a professional coach, and the scout is marketing the Bulls' professional setup to amateur players while they are still in school? Or that the coach's story, designed to demonstrate the difference between professionalism and amateurism in South African rugby, in fact depends on the complication of that very distinction, by a player using the love and camaraderie of amateurism—love and camaraderie that ought be dead or dying in professionalism—as a tool to motivate his professional teammates to perform better as professionals? Or that the coach and player who are explicitly venerating amateur rugby at the expense of its professional counterpart are themselves professionals?

The present chapter proposes that those apparent contradictions can be resolved if we do not view amateurism and professionalism as hierarchically ranked positions (with the former being "purer" than the latter or with the latter being more "rational" than the former) or even as two distinct categories. Rather, resolution requires regarding them as two competing yet fundamentally intertwined responses to the autonomy of rugby. Elaborating on the argument of chapter 1, I argue here that rugby in South Africa unfolds within an autonomous frame that has an important measure of conceptual stability. For rugby's brand of uncertainty to unfold, it must occur in certain places and not others, it must follow a specific temporal schedule, it must be moderated by an allegedly unbiased and all-knowing supervisor, and its players must accept the sport's arbitrary rules and regulations. A proper match should not take more than 80 minutes. If it does, it can only proceed under precise conditions. Players and officially deputized persons may enter and leave the field during a match, but spectators must avoid the field at all costs while the game is being played. Within the designated space of the field and the time of the match, players are permitted—by the world around them and by one another—to use violence and to pursue the ultimately arbitrary goal of carrying a rubber ball from one end of the field to another. Affirmed consistently through each performance, those conditions confirm the conceptual autonomy of rugby as a social phenomenon.

This chapter draws particular inspiration from the work of Theodor Adorno and Arthur Danto. As I showed in chapter 1, Adorno takes special interest in the formal politics of the autonomy of art. Articulating his position with particular clarity in his article "Commitment" (2007a), Adorno argues that the art object's autonomy is sufficient to actually disrupt the political messages and sentiments—both formulated in everyday experience—that artists attempt to insert in their work. Danto shares that perspective. In his work, he sees autonomy as an interpretive framework, which separates an art object from an identical object in everyday use; autonomy is what authorizes the identification of an object as "art," which, in turn, allows viewers to search for special significance in that object. For both theorists, conceptions of art and its significance that fail to pay heed to autonomy are inevitably incomplete, because they are unable to explain why an artwork is an artwork rather than something else (cf. Goehr 2008, 84–86). Also for both theorists, such failure comes with real-world consequences. To Adorno, it explains the shortcomings of "political" art; a slogan that appears as a work of art is not perceived by its audiences like a slogan shouted in the street. To Danto, the failure explains why philosophers and art critics struggle to condemn morally reprehensible artworks: they already accept those artworks as a particular kind of thing, often useless or harmless, to which their otherwise well-defined rules of morality do not, cannot, or should not apply (Danto 1988).

Elaborating on the work of those theorists of artistic autonomy, I show here that both professionals and amateurs acknowledge rugby's social autonomy, but only partially. Professional coaches and scouts claim to collapse rugby into the world of everyday economic relations. They want to make the sport a job like any other and to run their teams like businesses. The reduction of players to tokens of value that can be bought, sold, and traded is invariably undercut, though, by the players (on whose performances rugby ultimately relies) and by professional coaches and management (who abet their players by "binding the group together" to encourage strong performances). Avowed amateurs, among whom high school administrators figure prominently, argue, in contrast, that rugby ought to operate independently from economic and political concerns. They see worldly things as undermining not just the joy of playing rugby but the rituals and relationships associated with the sport. The dreams of those amateurs, like the longings of their professional antagonists, are also undercut. Rugby can never be fully detached from the world from which it emerges and to which it is fundamentally beholden. Families eager to benefit from the talents of their sons sign them to junior contracts, and some high school teams recruit young players with a tenacity that rivals their professional antagonists. In those respects, rugby in

South Africa has much in common not just with rugby in other places and times but with other sports and other apparently autonomous social forms.

If the discourses and practices of amateurism and professionalism continually cut across and meld with each other, it is worth considering why those categories need be used at all. As Adorno demonstrates so poignantly with his claim that poetry could no longer be justified after Auschwitz (Adorno 1967, 34; Ray 2005, 64), formal politics always unfold within an established political field. A rush to abandon categories like amateurism and professionalism—which frame rugby as autonomous or not—would necessarily overlook the social hierarchies and political inequalities mobilized when those categories are used. High school administrators thus have the luxury of recognizing and valorizing rugby's autonomy when it suits their vision for sport's role in a young man's education. They are permitted to disregard it, professional scouts suggest, when they want to achieve success. Similarly, professional teams consider their rugby to be a component of a broader economic system when they negotiate deals with players or substitute one player for another in a team's lineup, but they fall back on the language of loyalty when they need their players to perform together on the field. If players are not amenable to either of those contradictory approaches, they are easily replaced.

Autonomy, furthermore, has a history of its own. Placing the negotiations that occur in South African rugby in a broader historical context reveals that notional debates about autonomy are an extension of a much longer series of debates, dating back to Europe in the 18th and 19th centuries. The broader historical context shows that conceptions of amateurism and professionalism, like conceptions of autonomous art, are inherently political because they are based on implicit distinctions between people who are free to play and people who are obliged to work. Far from undermining the uniqueness of South African debates, the historical context makes that uniqueness yet more explicit because it requires us to recognize that the construction, policing, and deconstruction of autonomy has always occurred and still occurs against the backdrop of contextually specific forms of racial and class prejudice. This chapter shows that a consideration of the politics of rugby's social autonomy—of whether players are seen to be sons or commodities, as well as of the social positions against which that distinction is drawn—reveals much about the relevance of colonialism and apartheid in South Africa's contemporary moment. This chapter also shows that autonomy does more than efface the ways that politics and economic conditions inform the performance of rugby. Debates about amateurism and professionalism center ultimately on the appropriate boundaries of work and play, and situations occasionally arise when work and play appear side by side. In such situations, rugby becomes a potent performance of history. The shifting logics of amateurism and professionalism freeze temporarily, and the political conditions that sustain rugby's autonomy in South Africa—including both the unequal distribution of work and play and the historical framings of work and play that make such a distribution difficult to consider—come clearly and poignantly into view.

SELLING SOULS:
AMATEURISM AND CONTESTING RUGBY'S AUTONOMY

South Africa's professional rugby teams have depended on high schools to provide them with talented athletes since the dawn of formalized professionalism in 1995, but teams have recently begun to modify the terms of the arrangement to better suit their needs. Some teams now offer contracts to promising high school players on the condition that they relocate to a school, selected by the team, within that team's home region. That strategy has met significant opposition from a number of coaches and administrators who work at the high school level. In a 2011 article published in the Afrikaans newspaper *Rapport* and entitled "Schoolboys 'Raptured' by Blue Bulls Rugby" (Jansen 2011), a group of headmasters in Western Cape Province expressed concerns about what such a practice might do to the players involved. They said that those actions broke up families and damaged relationships between schools. In conversation with me, a high school rugby administrator used even more explicit language to describe the situation: "One of our players was bought by a team and [now attends a new high school]. I mean, he was bought for his rugby talent, not for what he was as a leader or whatever. They bought him for rugby. And he sold his soul and off he goes. And the dad is happy because he's getting payment for his boy, so that's just a different sort of slavery. That's slave trading!" The administrator added that to make a bad situation worse, a newly purchased player often takes a spot away from a player who had played rugby at the school since the day he enrolled. "We have no control over anybody that wants to come here of his own accord," he averred, but his stance of recruiting players from other schools was clear: "We don't scout players. [When one does scout players, one] cannot explain to a boy what loyalty means."

That administrator's precise terminology and its racial connotations are elaborated later in this chapter. For now, it suffices to observe that referents like "slavery" and "the selling of souls" help administrators conceptualize the implications that stem from the financial reimbursement of young rugby players. While young players may view professional rugby as a dream come true, administrators—like the coach whose warning opened this chapter—know better. Traditions and loyalties, they believe, fall to the wayside when money and fame take precedence. At that point, rugby becomes a hard, short, exhausting career.

When administrators and coaches posit a definitive separation between athletic performance and other forms of labor, they partake in a very old argument. A number of theorists of sport attribute the drawing of that distinction to the increased importance that sporting activities acquired in England's elite "public" schools during the middle of the 19th century. Those schools, which had long been devoted to the education of the English aristocracy, underwent an appreciable change as they began to incorporate the children of England's middle class. Shaped by dynamics located inside those schools (e.g., a new class of headmasters, a new curriculum that emphasized physical and moral as well as intellectual education, and new expectations for disciplined behavior) and by forces extending far beyond them (including the British Empire's need for administrators and the increasing prevalence of social Darwinist ideology), recreational games became a powerful and effective means to educate boys about how to act as men (Mangan 1981). In pursuit of that goal, headmasters imposed standards of play that sought to protect the conditions that facilitated social integration and character development (Huggins 2006, 17). Players were encouraged to win, but within the rules. The masculine ideal that developed in that context (which Mangan has identified as "athleticism") required players to strike a difficult balance between aggression and fairness (Huggins 2006, 17), and games exploded in popularity. "This unique educational ideal," McDevitt writes, "was promulgated throughout the British Empire; the belief that games created the hardy, quick-thinking men who would run the Empire, dominated elite education throughout the realm in the second half of the nineteenth century through World War II" (2000, 11).

That conception of masculinity required players to pursue their sporting activities in good faith, though, and money seemed to call that good faith into question. The reference to "loyalty" by the South African administrator quoted above, shows why that questioning might occur. In his perspective, schools should value players because they have watched them grow and develop. The player chooses to attend the school and invests time and energy in his rugby, and the school—demonstrating a reciprocal commitment to the player—rewards that investment with playing time, social prestige, and facilitates to aid his development. The administrator's remark about "explaining loyalty" suggests that the school models loyalty for its players, who learn to show loyalty to one another, in turn. Should a school decide to "buy" players, the cultivated and learned relationships are short-circuited or even undercut. Debt and obligation are produced by economic means (rather than by means of relationships cultivated over time), and the players in question never learn how to properly appreciate their teammates or the teams for which they play. Neither party feels loyalty to the other, and responsibilities are extracted in payments of cash. A retired professional player I knew described his abrupt transition to professional rugby in much that same way. When rugby professionalized, he said, he was astounded to discover that his prestigious provincial team was interested in paying him for his play. He recalled being so excited and honored that he would have paid the team to let him join. Once he signed the contract, though, he felt an immediate and pronounced change in his relationship with the team. He found, to his chagrin, that the team could make demands on his time whenever it liked. He was treated as an employee, rather than a player, and he performed for the business rather than for his own enjoyment. He felt, as he put it, "owned."

In the 19th century, advocates for amateurism, an ideology named after the Latin word for lover—*amator*—and premised on the value of "playing just to play," justified their distinction between sport and labor on similar grounds. Although many different arguments were used, a central component of all of them was the notion that "the element of compulsion inherent in professional sport by virtue of its occupational character would . . . decrease the enjoyment afforded to players by the activity itself" (Dunning and Sheard 2005, 138). Concern with compulsion, resonating above in the administrator's remark about the consequences of "buying" players and in the professional player's comment about feeling "owned," justified a range of fears, not only about competing for championships and paying players outright, but about offering players compensation for their time away from work (discussed further below) and about recruiting talented players to play rugby and "work" for local businesses. Theorists of amateurism found the charging of admission to matches dangerous as well, believing that players would feel a sense of obligation to perform for their paying customers rather than for themselves, their teammates, and their love of play itself. If a South African high schooler could "sell his soul" and enter into sporting slavery, English players might also become slaves of supporters who paid to watch them (cf. Holt 1989, 104).[1]

Sports were not the only sphere of life that had to be distinguished from economic concerns during the 19th century. Art did as well, for similar reasons. Regarding moral pedagogical value, advocates of amateurism were much less ambiguous about sports than advocates of aestheticism were about art, perhaps because of the deep ties that bound British sports to education and muscular Christianity (Putney 2001). Both positions nevertheless emerged from concerns about the deleterious consequences that money might carry for the self and its interests. Noël Carroll, for example, has argued that, in European aesthetic theory, the category of art (which once described the mastery of a particular skill) came to be associated with "a form of play, contemplative play free of social needs and interests," as artists performed "defensive maneuvers" to protect the sanctity of art against "vulgar materialism" (2008, 92–93). In the process, he adds, the valuelessness of art itself became a form of value. Art functioned as "a sign of conspicuous consumption—a badge of social distinction for the bourgeois consumer" (94). Raymond Williams, too, has observed that the European categories of art and the aesthetic came to be linked with particular artistic conditions. Though the body of works that could count as "literature" was never fixed or stable, he writes, "the specialization of 'literature' to 'creative' or 'imaginative' works . . . is in part a major affirmative response, in the name of an essentially general human 'creativity,' to the socially repressive and intellectually mechanical forms of a new social order: that of capitalism and especially industrial capitalism" (1977, 49–50). Having been recognized within those conditions, Williams concludes, resultant artistic works could be "seen as separate from the dominant bourgeois productive norm: the making of commodities" (153).

For the theorists just quoted, "autonomy" (i.e., art's apparent freedom from the economic and political conditions of the world that surrounded it) was not a quality inherent in the category of art itself. Indeed, as Theodor Adorno reminds us in "Commitment," autonomy could never be inherent to art. Proponents of art's full autonomy, he observes, forget that no artwork is created out of nothingness. Its materials, its representations, and even the imagination of the artist emerge from the social world that the completed artwork is supposed to have escaped. "There is no material content, no formal category of artistic creation, however mysteriously transmitted and itself unaware of the process," Adorno writes, "which did not originate in the empirical reality from which it breaks free. It is this which constitutes the true relation of art to reality, whose elements are regrouped by its formal laws" (2007a, 190). Artists may believe that their artworks are so fully detached from the world that those works cannot carry political content of any kind, but that belief is a product of a selective vision that confuses the social reality of art's autonomy for full autonomy. In doing so, it overlooks, at the very least, the conditions of artistic production, consumption, and circulation in which the artist works. In other words, the theory of art's full autonomy does not prompt artists to realize that they are free of all sociopolitical obligations as much as it invites them to partake in an obtuse form of obligation that conceals the political position they have chosen to adopt.

Jannie, the professional scout accused of "rapturing" young South African rugby players, seemed to share that view. He was adamant that the coaches and headmasters at high schools with top amateur teams were, at best, inconsistent in their commitment to the values they espoused. Those schools hire professional coaches and trainers to put their players through rigorous training sessions, he observed, and they play intense schedules that supplement local derbies with matches in distant locales. Some matches require hours of travel and days away from the classroom. South African high schools, seen from this perspective, do not protect the sanctity of sport and fear its demise as much as they use the language of sanctity, purity, and loyalty to artificially delineate the category of sport from social practices that are compelled, by history and circumstance, to disclose their underlying economic motive.

Somewhat like Adorno, who argued that artworks would actually reject an artist's attempt to make them fully autonomous and "throw [those 'intellectual creations'] back on themselves" (2007a, 190), Jannie believed that hypocritical amateurs were doomed to fail. High schools and professional teams that accept that the future of rugby lay in economic investment would leave behind schools with anxieties about "loyalty" and "enslavement." While other teams continued to stagger under the weight of amateurism and its artificially imposed obligations, Jannie felt more than justified in sloughing off that burden in order to keep his team on the forefront of the race to competitive success. Instead of signing and relocating a single high school player here and there, as most professional teams did, Jannie moved 17 players simultaneously. That aggressive strategy, he supposed, had prompted the negative article about him in *Rapport*, but Jannie interpreted the aggrieved reactions in terms of his own understanding of amateur hypocrisy: they were upset with him, he told me, because he was beating them at their own game.

CUTTING TAILS: PROFESSIONALISM AND THE ERASURE OF
RUGBY'S AUTONOMY

For Jannie, the task facing rugby administrators in South Africa was simple: abandon autonomy and turn rugby into a profitable industry as swiftly and thoroughly as possible. Other professional coaches and administrators made similar claims about amateur rugby and offered remedies that mirrored that perspective. Two longtime Bulls employees told me independently that they responded to the advent of rugby's professional era with a systematic reevaluation of their institutional practices. One manager said that he woke up "the morning after the 1995 Rugby World Cup and suddenly everyone was professional."[2] He immediately met with the head coach and gave him an ultimatum: he could work or he could coach the team, but he could no longer do both. The players were made to choose as well, and he insisted that they be ready to train all day, watch their diets, and attend video sessions. Activities that had once been optional or negotiable became explicitly mandatory, and that manager began to devise the team's first weekly schedule so that he could better coordinate practice sessions and workout regimes. Another administrator applied the same model to the boardroom and explicitly credited the success of the Bulls in the professional era to the team's rapid transition to professionalism. The Bulls, he said, sold 50 percent of their shares to South African Investments, Ltd. (SAIL), a sports and entertainment firm that was qualified to manage the risks and structural changes that came with running a rugby team as a business. Other teams that were slower to adapt, he said, discovered only belatedly what the Bulls had suspected all along: that the self-righteous rugby men of the amateur era were ill-prepared to manage professional teams and the influx of cash that professionalism brought with it.

Those professional men dismissed the claims of their amateur colleagues as disingenuous and prone to failure, yet they believed that amateur claims about rugby's autonomy produced concrete effects, harming teams and their budgets and significantly impacting the perceptions of young players. In the opinion of many professional coaches and scouts, amateur ideologues convince players that rugby really *is* autonomous, and that flawed perspective prevents players from readying themselves for the realities of a professional career. One administrator told me that while young players tend to believe that their first junior contract signals the beginning of a long partnership with a professional team, established senior players hold on to their designated positions for years, barring retirement, relocation, or injury. If a new player finds himself in the unfortunate situation of playing behind an especially talented player, he might never even see the field. Although a team fields 23 players on a given game day, the true number of available roster spots will be fewer than many young players imagine. Young professional players also tend not to realize that professional teams sometimes prefer hiring a proven high-level player from another team over offering a senior contract to an unproven junior one. Even if a young player finds himself in a nearly optimal scenario and moves swiftly up the junior hierarchy to play with senior-level teammates when he is relatively fresh out of high school, the tables can quickly turn on him if an accomplished player on another team suddenly becomes available. In such a situation, a once-promising star-to-be quickly becomes a backup option and then, eventually, entirely replaceable. The administrator who explained these points to me was candid about the extent of his concern for young players and their struggles. He said, "I don't give a damn about them. I just want to win trophies with them."

Jannie was characteristically upfront about his concerns about amateur administrators and the effects that their stories had on young players. "The problem," he explained to me, "is that the old generation tells the guys that the game should be for fun, and the [young players], they see rugby as a cocoon. Then, all of a sudden, they have to go and compete against [veteran stars on professional teams]. When they get to professional rugby, they're competing not against their school but against the whole country. Some guys just don't understand it." He added, "A team must have depth. Players need to be prepared to compete." A colleague of Jannie's agreed, complaining that young players "don't understand how [professional rugby] works. When you are [signed to a junior professional contract at] 18 years old, you compete against other 18-year-olds. When you are 20 years old, you compete against 18-, 19-, and 20-year-olds. When you are a senior player, you are up against guys who are 5 and 10 years older than you. You have to work, and these guys aren't necessarily prepared to do that. If you can't beat out a [talented senior player] at your position, you must hang up your [rugby boots]. Become a businessman or something."

Professional coaches and administrators do not just lament the "cocoon" of autonomy among themselves. As the introduction of this chapter demonstrated, coaches sometimes try to dispel South African rugby's mystique of amateurism by speaking directly and forcefully to players. One longtime professional coach I knew likened the process of bringing a young player into professional rugby to "cutting the tail off a puppy." If you cut the tail slowly, he said, the dog will die from the pain, but if you do it quickly, it is all over. He applied that rule across the structures of his team—the offices of the head of contracting, the physiotherapist's table, the gym, the video session room, and the field on game day. Both the phrase and its systematic deployment implied that the transition to professionalism must be swift and complete or it will never occur at all. Another coach I knew outlined the situation to his team in no uncertain terms. The team had been playing poorly, and he could not afford to flatter them. Their performance the previous week, he told them during a video session, simply had not been good enough. "It's a tough world we live in," he said. "If things don't go well for us, the bosses will say 'cheers' and find people they think will do the job." That observation came from his own experience: "One time, we were playing a team and they [immediately scored easily on us]. It was two minutes into the game, but it haunted us. The coach dropped me then. He was right to do it, but it hurt. He told me, 'We think [two other players] are the way forward.' I knew it was coming but it still wasn't easy." He told the assembled players, "You all deserve a chance, but the way we're performing isn't doing any of our careers any favors. I have to be honest with you: this ship is sinking at the moment, and they will buy someone else. There are no loyalties in this company." The coach continued, "It seems fine to lose a game or two, but a few bad ones will haunt you for your career." He knew all about the psychological and social costs that come with holding on to amateur dreams in a professional reality, and he was not about to let them suffer the same fate as he had experienced during his own career.

From a professionalized perspective, perhaps the best way to avoid the problems produced by amateur dreams would be to prevent those dreams from developing in the first place. For his part, Jannie planned to respond to the vacillations of high school administrators by recruiting players at increasingly young ages. Although, at the time of my fieldwork, he had not yet signed a player who was younger than 14 years old, he told me that he expected it would not be long before teams began to contract players from primary school and train them in dedicated academies, as European professional football teams do. Considered within the context of Jannie's other statements as well as those of his colleagues, the appeal of that vision for South Africa's rugby future stems from the fact that it promises to "cut the tails" of players so early that they know no other life. In effect, teams will rear their own competitors from childhood. High school headmasters and administrators may continue to use terms like "selling souls" to express their discontent with this

Fig. 1. A mock press conference backdrop, assembled at a rugby festival for seven-year-olds. (Photograph by the author.)

vision of rugby's future, but Jannie seems to have a ready response: if there was ever a time when rugby was independent of economic concerns, that time has passed. Even the contradictory behavior of the "amateurs" suggests that rugby is now a fully professionalized activity. Rugby is changing quickly, and those who want to play it at a high level must acknowledge the situation or risk becoming obsolete.

TREATING SONS AS COMMODITIES: FINDING POLITICS IN RUGBY'S AUTONOMY

While Jannie and his colleagues seem able to dismiss amateur critiques without much effort, the opinion of one professional coach I knew would perhaps prove more difficult to explain away. This coach, Charl, made his stance on the matter of "cutting tails" clear during a vigorous debate with one of his colleagues. The colleague in question had decided to replace a player on his team with that player's younger brother, and he defended his choice on the grounds that both brothers played the same position. In that coach's opinion, the younger player was better suited to the team's goals than his sibling. In the present parlance of professional rugby, it was in the team's best interest to "fast-track" the younger brother by putting him on a team that competes against more physically developed players. He would learn to play a faster, more competitive game at a younger age and would thus be prepared for success later in his career. Conceding that the involvement of the older brother made the decision more difficult, the coach nevertheless asserted that it made sense to replace him no matter who his replacement happened to be. The coach's perspective was, in short, identical to that of Jannie and the men cited above: players should understand that they play at the whim of the team that contracts them. If the team decided to offer contracts to a pair of brothers who then signed their contracts, the team was free to play them how and when it chose. From the team's perspective, the bond between the brothers should be no more relevant to its process of player selection than concerns about "rapturing" were to the team's strategies of recruitment. If swapping brothers put the better player on the field, the brothers should be swapped.

Charl disagreed vehemently with that logic. He rejected the "fast-tracking" model. Even if the younger brother was better than his older sibling in some respects, he said, it made more sense to let him "mature" alongside his younger teammates. That process of maturation concerned the player's development as both an athlete and a person. As Charl explained to me in a different moment, young rugby players need space and latitude to exper-iment and make mistakes if they are going to grow. The team hoped that the crucible of high-level rugby would harden the young player quickly, but Charl feared that it would burn the player up. Charl also did not believe that the elder brother would be easily replaced. In responding to his colleague, Charl drew an explicit parallel between the well-being of the brothers and that of the team as a whole, predicting that the coach's reasonable decision would bring dire consequences for all involved: "Neither brother trusts us now. You win finals with a family, and we caused a conflict within their fam-ily. Their literal family!" While another professional coach might believe that "giving a damn" about a player would prevent him from "winning trophies" with that player, Charl's remarks suggest that a team must learn to care about their players, because a neglected team will be a team that loses. If players are scared or disenfranchised or feel as though their jobs are at risk, their perfor-mances will become artless and flat.

The everyday practices of the professional teams I spent time with sug-gest that there may be some truth to Charl's perspective. Professional coaches and administrators, I found, generally appeared to maintain businesslike attitudes in boardrooms, selection meetings, and contract negotiations, but references to reciprocal obligations that look something like loyalty tended to emerge when teams prepared to take the field. During one halftime speech I heard, for example, a coach reminded his team that he and the coaching staff were "going to learn a lot about which players performed in the remainder of the match." In doing so, he intimated the contingency of a player's future selection—and, by extension, his rugby career—on the next half of rugby that he played. In nearly the same breath, though, the coach tempered his thinly veiled threat with references to each player's pride in himself and responsibility to the others. Such schoolyard rugby language produced the contradictions articulated at the start of this chapter: it could make professional players long for a more meaningful past and prepare them for a match at the same time. While Jannie and his colleagues dismiss high school headmasters and administrators who believe too fervently in amateurism, the sudden appearance of an amateur ideology during a professional team's halftime speeches and pregame motivation sessions suggests that amateurism is not so easily effaced. One scout I knew acknowledged the salience of such language in a comment that may have been intended to put the final nail in amateurism's coffin but inadvertently hinted at professional rugby's reliance on the corpse concealed therein. "The love of the game still exists," he said, "but now it's just a thing to get professional players into work each day."

Although that scout described "the love of the game" as something of a useful remnant of rugby's past significance, Charl's perspective offers a more robust interpretation. For him, teams cannot afford to reduce players to exchangeable quanta of economic value. He feels that way not because he believes that rugby should be independent of all economic considerations or that money undermines the relationships between players and teams but because he believes that a successful rugby team depends on the creativity of its players. Like advocates of artistic autonomy, Charl believes that creativity emerges from within the players themselves. Unlike those advocates, though, he thinks that creativity can be marshaled toward economic ends if a player's social being is acknowledged.[3] Charl's debate with his colleague about the nature of the team as a "family" demonstrates that view, as does an exchange Charl had with me. We were driving together one evening, and he, ever busy, used the moment of relative quiet to speak with a player's parent on the phone. He assured the man that the player was still in the team's plans. The player had not played much lately because he was suffering from nagging injuries, and the team wanted him to take it easy until the medical staff was certain that he would be able to perform up to his potential. When Charl hung up the phone, he snorted and shook his head. "You've gotta treat these guys like your sons, not like flippin' commodities!" he told me, gripping the steering wheel tightly. With that, he turned his attention away from the player's father and toward the rugby industry as a whole: "We're not in a commodity business, we're in a human business. You can't talk up a player; you must coach him. They're all kids! All of them. They need mentors!"

If Adorno's "Commitment" places Jannie's critique of amateurism in a broader theoretical context, demonstrating that amateur administrators are actually theorists of autonomy who deny rugby's politics in their commitment to autotelic sport, it does the same for Charl's critique of professionalism's dominant logic. Adorno writes that proponents of politically committed art, such as Jean-Paul Sartre or Bertolt Brecht, take on for themselves a superficially laudable but ultimately impossible task. On the one hand, political artists want to persuade their audiences of the urgency of their causes. To do so effectively, they must break down the barrier that has historically separated art objects from everyday objects. Art must be "of the world" if it is to be taken seriously. On the other hand, the same artists can become so dedicated to their political projects that they forget to recognize how artistic autonomy distorts the statements that pass into it. "Even an ordinary 'was' in a report of something that was not," Adorno notes, "acquires a new formal quality from the fact that it was not so" (2007a, 178). While Jannie believes that amateurism will ultimately culminate in performative failure, Charl warns the same about a thoroughgoing adherence to an economic logic. Professional coaches and administrators want to make rugby like any other form of work until they find themselves in the tense moments when rugby's performances are particularly close at hand. At that point, they suddenly recognize that their players are social beings, rather than rugby-playing bodies that coaches and administrators can manipulate in the clubhouse, trade for one another, and relocate to schools of teams' choosing.

For Adorno and Charl, there is an inescapable minimal difference between autonomous objects and objects of other kinds. The two men may seem to theorize those differences in distinct ways, with Adorno thinking in terms of formal qualities and Charl in terms of creativity, but that theoretical distinction fades away when we remember that Charl's definition of creativity is contingent on a player's capacity to perform a unique and arbitrary set of athletic tasks. As Andrew Edgar (2013) has argued, sporting actions require participants and observers to understand those actions as something other than they appear to be. A moment of contact must be understood as a rugby "tackle," rather than an assault, for the game to exist at all. In that respect, Edgar builds on Arthur Danto's famous conception of the "artworld." Faced with Andy Warhol's *Brillo Box*—which looked almost exactly like a "mere real" (1981) Brillo box but had undoubted status as a work of art—Danto observed that it could only exist as a work of art because a mid-20th-century Euro-American "artworld" had cleared the conceptual ground for it to be interpreted as such (1964; 1992, 37).

Although Danto sometimes expresses skepticism about the possibility that sporting actions can be performed in such a way as to mean something beyond themselves (2013, 51), his *Transfiguration of the Commonplace* suggests that productive commonalities exist between art and a range of other activities that appear, in many circumstances, to exhibit a kind of autonomy from everyday life. Apropos of the argument in chapter 1, Danto observes, "There are close conceptual ties between games, magic, dreams, and art, all of which fall outside the world and stand at just the same kind of distance from it which we are trying to analyze" (1981, 18).[4] Perhaps elaborating on that point, Edgar (2013, 37) posits that participants in sports must be aware that they are participating in a "sportworld" that makes their tackles legible as such. I explore some of the implications of that legibility in the chapter 3 of the present study. Here, it is sufficient to note that the existence of a "sportworld" encourages spectators and participants to draw a small but significant conceptual distinction between sporting and nonsporting actions, a distinction that remains in place whether teams pay their players or not.

"SISEBENZA": AUTONOMY AND THE PERFORMANCE OF SOUTH AFRICAN HISTORY

Several moments in my fieldwork brought into clear view the margins of South Africa's rugby "sportworld" and the political and social context that made that "sportworld" thinkable in the first place. On one occasion, I stood at the edge of a field and watched a team of high school players make its way through a rigorous preseason workout. It required the players to do pull-ups on a bar that was situated next to a shaded nook where the school's groundskeepers took their breaks. For a few minutes, the boys (almost all of whom were white) exercised in the sun, hoisting themselves in the air and groaning, and four or five groundskeepers (all of whom were black) stood together and watched them with mild interest. During the exercise, one of the groundskeepers shouted a word of encouragement to the boys. The boys fought with their various exercises for a moment longer until they finished, at which point one of them turned to the groundskeepers and told them, in isiXhosa, "Sisebenza" (We are working).

To elucidate the broad political significance of that player's offhand remark, it is necessary to situate it within a context marked not only by autonomy and its formal politics but also by the framings of race and class around and against which that autonomy was theorized. To amateurs and professionals who sit at the center of South Africa's rugby circles, the meaning of the remark would seem relatively clear. A proponent of "cutting tails," for example, might laud the player for the seriousness of his approach to rugby. Professional teams in South Africa are recruiting players at younger and younger ages, high school fitness coaches can report about a player's work ethic to professional scouts, and there are occasionally situations—like the one that opened this chapter—in which a player's high school coach is a junior professional coach. At a time when South Africa's rugby is growing increasingly professionalized and when the boundary between contracted player and high school student is increasingly fluid, it could make sense for a player to claim his exercise as work. The player's headmaster might lament (as I heard some people do) that rugby is now approached with such seriousness that players lack the opportunity to pursue other extracurricular activities that could help them become well-rounded human beings. Jannie would perhaps respond that the boy was "working" because his school had sponsored the preseason program, which it did because it wanted to offer players a rigorous sporting experience and, ultimately, to remain competitive in South Africa's increasingly professionalized rugby landscape. Even if the player had not yet signed a professional contract and even if a fitness session is not identical to a live rugby match, the player's statement about the meaning of his movements seems to shed inadvertent light on the contradictions that lie at the heart of amateur high school rugby in South Africa.

The player may have lent credence to Jannie's critical perspective, but he also exposed much deeper contradictions. As Williams and Carroll demonstrated, the dominant European conception of the autonomous artist and the autonomous objects they created developed in conjunction with the formation of a middle-class subjectivity. The formation was a component in a double move, in which the articulation of that subjectivity was made to appear natural and inevitable by means of a simultaneous disavowal of political interest. For Carroll (2008, 92), the disavowal targeted all forms of interest, whether political, economic, or ethical. For Williams, art's autonomy served as a creative refuge from the oppressive conditions of industrial capitalism. Terry Eagleton, working in the same tradition as Williams, has theorized the construction of autonomy more explicitly: "The idea of autonomy—of a mode of being which is entirely self-regulating and self-determining—provides the middle class with just the ideological model of subjectivity it requires for its material operations" (1990, 9).

Seen in that context, the player's remark calls attention not just to the work of rugby (as Jannie would have liked) but to the conditions that allowed the player's work to manifest as play. In that respect, the player's statement—like those of 21st-century amateur administrators who spoke of "slavery" and the "selling of souls" to defend rugby's autonomy in South Africa—found unexpected echoes in the past. Working-class players in late 19th-century England seemed to have been acutely aware of the politics of autonomous sport. Eager for remuneration for the time (and energy) that serious sporting participation required of them, those players contested amateurism from the moment it was espoused. They demanded that England's Rugby Football Union recognize and legitimize payments to players for time spent playing rugby rather than working (called "broken-time" payments). In a letter to the editor of the *Times* in September 1897, a man who signed off as "One of Many Who Love 'The Making of English Men'" described the struggles of working-class rugby players.

> The players who are chosen for away matches, sometimes played at long distances from home, have to leave work early or perhaps are unable to go to work at all, and thereby forfeit a portion of their wages, so the wife and family have to suffer from the lessened wage; and the player has to make a double journey and to play a fatiguing game in a semi-fasting state, unless he spends on himself what should be spent for the whole family. As regards the latter condition it may be argued that clubs have power to provide refreshments for teams. No, Sir, all clubs have the will to do so, but unfortunately all have not the power, not being rich enough to do more than supply a "plain tea," that is to say a tea without meat, after the game is over, and in some cases they are not able to do even that; they might, however, be able to help with a small payment a few of the players most in need of it. (One of Many Who Love "The Making of English Men" 1897)

Remuneration requests laid bare the political construction of rugby's autonomy, in several ways. First, by requesting broken-time payments, players emphasized that they had families to care for and jobs to keep. Far from being notional "self-regulating and self-determining" subjects (Eagleton 1990, 9), they presented themselves as social beings with obligations and responsibilities. Second, working-class players found nothing immoral about playing rugby for cash. Collins writes, "Working-class men . . . brought with them [to rugby] a range of cultural practices which were based on the necessity of selling their labour power in whichever way was the most lucrative, including the utilisation of sporting prowess." He adds, "A greater clash with the ideals of public school sport could not be imagined, especially for those who sought to utilize football as a medium for moral improvement" (1998, 34–35; cf. Pope 1996). That approach, which seemed so commonsensical to poorer players, implicitly challenged the amateur vision of sport as a form of labor that should only be pursued as an end in itself. Finally, the requests for payment and compromise laid bare the gulf between amateur ideology and social reality. Some players, Dunning and Sheard write, were already receiving a range of different kinds of payment, so stigmatized that all forms of financial remuneration were shrouded by a "conspiracy of silence" (2005, 129).

To argue that the work of rugby is shaped by the intersections of class, history, and power is not to say that sports ought not be played for cash. For such a claim to be valid, one would have to visualize a space for sports that was fully independent of other forms of work. Theorists of amateurism attempted to make that claim, and as this chapter has shown, an unexpected alliance of art theorists and advocates for professionalism recognizes that the claim does not escape the burden of money (cf. Walsh and Giulianotti 2007). It merely pretends that such burden does not exist. Peter Donnelly has demonstrated the same perspective with particular poignancy. In a 1997 essay, he suggests that important parallels may exist between the strain that youthful bodies experience in highly competitive youth sports and that which they encounter in child labor. His argument is extremely and intentionally provocative. As Donnelly notes, drawing such comparisons highlights both the privileges associated with highly competitive youth sports and the sheer difficulty of thinking of sport as work (1997, 392–33; cf. J. Ryan 2000, 11). Danto, Adorno, and Edgar help explain why the latter difficulty exists: to "think" of autonomous activities as work involves breaking down the historically produced (and therefore political) conceptual barriers that delineate autonomy in the first place.[5]

Those conceptual barriers were never constituted around class alone, as genealogies of autonomous art make clear. European art theorists "discovered" the autonomy of their art objects by means of a strategic effacement of race as well as class. For the purposes of the present argument, the most relevant consideration of that process is almost certainly the analysis by Elizabeth Williams of a 1928 exhibition of pre-Columbian art at the Louvre. As Williams notes in her recounting of the historical backdrop for the exhibition, 19th-century curators were uncertain about how to categorize "ethnographic collections." Did they belong in museums of natural history or in museums of art? One curator in 1831, E. F. Jomard, determined that "there is no question of beauty in these arts . . . but only of objects *considered in relation to practical and social utility*" (Williams 1988, 147; emphasis added). Although Williams seeks to recuperate the art value of those objects, it is sufficient to note here the work that Jomard is able to accomplish with his rejection of "utility"; both pre-Columbian art and European objects of everyday significance are excluded from his category of autonomy. In other words, both race and class politics were both artfully concealed, if for different reasons.

Whether non-European objects were regarded as too useful to be beautiful, as curiosities that required scientific analysis and collection (Fabian 2004; Price 2001), or as artistic creations that lacked style or history, available as sources of inspiration for European artists who wanted to dismantle and reconstruct European modernism (Gikandi 2006), the autonomous art object was theorized into being in Europe as part of a dialectical process, in conversation with assessments of the aesthetic value of objects produced by other people, elsewhere in the world. Those judgments helped to constitute— explicitly or implicitly—the grounds on which European art was to be valued. Once value had been found and once autonomy was identified as its source, the art object appeared to stand for itself, independent of all ties to social conditions. It thereby strategically effaced the very processes by which and the political conditions in which it became autonomous and valuable.

Discourses about "slavery," mobilized by amateur administrators in the interest of protecting the "sanctity" of high school rugby in South Africa, serve as potent reminders of the deep and fundamental presence of theories of race in sporting autonomy as well. The concept of slavery as administrators employ it does not merely point toward anxieties about class identity, cash, moral obligation, and labor; nor, as Kopytoff puts it, does it serve only as a ready metaphor "when commoditization threatens to invade" spheres of human life thought to be beyond price and market (1986, 84). Slavery and enslaved persons were and continue to be mobilized in the service of placing sport into that very sphere of human life, beyond price and market. Because the perceived autonomy of sport is, as shown above, intertwined historically with the perceived autonomy of those who play it, that rhetorical move should be read as mobilizing slavery and blackness as a means to valorize a specifically white and European bourgeois subject (cf. Trouillot 1995, 76–77; Stoler 1995, 123–24).[6] Theories of non-European "primitivism" add to that reading, in that, as Carrington has artfully shown, the construction of a primitive Other (as raw, simple, emotional, and childlike) cleared the space for European men to recognize themselves as engaged in physical activities that they believed could demonstrate their rationality, their modernity and civilization, their maturity, and their restraint (2010, 41–46).[7] Once properly educated, European men felt justified in carrying sports to colonies and using them as a means to "civilize" and "discipline" colonized persons in their image (Alegi 2010; R. Foster 2006; Holt 1989; Stoddart 1988). That colonized groups fell invariably short of colonizer expectations is unsurprising, given (1) that they played sports for their own reasons and (2) that the very purpose of sports education—and its underlying values and principles—was premised on a racist misreading of those groups, their identities, and their capabilities. In the eyes of their instructors, they could never fully learn the "lessons," because they were not already wealthy, white, and male.

The result was a dominant model of sporting autonomy that wove together class exclusion, gendered power, and racial superiority. In South Africa, that colonial model came to be ratified, during apartheid, by violence and systematic legislated racism—cloaked in a guise of established "custom"—that degraded nonwhite sporting participants and denied them the resources and opportunities necessary for success and recognition. Thus, when apartheid administrators such as Eben Dönges and Piet Koornhof insisted (in 1956 and 1975, respectively) that sporting codes were organized autonomously, with minimal government interference (Rademeyer 2014), their approach absolved the state of responsibility for both its explicit interventions in sport (described throughout this book) and its interventions via its specious notion of "custom" and the racist policies extending from that notion. Anything that challenged the primacy of apartheid "custom"—whether a boycott, a protest, or the inclusion of a nonwhite player on a foreign team slated to play white teams in South Africa—was framed in official discourse as an unwelcome political intervention in apolitical, autonomous sport. In explicit rejection of that position, the South African Council of Sport argued that there could be "no normal sport in an abnormal society"—that the racism of apartheid infused sports in South Africa at a fundamental constitutive level, just as it infused every other aspect of South African social life.

Even today, underrepresented players and coaches in South Africa are well positioned to recognize the political conditions that undergird rugby's autonomy. One former player who identified as black told me that rugby was an "expensive" sport in South Africa. The "expense" he referenced, he explained, was not the cost of equipment or the maintenance of fields but the

fact that the institutions controlling rugby's highest levels are extremely difficult for most black South Africans to access. Like many of his colleagues, that
player recognized the tightness of the margins for error in competitive rugby.
If a player wants to win a professional contract, he must play serious rugby
from a relatively young age. Like the high school player referenced above,
he should attend preseason training sessions. He must also travel with his
team to rugby festivals in distant cities and even invest in a personal fitness
instructor or coach who can privately teach him the skills associated with his
position of choice. Each of those efforts comes with a cost, perhaps the heavi-
est being the cost of attending one of the country's premier rugby-playing
high schools. As I show in chapter 4, those schools tend to be some of the
most expensive in the country.[8] When amateur administrators lament the
damage done to players who are "bought," "sold," and "enslaved," they are also
lamenting the harm done to a conception of sporting autonomy that allows
administrators to conceal the same inequalities of race and class that they use
to control young players and the work their bodies do for the schools that
recruit them.

Marginalized and underrepresented players find that structure replicated
in professional rugby, albeit in an inverted form. While amateur administrators overlook the expense of their school and insist that they accept any
player who wants to attend, professional administrators and coaches say that
they will hire and play any player—no matter their background—who is good
enough to deserve a contract. Because professional rugby is an outgrowth of
South Africa's high school system, its cutthroat and "meritocratic" approach
to the sport is no less marked by the raced and classed "expense" than its
amateur counterpart. While amateur administrators condemn players (and
their families) for profiting off their sporting abilities, thereby strategically
ignoring the hardships players might face off the field, some black, African,
and coloured professional players believe that professional teams are willing to turn their disadvantages against them too. Several current and former
players shared with me their belief, for example, that South African teams
pay nonwhite players less money than their white teammates, based on the
assumption that nonwhite players are bound to be poorer and, as such, more
willing to compromise on their salaries because they are desperate for the
opportunity. Whether or not those suspicions are true, they indicate where
players locate themselves within professional organizations. Where professional administrators and scouts see a fair and fundamentally apolitical economic logic, players see a system that is deeply political because it mobilizes

them selectively on the basis of their historically constituted positionalities as raced and classed subjects.

When we keep those perspectives and the politics of artistic autonomy in mind, the real stake of the aforementioned player's "Sisebenza" comes into view. That player may have sought merely to point out the seriousness of his exercise, but his remark occurred in a context thoroughly structured by race and class inequality. His exercise was expensive. As such, it was exclusive, limited to only those South Africans (most of whom were white and wealthy) who could afford to perform it in that place and at that time. Moreover, his exercise was exhaustion for its own sake. It was a form of work that had been constituted as autonomous, formally conceived in opposition to the very sort of manual labor that the adjacent men performed to make their livings. His remark, then, was not just elitist but also replicated a process—one that reemerges with some regularity in the social histories of sporting and artistic forms[9]—of strategic effacement. The young player acknowledged the labor of the neighboring groundskeepers, claimed that labor for himself to emphasize how hard he was working, and erased its ties to its source.

Another situation, on a different day but on the same grassy patch, further underlines the salience of that reading of effacement. In two photographs (fig. 2), a trainer, not visible in either image, is putting a group of athletes through a series of exercises. In one of the elements of the routine, the athletes exhausted their upper arms and shoulders by repeatedly smashing heavy sledgehammers against a large rubber tire. That exercise is visible in the left photo, halfway concealed by a small tree. In the foreground, prominently featured in the photo on the right, a man stood neck-deep in a hole, hacking away at a piece of PVC piping. A few moments after the photos were taken, the boys finished their exercises and left the field. A few moments after that, I heard the same, dull thud of hammer against tire. It wasn't a player finishing an exercise; it was one of the groundskeepers. He smacked the hammer against the tire four or five times before he set it down and walked away.

When considered in the context of this chapter as a whole, the sound of the hammer bonking ineffectually off the rubber tire served as a brief but poignant sonic reminder of the unproductivity of the boys' labor. While that remark of "Sisebenza" from the player registers as a concealment of differences in raced and classed identities, as a means of dictating the terms in which his body enters the labor market and of protecting his own wealthy, white masculinity from political consideration, the worker who hammered the tire used his own body to identify the performative similarities between

Fig. 2. Labors juxta-
posed. (Photographs by
the author.)

work and exercise and, in the process, to call attention (however briefly)
to the autonomy of those exercises. In so doing, he, like an African artist
rereading the impacts of African art on European modernism (Gikandi 2006,
56), created an opportunity for an alternative telling of history, not only one
that links his gesture to the letter of an advocate for working-class players in
19th-century England who associates the fatigue of rugby with the fatigue of
work, but one that troubles the boundaries that separate sporting exercises
from work in South Africa in particular.

With that telling of history in mind, it is perhaps unsurprising that the
conceptual barrier that separates rugby from work in South Africa is rarely
contested directly. Although athletic training and paid manual labor may
seem so self-evidently different that their similarities are difficult to recognize,
the argument of this chapter suggests that the barrier might also go unrecognized because of the politics of its construction. Calling attention to the
conceptual barrier that surrounds rugby therefore requires attending to the
conditions that shape athletic performances in South Africa—the "expense"
of rugby's performance in elite and historically white schools, the impossibility of a white schoolboy's sporting labor being equivalent to the work of a
black groundskeeper, and the histories of racial segregation and violence that
make such equivalences impossible. As rugby's class profile in England was
shrouded in a "conspiracy of silence" (Dunning and Sheard 2005, 129), South
Africa's long-standing regime of racial discrimination is similarly concealed.

In point of fact, I can recall only one instance in my research when training and work actually intersected rather than running on parallel tracks. That

moment, like the two described above, centered on an encounter between players and laborers, though the players in question were under contract with a professional team. The players were busy with a circuit of "strongman" exercises. Much loved by coaches and much hated by players, these exercises involve building strength by moving extremely heavy weights across relatively short distances. In one section of the circuit, two players (again, male and white) were using ropes to pull a weighted metal sled back and forth between them. One player would pull and pull until the sled lay at his feet, at which point the second player would take over from the opposite end and pull the sled all the way back. It was clearly a grueling exercise, and the players' enthusiasm was well on the wane when a groundskeeper (again, male and black) walked past them on his way across the field. One player, having dragged the sled all the way to his side only to watch it slip away yet again, collapsed on the grass in dismay and rolled to face the groundskeeper.

"Come pull this thing for me, man!" he moaned. "I'm dying here."

The worker, interested and perhaps amused, came closer and asked the player if he really did need help. By that point, the sled had nearly reached the feet of the player's teammate, who was struggling mightily as well. The begging player, still lolling dramatically on the ground and apparently recognizing an opportunity to use the laborer to manipulate his friend, told the laborer that his help would be very much appreciated. The groundskeeper approached the rope and started pulling the sled back toward the downed player, effectively initiating a game of tug-of-war with the player's partner on the other side. While the player on the laborer's side tossed on the ground in gales of laughter, his teammate was furious.

"*Nee man!*" the teammate exclaimed. "Are you stupid?"

The groundskeeper stopped pulling and cast a look in the direction of the player who had asked for his assistance. The player, evidently reading the worker's reaction as a request for guidance, grinned and nodded, encouraging the man to resume pulling. The groundskeeper readied himself to pull again when the distant teammate shouted, "Stop! I'll *fokkin' bliksem jou* [fuckin' smack you]!" He yelled with such rage and intensity that the groundskeeper dropped the rope and hurried off the field.

Although an observer could perhaps argue that the aggravated player's anger stemmed solely from the fact that the groundskeeper's actions were undermining his efforts to pull the weighted sled, that sabotage can hardly be said to explain, let alone justify, his threat. Why did he not condemn his teammate, who had initiated the situation? Why did he not drop the rope?

This chapter suggests an answer to those questions: this player's threat of violence was a deliberate (if not necessarily conscious) attempt to close the space of reflection—a space for the consideration of history, politics, race, and class—that his teammate had inadvertently opened when he invited the groundskeeper to help him pull the rope. In the split second when work and exercise briefly intersected, it was no longer clear what was occurring or why. Was it exercise for its own sake, manual labor for the sake of economic obligation, or neither?

What appeared in that moment was nothing like a synthesis of the two activities. If anything, their proximity made the conceptual distinction between them and the historical and political obstacles to their synthesis more painfully obvious. The groundskeeper may have given his labor willingly to the autotelic project, but he (unlike the groundskeeper who hammered the tire) was ordered into the conceptual space of exercise by the white player, like a boss might order a worker. Much as a professional coach can frame rugby in terms of collegiality in one moment and salaries the next or as a young white player can thoughtlessly claim his playful exercise as work, the white player initiating the strongman encounter was able to demonstrate his authority, granted to him by a long history of racial inequality, by manipulating rugby's frame—carelessly and playfully controlling the boundary between work and play at someone else's expense. The second player's reaction to the prank affirmed the authority (in the fact that he condemned the groundskeeper rather than his friend) and revealed the social violence concealed therein; he too played the role of the boss or the soldier or the police officer, ordering the groundskeeper out of the exercise with a threat of force. The violence of his command put an end to the spatiotemporal transgression of the categories of work and play. The white players returned to their "expensive" careers, the black groundskeeper went back to his manual labor, and the "proper" (i.e., the historically and politically normalized) distribution of work and play was definitively restored.

CONCLUSION

Having gone to great lengths in "Commitment" to show that both "art for art's sake" and politically committed art fail to meet their own criteria for aesthetic success, Adorno offers his own vision for political art. In his conception, the failures of those alternative positions stem directly from an ambiguity that lies at the heart of the European category of art itself. Art, he claims, is equal parts autonomous and worldly. That equivalence is unavoidable because art comes to its autonomy from a thoroughly social position. Not only do political artists and artists working "for the sake of art" articulate their stances on autonomy from standpoints that emerge from an already existing social world (a world that, as Carroll, Eagleton, and Williams show, was profoundly shaped by the disorienting effects of industrial capitalism). They also create artworks that cross into autonomy from a world of material limitations. With those constraints in mind, artistic autonomy is, for Adorno, neither a natural fact nor an obstacle to commodification; it is more appropriately imagined as a constructed surface through which artworks in a European tradition must pass (2007a, 190). Like a stick that stands upright in a still body of water, the artwork encounters the surface of art's autonomy and refracts sharply in directions that uncritical artists do not to anticipate. The aesthetic failures of advocates of committed art and "art for art's sake" can therefore be traced to the fact that neither group properly theorizes the terms of that refraction. Neither group even acknowledges that the refraction occurs.

If the critiques by Jannie and Charl are sincerely meant, the same could be said of South African rugby as well. Advocates of "art for art's sake" believe art to have always already broken with the world. Rugby's amateur administrators, when confronted with economic value, make a similar claim. As Jannie observed, though, those administrators do not truly want rugby to exist autonomously. Not only do they want to develop loyalty in their players—which they would necessarily expect to see exhibited off the sporting field, in everyday life—but they want successful teams and will recruit and train top talent in order to produce them. In the pursuit of success, the administrators, like 19th-century amateurs before them (cf. Huggins 2006), find themselves making strategic compromises with their own values in the pursuit of athletic accomplishment. Committed artists, in contrast, try to dismiss that breakage entirely. Amateur administrators may chafe at that vision, but Charl articulated a subtler critical objection. Rugby teams, he realized, can never fully transform their players into laborers, because teams rely on the creativity of their players for their success. Emphasis on human creativity is, as Carroll shows in the case of art, itself a product of autonomy. Thus professional teams also embrace a strategic compromise: they negotiate with players in the language of professionalism and motivate them in the language of amateurism. Ultimately, autonomy forces both amateurs and professionals to compromise their visions, and their resulting projects—to use Adorno's words—"[slither]

into the abyss of [their] opposite[s]" (2007a, 189). That those compromises seem to do little actual harm to teams and schools stems largely from the fact that well-positioned administrators and coaches understand how to use the compromises to efface forms of class and racial exclusion and, in doing so, to attract committed players and squeeze better performances out of them.

In Adorno's view, the best way to appreciate the aesthetic and political consequences of autonomy is to look closely at the moment of breakage. Arthur Danto performs a similar maneuver. When faced with Andy Warhol's *Brillo Box*, Danto sought to identify "whatever it [was], which clearly [did] *not* meet the eye, which [kept] art and reality from leaking hopelessly into one another's territory" (1973, 5–6). In Danto's case, the *Brillo Box* was made conceptually recognizable by a preexisting Euro-American "artworld." Although Danto operates on the premise that certain qualities delineate the category of art in all places and times, he argues that those qualities are not always readily apparent. Instead, he writes, there is a history, enacted through the history of art, in which the essence of art—the necessary and sufficient conditions—are "painfully brought to consciousness" (1997, 95). For Danto, Warhol's *Brillo Box* marked just that moment. The history of the Euro-American artworld brought about the possibility that an artist could create an object that resembled a commodity almost exactly. In that moment, the question of what constitutes art became open for debate.

The high school player's "Sisebenza," the laborer's hammering of the tire, and the conflict between the professional players and the laborer over the pulling exercise can all be interpreted in similar ways. In 21st-century South Africa, the social conditions that produced those negotiations include not just the country's history of colonialism and apartheid, which brought the particular juxtapositions of manual labor and expensive play into being, but also the increasing professionalization of South African rugby as a whole. What began in earnest in 1995 has grown to incorporate television deals of greater and greater value, longer seasons, fitness and field sessions several times a day, scouts and agents, the recruitment and movement of players to new high schools, the project of starting dedicated rugby academies, and the general "cutting of tails" at progressively younger ages. Those trends could never guarantee that a junior player would try to explore the distinction between training in a gym and working on the grass, but they certainly could have made the prospect more "thinkable" than it would have been in years past. Had social conditions permitted those sporting actions to be seen as labor, there would have been no tension to dispel.

Had there been no visible or audible similarity between those actions, though, no comparison would have resulted. Nobody would have felt the need to say anything about work, because it would have been obvious that they were doing nothing of the sort. As with Danto's assessment of Warhol's *Brillo Box*, the political significance of those encounters owes a debt to autonomy. The case of the boy's "Sisebenza" is emblematic in that regard. Much like the fate suffered by producers of committed art, the autonomy of sport threw quotation marks around the boy's "work" and gave it a new (and likely unintended) formal quality. It bent his movements away from the labor they might have initially appeared to resemble. In that situation and in the examples that followed it, formally similar activities were placed side by side on rugby fields in South Africa, and a conceptual difference, supplied by the particular chemistry of history, race, and class in South Africa's preexisting "sportworld" (Edgar 2013), set them apart.[10]

That sporting autonomy called attention to the lingering similarities between sport and work demonstrates rugby's (potentially significant) contributions to South Africa's post-apartheid present. One of Adorno's most provocative points about the political potential of art is instructive here. Although it is true, he concedes, that artistic works necessarily conceal the labor that was required to produce them, "the social isolation of the work of art from its own production is also the measure of its immanent progress, that of its mastery of its own artistic material. All the paradoxes of art in high capitalism—and its very existence is a paradox—culminate in the single paradox that it speaks of the human by virtue of its reification, and that it is only through the perfection of its character as illusion that it partakes of truth" (Adorno 2005, 73). When applied to rugby, that statement productively reframes the politics of the sport's performance. Rather than allowing rugby to become political only in those situations when the sport is used to make explicit political statements, it suggests that rugby is (like art) political even in its existing social autonomy. Indeed, in the situations outlined in this chapter, it was precisely that autonomy—to reframe Adorno's observation about Paul Klee's painting *Angelus Novus*—that allowed the politics of each moment to speak (Adorno 2007a, 195).

CHAPTER 3

Residual Uncertainty

Play, Injuries, and Rugby's Masculine Ideal

In chapter 2, participation in rugby appeared as something of a contractual agreement. Andrew Edgar's sportified reading of Arthur Danto's artworld hinges, in that regard, on the idea that the players involved in a sporting situation understand and sign off on the terms of the games they play. For sport itself to exist, players must recognize their situation as a sporting one (Edgar 2013). That conception makes some intuitive sense. If one group of players on the field attempts to perform some sporting task and their notional opposition wants to do something entirely different, the game cannot go forward. Both teams must accept the rules, the arbitrary goals, and the consequences that come when rules are broken and when goals are not achieved. The same logic extends to nonplayers who find themselves in the middle of a contest. If a nonplayer picks up a football and runs away with it during a game, the nonplayer can be accused of being a "spoil-sport" (Huizinga 1980, 11), of ruining the game for its players and spectators, but they could hardly be accused of committing a handball penalty, because they never accepted the terms of the game in the first place.

That conception of sporting participation has affinities with Gregory Bateson's (1972) account of the metacommunicative dimension of play. Playful fights, Bateson observed, are only possible if the participants in the moment are aware that what they seem to be doing to one another is not what they intend to do. They may appear to be attacking one another, but an attack is not their true goal. Their "play frame," like Edgar's "sportworld," depends on consent.[1] Bateson is aware that consent may not hold at all or even for very long. The play frame can collapse if the participants in that frame mistake fake attacks for real ones, think that fake attacks seem too real to be fake, or use a fake attack as the perfect opportunity to sneak in a real one. If one of two participants thinks that they are playing at fighting while the other participant is intent on having a real fight, a real fight will usually result. Yet a testament to the strength of the play frame and to its capacity to communicate about the communication it frames is that fake attacks (nips and bites in the case of animal play) do not register immediately or inevitably as real ones. In the case of rugby, a player can tackle another player only when that other player could conceivably "expect it"—that is, when the rules of the game invite that possibility. Should that player tackle a nonplayer (either on or off the field) or tackle a fellow player when the rules of the game forbid that action, the tackle becomes something else entirely. The same action gets transformed into an explicitly violent act, made all the more malicious by the fact that it masqueraded as a tackle.

For Bateson, the play frame depends on more than just the artificiality of apparently real bites. "Not only does the playful nip not denote what would be denoted by the bite for which it stands," Bateson writes, "but, in addition, the bite itself is fictional. Not only do the playing animals not quite mean what they are saying but, also, they are usually communicating about something which does not exist" (1972, 182). Bateson finds the same logic at work in human animals in trompe l'oeil painting—a genre in which artists devote significant effort to dazzling observers with paintings that present the painted work as something real (i.e., the artists prefer to make "fake" things look "real" rather than to make "real" things in the first place)—and he further suggests that those fictions can become, "in the dim region where art, magic, and religion meet" (183), so powerful that they acquire a reality and substance all their own. According to that conception, a bite gives real depth and seriousness to a nip, even if that bite is merely fictional.

The magical reality of playful fictions is plainly relevant to the premise of the present book, insofar as its central argument is that rugby takes on a life of its own as its players engage in the inherent uncertainty of the sport's live performance. Mangan and a number of other historians and theorists referenced in chapter 2 of the present study argued that the ethos of amateur athleticism depended on one's willingness to play as though the results of the sporting contest carried no larger significance. If a contest is to be truly playful, the match and its struggles must end when that playful contest ends—at the final whistle and the edges of the field. Those temporal and spatial boundaries were part of the reason that amateurs in 19th-century England felt threatened by the allocation of payments to players in exchange for their participation.

Amateurs feared that payments would so undermine players' commitment to performing in good faith that rugby's autonomy would be broken and that the sport would, as Dunning and Sheard (2005, 139) put it, "be transformed from a 'mock fight' into a 'real' one." "Professionals," the amateur argument therefore asserts, "cannot be expected to show such good faith since their livelihood is at stake. Hence, for [professional players], Rugby ceases to be a 'sport,' a form of 'play,' and becomes a form of fighting in earnest" (139).

In that conception, rugby draws much social significance from its fictional bites, because the player's quality as an amateur athlete was bound to his capacity to both recognize the limits of violence during play and set aside that violence once the play had finished. Playing properly was a measure of his forbearance. Indeed, in their 1959 *Report on Rugby*, Morgan and Nicholson remarked that one of the wondrous things about the sport was the willingness of players to abandon their conflicts at the match's final whistle. The authors quote Sir Wavell Wakefield, who wrote, "It may be that Rugger has an element of danger about it, and people often ask whether it is worth risking serious injury in what, after all, is only a game. It would, I think, be a poor sort of game that had no sort of risk to be faced, and it is one of the glories of Rugger that you can put your shoulder into a man with all your strength and bring him down with a crash, knowing that if you stave in a rib or two of his he will bear you no grudge, while if he knocks your teeth out in handing you off it is merely your own fault for tackling him too high. Such accidents are relatively rare, but when they do happen they are just the fortune of war" (131).

That conception of sporting violence is grounded in consent, in a manner consistent with Edgar's conception of the "sportworld," in that players feel free to pursue their violent courses of action because they know that their opponents will "bear [them] no grudge." At the same time, Wakefield also acknowledges the consequences that sports can carry even once a match has finished. A tackle is not an assault, just as a nip is not a bite, but a tackle can leave marks on the body that resemble assaults. Players leave matches with broken bones, torn ligaments, lost teeth, blackened eyes, and myriad bloody scrapes and bruises. Bodies break under new injuries and carry old ones for decades. Even the strongest players begin to feel rugby's autonomous "nips" as "bites" over the course of their careers. Though games can, under ideal circumstances, end peaceably and take animosities with them, apparently banal observations about pain and injury suggest that, in practice, injuries form something of a troubling reminder of the supplemental element, or residue, of play. They are a reminder, as Adorno put it, of "the empirical reality from which [artistic creation or, in this argument, athletic performance] breaks free" (2007a, 190).[2] Most notable about Wakefield's remarks, from that perspective, is the way that they artfully fold rugby injuries back into the danger and glory of the sport. To risk injury is to have the opportunity to act courageously on the field and to demonstrate the very forbearance that, in an amateur ideology, marked rugby as a form of play in the first place.

All the players, coaches, and medical personnel that I worked with in South Africa shared an appreciation for the playful dimension of rugby, but the respective positionalities of those groups prompted them to interpret that supplemental element in broadly different ways. Coaches may have cared deeply about their players, but they placed a premium on dynamic performances. In keeping with the Bulls' *maak vas* style, which can be beautiful and compelling when it momentarily overcomes uncertainty, coaches valued players who seemed to be able to play their sport with a special degree of independence and control. Confronted with unpredictable situations, the most desirable players were those who appeared able to act, rather than react, on the field. In their most idealized form, this player would be immune to even the most unpredictable of injuries.

The Bulls may have exhibited a strong attachment to that conception of sporting agency, partly because of the team's relationship to apartheid and its politics, but as I demonstrate in this chapter, that perspective owes an even deeper debt to history. I argue that when coaches in post-apartheid South Africa expect their players to control rugby during the liveness of play, those coaches are holding their players to a standard of performance that has its origins in the idealized political subject of the Enlightenment tradition (cf. Schneewind 1998). Drawing from the work of Judith Butler and Seyla Benhabib, I show that subject (introduced in chapter 2 of the present study as a white and economically self-sufficient Briton) to be inherently gendered, insofar as it is assumed to act from an "autonomous"—decontextualized and disembodied—position. Investigating contemporary manifestations of that gendered ideal in South African rugby, this chapter shows that even though no such player could ever exist in practice, coaches still used him as a standard against which actual players could be measured.

The rugby players I knew appreciated the efficacy of that subjectivity as much as their coaches but were uniquely positioned to recognize how elusive (even false) that vision of perfect agency was. When coaches viewed injuries as the product of mental or physical weakness, players called on their own embodied experiences to point out the artificiality of that logic and, in doing so, to insist that resources be devoted to preserving their well-being. Medical personnel, being the people who provide those resources, were likewise capable of apprehending players as vulnerable bodies. They did not take to the field themselves, but they certainly saw the real material damage that rugby's "nips" could do. Ultimately, this chapter demonstrates that injuries, viewed as a residual element of rugby's play, shed light on both the gendered standard of performance to which professional players in South Africa are held and the conflicts that result when players (inevitably) fail to embody that impossible ideal.

RUGBY, UNCERTAINTY, AND THE POSSIBILITY OF INJURY

Compared to the lush conditions of the Bulls' manicured home field, the atmosphere on this particular game day was harsh and unforgiving. Twilight was setting in, both because winter was shortening the days and because the day itself was overcast and damp. The field was equipped with concrete steps rather than seats and with mud patches rather than concrete parking lots, and the Bulls' opposition had no gigantic floodlights and no massive pavilion. The ground was already growing so dark that it seemed likely to me that the players would struggle to see the ball when the game finally began. The game itself was only a semiformal contest, but the Bulls coaches approached it with seriousness. One coach warned his players in the team's huddle that their opponents would be keen to show the Bulls that they could compete with them, because none of them had attended prestigious rugby schools or played for top teams. That meant, he said, that the game might turn dirty. Apropos of the argument of the chapter 2, the coach reminded the players that if things did get dirty, they remain committed to a professional mindset. "You must be professional," he repeated to me, once the players had taken the field. "It's the difference between us and them," he added.

If the field, the light, and the opposition presented difficulties (both real and imagined) for the Bulls and their professional attitude, the situation became yet more challenging when the coaching staff realized that there was no ambulance at the game. There seemed to be no medics present either. The medics were eventually found, but the team doctor for the Bulls was perturbed to notice that the medics' backboard—a tool for stabilizing players with neck injuries so that they might be carried off the field—had no straps attached. That absence defeated the purpose of the board, the doctor explained, because an injured player's body would slide around on the board if it were not held fast. I was standing aside with the Bulls coaches as they debated how to proceed. All were concerned, but one was especially upset. He kept calling the whole thing "flippin' *onaanvaarbaar* [unacceptable]," and he observed loudly that South African rugby's protocol for injury prevention dictated that teams must never play a match without an ambulance present. The club president for the opposition responded that his team was poor and could not afford to bring an ambulance to the field for a semiformal match. His club didn't even *want* the games, he added. The Bulls youth team would destroy his youth team ("They're just kids!" he said of his own players, many of whom were older than the Bulls players), and beating the Bulls in a practice match was not their priority. The angry Bulls coach responded, "This isn't about your players or our players. It's about all 30 of those guys out there and keeping them safe." By the end of the conversation, everyone on both teams seemed equally frustrated.

Scholars who write about suffering in sport often distinguish between pain and injury. In their conceptions, the term *pain* covers a wide swath of different experiential conditions that include everything from the exhaustion of training, to the shocks that the body encounters in the playing of high-impact sports, to the aches that players experience in the hours and days following a contest. The term *injury*, meanwhile, describes situations in which the physiology of the body breaks down. Those positions, scholars recognize, are not dichotomous. Rather, they are fundamentally intertwined (cf. Malcom 2006; Waddington 2004). Players will mistake an injury for everyday pain. They will train so hard through their pain that they drive themselves to injury, and their injuries will linger on as pain long after they have allegedly healed. Coaches will fail to recognize an injury and decide that a player is unwilling or unable to train through pain. They will also, on rare occasions, hope that pain really is an injury, so they need not go to the trouble of cutting underperforming players on account of their play on the field. All of those conceptions of pain and injury were present in my fieldwork, as I show in this chapter.

The preceding remark by the Bulls coach is particularly interesting, though, because it presents rugby itself as an unsafe situation. Rugby is a sport that requires its players to slam their bodies into one another, repeatedly and at high speeds. Under such conditions, players can harm each other in all sorts of ways. Emergency medical personnel must be present and properly prepared, because nobody can anticipate the dangers that a live rugby match will bring. Scholars who write about other conflict sports have made similar observations. Works by Sharon Mazer (2005) and Heather Levi (2008) on professional wrestling link injuries explicitly to safety, anticipation, and uncertainty. For both authors, analyses that focus on the scriptedness of professional wrestling often overlook the fact that no script and no amount of preparation can protect participants from injury. As is the case with rugby, professional wrestling is less a situation in which humans do violence (or simulated violence) to each other than a live and unpredictably dangerous environment into which human actors enter. In such environments, a real "bite" can emerge from a series of fake "nips," with almost no warning at all (cf. Mazer 2005, 83).

That view about the dangers associated with rugby's unpredictability was shared quite widely among people in my field sites. Often, those dangers were articulated (and justified) in terms of the unpredictability of life itself. Although parents were not always thrilled that their sons played rugby, many said that there was no reason to agonize about an injury on the field. Injuries happen, I was told, no matter the place. A young man could get hurt riding a motorbike or walking to school. One parent I knew felt that his son's rugby injury had been preordained—that the player would have gotten the injury no matter what he had done in life. Players, young or old, tended to have similar views on the possibility of injury in rugby and everyday life. One dismissed his serious knee injury in terms of rugby's risk. It was nothing more than a freak accident, he said. He had been in the wrong place at the wrong time. He concluded, "Sports always have injuries. You could get hurt driving a car. There are always risks."[3] Even medical personnel—who, as I show below, know the workings of the body extremely well—used chance and risk to explain the origins of rugby injuries. In one instance, a player was sitting in the doctor's office for the Bulls and lamenting his injury, which I had seen; he had been sprinting down the field when, suddenly and without apparent provocation, he fell to the ground. "*Ek het my enkel uitgekak!*" (I just fucked up my ankle!), he yelled, writhing on the grass. As the doctor fitted him with crutches, he shook his head and observed, "Just my flippin' luck. Every flippin' year." Neither the doctor nor I knew what to say. Eventually, the doctor told him, "It's just the way of the game, apparently."

To claim that uncertainty is the mechanism by which injuries enter rugby is not necessarily to imply that players do not author their own acts of violence and produce their own pain. They throw themselves into tackles, of course, but they also stomp on and knee other players. They twist each others' arms behind their backs and over their heads. Sometimes players bite one another and punch or kick each other in the groin. Yet, though authorship can sometimes appear clearer in those foul moments than in ordinary violent ones, the capacity of those players to determine a particular course of action remains relatively limited. They move their own bodies and perform those actions themselves, but they can never fully predict the trajectory of any given sequence of play. When one player aims to harm another, he cannot control where the other player will be, how that player will orient his body, or whether the effort to harm will be noticed before it is undertaken. Acts of violence also often occur within a narrative flow that develops within the unfolding uncertainty of the match itself. After an opposing player tackles a ball carrier with particular force and poignancy, the tackled player might respond, in the next available moment, by charging yet harder at another player. That hit can produce yet more reactions, culminating in a stoppage of play by the referee or a full-on fight. Although the "play frame" of a match can break and be deliberately broken (as I show in chapter 5), the existence of the frame itself is the product of a contingent and collective narrative that players produce but only minimally control. During the flow of the match, "in the dim region where art, magic, and religion meet" (Bateson 1972, 183), the game takes on a life of its own.

GENDERED AUTONOMY AND SPORTING PERFORMANCE

As I argued in chapter 1 with respect to the Bulls' *maak vas* style, the occasions when one momentarily seems to control rugby—an entity one has conjured into being in concert with one's teammates and opposition—possess an unexpected beauty and power. Those qualities stem partly from history and social relations but also from the struggle with rugby's inherent unpredictability. To act definitively on the field is, I suggested in that chapter, to appear to overcome chance itself and, in doing so, to become something more than human. Richard Pringle's rugby-playing informants in New Zealand seem to recognize that quality as well, for they claim to experience great pleasure and satisfaction in the moments when they extract authoritative performances from the sport's dominant conditions of danger and risk (Pringle 2009, 221). Orin Starn, writing of Tiger Woods, has made a strikingly similar claim about a completely different sport. As a prelude to his account of Woods's infamously public sex scandal, Starn describes the grounds on which Woods became a larger-than-life presence in golf in the first place. That status was not due merely to Woods's racial identity or to the fact that he won an astounding number of tournaments. It was also, Starn proposes, due to the difficulty of golf itself. For Starn, the joy of golf stems from the unlikeliness of accomplishing the task that the sport sets for its players. When a golfer is able to put golf's small white ball exactly where they intend it to go, he suggests, the golfer experiences a pleasurable illusion of power. It feels, Starn writes, like "a small brush with the sublime" (2011, 15). While the common golfer is able to feel that sensation only rarely, Woods's talents made it appear as though he could experience sublimity whenever he chose. In golf's heightened conditions of performative uncertainty, he was nearly godly in his apparent capacity to dictate the future for his ball.[4]

That interpretation of the power of apparently unconstrained human action resonates not just with the Bulls and their approach to rugby but also with Terry Eagleton's observations about aesthetic autonomy, discussed in chapter 2 of the present study. In Eagleton's conception, that autonomy emerged as a symbolic solution to an ultimately intractable 19th-century bourgeois problem: namely, "how values are to be derived, in a condition in which neither civil society nor the political state would seem to provide such values with a particularly plausible foundation" (1990, 63). It cleared a social space for people to behave as though they, not the category of art, were autonomous and therefore independent of all social and political obligation. Tiger Woods's ability to place a golf ball wherever he likes or the Bulls' ability to play exactly the rugby match they desire, irrespective of their opponent or the weather, reinforces their apparent capacities to be, as Eagleton conceives it, "entirely self-regulating and self-determining" (9), as no ordinary person or team could be.

In my initial consideration of Eagleton's argument, I showed that working-class players who wished to be paid for their participation in sport contested the existence of that subject on economic terms. Feminist philosophers have added a gender as a second layer of critical nuance.[5] Seyla Benhabib is emblematic in that regard. She argues that the allegedly autonomous perspective is built on "the illusions of a self-transparent and self-grounding reason, the illusion of a disembedded and disembodied subject," and (perhaps most important in the case of rugby) the illusion of "having found an Archimedean standpoint, situated beyond historical and cultural contingency" (1992, 4). Those illusions, she writes, are gendered insofar as they serve to efface the networks of dependence and association that bind every subject, affectively and politically, to others. More will be said about those networks of dependence below. For now, it suffices to note that by concealing those ties, the political subject is transformed into a fictional but ideologically potent "adult male head of household" who does his business "in the market-place or in the polity with like others." Benhabib adds, "Since Rousseau, the demand has been to make 'l'homme' whole again" (50).

That conception of the political subject shares affinities with many theorizations of gender on the sporting field. Overman, for example, argues that the male body "tend[s] to be valued for performance" and, further, that the bodily form produced and celebrated in sports exhibits "self-mastery" (2010, 135–36). Performative self-mastery may not be identical to the reasoning subject produced out of the Enlightenment, but it is predicated on an illusion of contextual disengagement, insofar as the successful male athlete demonstrates his capacity to discipline his body until it allows him to triumph over the conditions of competition. Messner has made a similar observation. Following Connell (1985), who argued for a theory of masculinity that both acknowledged a plurality of male identities and recognized that some masculinities are valorized and normalized over others, Messner analyzed the cultural significance of the violence of sport. In his conception, sporting violence contributes to the production of a gendered hierarchy that separates "men" who can "give" and "take" violent hits and those people (irrespective of gender) who cannot. Because "giving" and "taking" hits amounts to a person's capacity to resist, to the best of their abilities, succumbing to the agentive force of another body, that measure also reflects a player's capacity to reject dependence and, at the most general level, contingency. In the case of American football, Messner explained, those gendered distinctions can be quite explicitly drawn: "In contrast to the bare and vulnerable bodies of the cheerleaders, the armored male bodies of the football players are elevated to mythical status" (1990, 213). In their study of rugby in an Australian high school, Light and Kirk have observed that though the sport requires its players to demonstrate both force and skill, the school's team invariably emphasized physical force when it was under pressure to perform: "Much of the training . . . featured drilling and disciplining of the body to make it an efficient weapon for the exercise of force and the domination of other young men" (2000, 169–70). Though Light and Kirk draw explicit connections between "aggression, suffering, and physical intimidation of opponents" (170) and the production of a hegemonic masculinity, Starn's observations about Tiger

Woods's apparent autonomy suggests that a skillful body can be emblematic of that hegemonic ideal as well. Burstyn, for her part, succinctly describes mainstream Euro-American constructions of sport: "Sport is a religion of domination and aggression constructed around a male godhead" (1999, 23). In Burstyn's usage, "godhead" comes to mean something like a source of divine validation, insofar as it permits athletes to participate in a surplus of masculinity that she (following Horowitz 1977) calls "hypermasculinity."

Important as those gendered critiques undoubtedly are, Benhabib and philosophers working in her tradition broaden them yet further. They suggest, in particular, that the sporting subject, like Eagleton's economic subject, may be hegemonic because it is a manifestation of an overarching conception of an idealized political subject.[6] Seen in that way, the idealized male athlete is ideologically disconcerting and coercive, not just because it insists on extreme self-mastery, violence, or aggression and intimidation, but also because it is modeled on a transcendent (and fully realized and therefore ultimately disembodied) ideal whose often-unacknowledged upper limit is that of God "himself." Thus, to elaborate on Burstyn's conceptualization, athletic performance may be constructed around a male godhead, but that godhead becomes a source of divine validation precisely because it offers a perfect ideal to which athletes are expected to aspire. Under such conditions, athletes can fail to achieve that godly ideal, provided that they pursue it with sufficient intensity and enthusiasm.

Rugby coaches in South Africa seem to take this Archimedean standpoint (illusory though it may be) very seriously as a performative ideal. On one perfectly prosaic occasion, two highly ranked Bulls officials discussed the appearance of their team's junior players as they prepared to play a visiting team from Wales. Even a casual spectator looking at the two sides would have noted the physical disparities. The Bulls players were young professionals. They were larger, visibly stronger, and much more disciplined in their pre-match demeanor than their opposition. In keeping with the team's preferred conception of rugby, the two officials praised the Bulls players for their physical dominance. The very highest compliment that a Bulls player could receive from those officials was to be called "*'n meneer*" (a sir), implying authority and command of the situation.[7] The Welsh players, who were comparatively small in stature and slight of build, were summarily dismissed. One player in particular, both men agreed, even looked "like a girl." The lively commentary by the officials continued for the duration of the match, as they watched the players they had recruited and supervised in training completely overwhelm their opposition.

Such moments of complete control, tantalizing though they may be, are generally few and fleeting. Games continually produce uncertainty, and teams and players will inevitably find themselves "on the back foot" (as rugby connoisseurs like to say)—that is, reading and responding rather than dictating and acting. As I showed in chapter 1, the Bulls respond to the inevitability of uncertainty by reaffirming their dominant strategy again and again. When rugby opens up possibilities, they almost always try to close those possibilities back down. The practical performance of masculine autonomy works in a similar way. Because displays of the perfect ideal are so rare, coaches and teams have turned the pursuit of the ideal into an index of masculinity as well. One morning, for example, I stood with a group of young players as they took to the field, frost still on the ground. It was 8:00 a.m. and the sun was barely up. The drill that the trainers and coaches had designed involved dividing the players into groups of three and having them (1) shuttle back and forth three times between cones placed five meters apart, (2) push one of their groupmates (who was holding a foam pad) five meters backward three times, and (3) tackle weighted bags three times. Each circuit, the coach said, ought to take the whole group roughly 15 minutes to complete. The team would keep that circuit going for 70 minutes straight. That duration, he added, was about double the length of time that the ball is in play in an actual game, so he intended it to be both a physical and a mental test. True to his word, players began to put their hands on their hips and stagger forward at the hour mark. The coaches exhorted them to go harder, keep their heads like they would in a game, and make sure that they continued to do their movements properly. As the drill progressed, players hit the ground and struggled to stand with greater and greater regularity. The precision of the groups began to break down, with each getting more and more disjointed and uncoordinated as players lost their bearings. Little dirt tracks began to form in the wet grass through all of the repetitions, and the players grew quieter as they entered what appeared to be their own little private places of exhaustion, pain, and weakness of limb. One player muttered in my hearing, "*Jy moet half-mal wees*" (You've got to be half-crazy).

After the session, the coach took his exhausted players inside to the film room and told them a story. Prisoners sent to Siberia by Stalin, he said, were made to stand for 36 hours at a time in packed train cars with no toilets, and only a cup of coffee to drink and a loaf of bread twice a day to eat. When the trains finally stopped, they marched for days in the cold to reach their destination. The key thing, he explained, was that the prisoners refused to crack, because "cracking was what the enemy wanted." He asked the players if the same thing applied to rugby. "Yes coach," they answered in unison. From the perspective of the argument of this chapter, the most striking thing about that training session and the lesson that followed it was that the coach did not downplay or dismiss the exhaustion of the training. In fact, he exaggerated it by comparing the session to a prison train and himself to Stalin. Such comparisons suggest, at the very least, that he wanted the players to acknowledge their suffering. While the ideal player might complete the exercise running at full speed and feel no exhaustion, the best possible realistic alternative would be for a player to keep running despite feeling absolute exhaustion. No matter what privations the coach or rugby imposed on the players, the coach wanted them to learn to hold themselves together, show no cracks, and pursue the elusive masculine ideal.

INJURIES AND RUGBY'S MASCULINE IDEAL

Given that coaches continually measure players according to their capacity to dominate uncertainty and that the ideal masculine body possesses no weaknesses and feels no harm, it would make sense that the masculine ideal would also inform how injuries are perceived. As one coach (and retired player) put it, life changes when you stop playing rugby. "People stop giving you things and your routine completely changes." He added, "You're not Superman anymore." His reference to Superman is fitting. The capacity of a player to self-regulate and self-determine should bring physical invulnerability along with it. Players embrace that perspective as well, as Howe's informants at Pontypridd Rugby Football Club demonstrate. Those athletes prefer to describe their experiences of bodily harm as "pain" rather than "injury," because injury carries the connotation of biomechanical failure. "The idea of injury," Howe writes, "detracts from a player's notion of *perfection* on the pitch" (2001, 295; emphasis added). A body that suffers when hit or that seems to fall apart as it performs an apparently playful action it has done hundreds or thousands of times before is not a body that can determine the shape of the world that surrounds it.

Should the inherent danger of rugby happen to break a body down, the injured player should (in the logic of the pursuit of an autonomous ideal) work as quickly and diligently as possible to repair it. In that regard, one coach complained to a group of coaches and trainers that one of his players was suffering from an overuse injury that seemed only to appear at practice time. He was magically healthy for his games. Another coach who knew the same player and had worked with him before offered some advice to his colleague and to the training staff: "Make him ride a bike for an hour and then go and swim for an hour. He must [throw up] every single time. He doesn't like training. If you kill him for three days, he'll make an amazing recovery." That approach to rehabilitation, sometimes called "inconveniencing" (Roderick, Waddington, and Parker 2000, 171), seeks to make rehabilitation so physically and psychologically exhausting that no player would want to do it for long. In the opinion of most of the coaches I knew, that strategy had no downside. If the player really is injured, he heals quickly. If a player decides to quit because the rehabilitation is too difficult or because his body breaks down yet more, professional coaches have a large and eager pool of potential players from which to draw.[8] If, finally, the player is merely pretending to be hurt, the inconvenient training has the potential to draw him back into the fold. When a trainer observed that overtraining might not be the best course of action for a player who claimed to suffer from an overuse injury, the recommending coach offered a logically consistent response: "Well, if he can't stay healthy, maybe he wasn't meant to play rugby." Whatever the outcome, the player's problem would solve itself.

As is the case throughout this book, the uncertainty of rugby extends outward from the field to other locations. Gym work, for example, becomes a means for coaches and trainers to test the limits of the injured player's body. A fit body should be able to assert itself over the weights presented to it.[9] By that logic, the failure to lift the requisite weight becomes threatening. Rather than the player moving the weight, with the same inevitability as a player controlling a match on the field, the body is dragged around by the barbell, the dumbbell, or even gravity. The rugby-playing body finds itself at the mercy of the exercises in question, and the body's vulnerabilities and limitations are exposed in the process. Sometimes that vulnerability is made palpably clear, as when a player loses control of a weight or needs to ask his teammates to free him from his burden. In a context in which rugby players are valued for their agentive capacities, the struggle of the player with his barbell becomes a struggle to demonstrate his own capacity for self-determination.

As a male-presenting body that occupied space in the gym but neither trained with players nor coached them, my presence brought the gendered norms into especially stark relief. Players frequently tested my strength, and I inevitably failed their tests. Some shoved me or punched me playfully, and some went further still. One day, for example, a player with whom I had developed something of a rapport walked over to me in the gym and pushed me back onto a large foam and rubber mat. I got up and pushed him playfully in return, at which point he tackled me hard onto the mat and ground his elbow against my jaw. The blow stung for a moment, and I lay there passively, elbow distorting my face, until the player grew bored and stopped. When we both stood up, he tackled me again. Players tested me in language too. They continually urged me to lift their weights, even though they seemed to understand, as I certainly did, that I would only get in their way in doing so. If I lifted with them, either I would have to take off and put back on so many weights at the start and end of my exercises that I would waste their time, or I would have to try to lift as much weight as they did and injure myself as a result. When I declined their invitations, some players were explicit about how they felt about me and my obvious physical vulnerability. One player dismissed me as a "cub," and another told me, with a friendly smirk, "Get out of here; we hate American pussies."[10]

Those actions against me were undoubtedly aggressive, the accompanying language notably crude. But the challenges still reinforce the salience of the vision of masculinity that I have articulated in this chapter. To be a successfully male body in the gym and on the rugby field is to be a body that can appear, momentarily, to embody the dreams of autonomy, free action, and self-reliance. Dropped passes, missed tackles, and failed attempts to lift appropriate weights may create opportunities for players (and coaches) to reflect on the impossibility of thoroughly autonomous performances, but more often than not, such errors are used to demonstrate a person's distance from perfection and, by extension, from the masculine ideal. As Benhabib writes of critical theorists who try to adopt disengaged political subjectivity, "Criticism [that purports to stand outside of the world] privileges an Archimedean standpoint, be it freedom or reason, and proceeds to show the unfreedom or unreasonableness of the world when measured against this [i.e., its own] paradigm. By privileging this Archimedean standpoint, criticism becomes dogmatism: it leaves its own standpoint unexplained, or it assumes the validity of its standpoint prior to engaging in the task of criticism" (1986, 33). Should a person fail, as I did, even to try to embody the desirable (sporting) subject position, that person abdicates all rights to masculine prowess.

They can be targeted with ridicule because they admitted their own vulnerability and voluntarily forfeited their subjectivity. Roderick, Waddington, and Parker have, perhaps not surprisingly, observed a similar hierarchical system in the valuation of injured professional football players: although the ideal player is a healthy one, "being prepared to play while injured is . . . a central characteristic of 'the good professional,'" and "by the same token, those who are not prepared to play through pain and injury are likely to be stigmatized as not having the 'right attitude,' as malingerers or, more bluntly, as 'poofters'" (2000, 169).

PAIN, PERFORMANCE, AND THE EMBODIED EXPERIENCE OF MALE RUGBY PLAYERS

As my experience clearly demonstrates, players valorize rugby's dream of masculine autonomy as much as their coaches do. At the same time, players possess an intimate and immediate familiarity with pain and violence that their coaches do not. In his work on mixed martial arts, Greg Downey (2007) found that competitors did not merely experience pain but learned to cultivate it actively in their training, in order to better understand it, adapt to it, and learn the limits of their bodies. That observation rang true in my research as well. Players appeared to learn, through trial and error, that pain never exists as a discrete abstraction that is present or absent (cf. Livingston 2012, 120). Pain and injury are always communicated or not, witnessed or not, and imbued with meaning of various kinds. Being socially situated, pain changes over time. As players struggle to manage their aches, pains, and injuries, they develop a kind of tacit knowledge of their bodies (Downey 2010; Samudra 2008) that helps them differentiate between kinds of pain that matter or do not, kinds that are acute or chronic, and how each kind of pain should be addressed. They come to recognize the physical tolls that attempting to "fully author" a sporting performance can take on a body. What a coach might be inclined to dismiss as a harmless "nip" is often, for a player, a painful or even debilitating "bite."

Predictably, contrasting conceptions of pain, sport, and the body lead to conflicts between players and coaches, as players insist on services that their coaches are unable or unwilling to provide. One day, for example, I witnessed a player arguing back and forth on the sidelines with his coach about the condition of the player's back. The player insisted that he needed an MRI, but his coach dismissed the condition as psychosomatic. The coach's position infuriated the player, who told him so: "You guys are so fickle. You hold young men's lives in your hands. Do you know how many talented guys come through here and sink through the system like sand?" A few moments later, the player received word from the training staff that he was permitted to get his MRI. He packed up his things and prepared to leave for the day. On his way off the field, he went down the line of coaches and training staff, shaking their hands and saying, "This is the first nice thing this company has done for me. Thank you to the company. Thank you to the company."

Taken in the context of the argument (made in chapter 2) about play and work in professional rugby, his gesture called attention to the contractual obligation that (in the absence of "real" loyalty) bound the player and the team together. Dripping with exaggerated deference and insincerity, the player's comments implied that if the team was not going to take care of him because it cared about him as a person, he was not going to thank the coaches and support staff as people either. He owed his gratitude, what little he felt, to the company for which he worked. His attitude further annoyed his coach, who responded by pointing down the line of the people that the player had just thanked. Every single person with the exception of one, he observed, was a consultant rather than an employee. Speaking the same language of subtext as the player, he suggested that they occupied positions no less perilous than the player did. If that message got through to the player, he was unfazed. He told the coach, "Tell you what, if I get this MRI and I'm okay, I'll be back to practice this afternoon." That promise, though aspirational insofar as medical procedures are rarely so efficient, was evidently meant to emphasize the player's confidence in his bodily knowledge. The coach shrugged and turned the player's own faith in his experiential knowledge against him. "You know in your head whether you can practice or not," he replied, suggesting with one sentence that he both tolerated the player's story and suspected that the injury existed only in the player's mind. The player left furious.[11]

On another, equally contentious occasion, this time during a management meeting, a team doctor reported that players who had been relegated from a higher team to a lower one were growing disgruntled because they received fewer services from their new team's training staff. The doctor, generally sympathetic to the needs of players, wanted the coaches and managers to know that the trainers did not believe the services necessary and were not trained to provide them in any case. The behavior of the players immensely frustrated one particular coach, who observed that the complainants had never requested the services before. He said that one player who wanted to receive a pre-match massage because he thought it would help him perform better had never actually played a match after receiving a massage, so he really could not know if massage made him a better player or not. The coach suggested that the trainers tell the players flat out, "We don't do that, and we don't think it's good for you before a match." The doctor was more tactful. While agreeing that the training staff should tell the players that the services they desired may not be useful and that the staff was not trained to provide them, she proposed that if the players pressed on, the staff should do its best. "If it works," she concluded, "let them have it. If it doesn't work, or if they complain that we made things worse, well, we told them the situation and they chose to go along." That position generally accepted, the meeting adjourned.

Several days later, I happened on a heated conversation between the frustrated coach and a player who quickly revealed himself to be the one who had requested the massage. The coach, apparently on message, encouraged the player to speak to the team doctor, but the player had grown tired of waiting for an answer. Predictably, in the context of the argument of this chapter, he justified his need for a massage on the basis of his understanding of his own body and its needs: "I can feel when my muscles are tight, when things are wrong. It's not like a heart problem or cancer or something. I know what's wrong better than you." The player announced that he was still going to get massages the day before his games, but he was going to visit an outside specialist and pay for them out of pocket while he waited for the team to get its act together. He said, "I want to be the best in the world at my position. I will do what it takes to be that, but I need support. The staff is there to make sure I can perform on the field, and I know what I need to perform."

"YOUR EYES CAN'T SEE WHAT YOUR MIND DOESN'T KNOW": PERCEIVING PLAYER PRECARITY

At first glance, this player's comment about staff responsibility reads, at best, as indelicate and dismissive of the work that staffers do. In the moment, it felt to me as though the player was attempting to depict his body as a finely tuned athletic machine, maintained by a legion of technicians and engineers. In time, though, I came to realize that the player's statement also indicated a profound dependence. The self that requires a pre-match massage, the self that the coaches privately thought was spoiled by playing for a higher team, was exactly the sort of self Seyla Benhabib sought to reveal beneath the "metaphysical illusions of the Enlightenment" (1992, 4)—a self sustained, from birth until death, by relationships with other subjects no less dependent (50). Judith Butler has made a similar claim about the dependent body. In *Frames of War*, she searches for a mode of engagement that can broaden how bodies are perceived and appreciated. She finds the term *recognition* to be unsatisfactory because a body can only be "recognized" if its status as living (and therefore as worthy of life) has already been decided. To escape the limitations of that category and the norms on which it is premised, Butler proposes that we theorize the perception of bodies by means of "apprehension," which she defines as the passing acknowledgment, or marking, of life (2009, 4–5). While the recognized body is implicitly imbued with rights that preserve its life (rights that make recognition of the body possible in the first place), the apprehended body can be perceived prior to those rights and, therefore, in its lived precarity.

Precariousness, which Butler argues is the acknowledgment that a body can die, is an unavoidable feature of life. Acknowledging the precarious existence of a body brings with it a collection of positive obligations that can preserve and sustain that life, irrespective of whether or not that life is actually recognized as valid, praiseworthy, or even human. For Butler, the obligations include "those basic supports that seek to minimize precariousness in egalitarian ways: food, shelter, work, medical care, education, rights of mobility and expression, protection against injury and oppression" (2009, 28–29). Apprehending a precarious body, Butler concludes, imparts an ethical responsibility to act. Though a pre-match massage is plainly not a grave ethical concern, the requesting player's argument adheres to the underlying logic of Butler's. Rather than depicting himself as an autonomous Superman, acting freely on the field, the player used his knowledge of his body and its needs to represent that body to his coaches and trainers as one that ought to be apprehended rather than recognized, as a dependent body in need of their support.

If coaches seem disinclined to apprehend the vulnerable bodies of their players, medical personnel tend to take them somewhat more seriously. Doctors, physiotherapists, trainers,[12] and other personnel are responsible for managing precisely physical concerns, of course, but Butler's argument about precarity suggests that the seriousness is attributable at least partly to the relationships that the support staffers have with players and their bodies. During the match mentioned at the opening of this chapter, a player did indeed get injured. Face dripping with blood, he came to the sideline to see the doctor. Tending to the injury was a thoroughly material process. The player's eyelid had split open, and the doctor worked quickly and efficiently to stitch the lid back together. She injected local anesthetic into the eyelid and then, using a hooked needle, drew some fine twine from one side of the cut to the other. With a few deft twists of a set of forceps that she held in her other hand, she pulled the cut shut and tied a knot. She instructed me to cut the twine, which I did clumsily, and to dab the blood away with a piece of gauze. We repeated the sequence again, and my second cut was better than my first. Throughout the whole process, which took no more than five minutes, the doctor kept up a running commentary with the player. She asked him to tell her about what had happened, to comment on the state of his vision, and—as she was stitching—to confirm that the anesthetic was working. Once she had finished, she fixed my first cut so that the twine didn't obstruct his eyesight, applied a dab of Vaseline to the stitches to stop the bleeding, covered the wound with a bandage, and sent the player back onto the field. Prosaic though the interaction was, it was entirely different from the interactions coaches tend to have with their players. The doctor was able to apprehend the player's body as injurable because she engaged the materiality of that body directly.[13] For a brief moment, she was literally under the player's skin, knitting his flesh back together.

On another occasion, the doctor articulated the consequences of her everyday familiarity with injurability. She had been called onto the field numerous times during a particularly bloody practice, and I remarked to her that she sometimes seemed like a person who was trying to keep a thousand plates spinning on poles. Just as she finished building one player up, another began to break down. "You must see these guys as walking body parts," I observed. "Do you even see the whole player anymore?" She laughed and said that she did still see the players as whole people. But then she pointed out a guy and commented on his running style: "Do you see how he runs funny?" He broke his tibia." This surprised me. "You know," I said, "you must look at these guys and see things about them that I would never see because I don't know them like you do and I don't know how the body works like you do." She nodded. "Your eyes can't see what your mind doesn't know," she told me.

The doctor's sentiment resonates, with uncanny precision, with Butler's argument about recognizing and apprehending bodies. To appreciate the significance of the slight hitch in a player's stride, one must first be able to per-

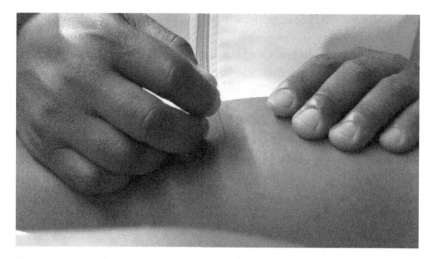

Fig. 3. A trainer applies acupuncture to the body of a player. (Photograph by author.)

ceive that player's body as susceptible to injury. Trainers, doctors, and support personnel are uniquely prepared to do so. They may not feel the violence of rugby directly on their bodies, but they are the first people to respond when a player suffers an injury. They look for the sources of pain and diagnose injuries, suture wounds back together, ask players about their physical and mental conditions, motivate players through exhausting training sessions, and track their progress through rehabilitation. They sit with players while they try to fathom the cause of an apparently inexplicable injury.[14] Familiarity with the materially vulnerable body by no means guarantees that support staff will take a player's subjective experience of an injury seriously,[15] but it acknowledges the possibility that a player's body can be permanently reshaped by the blows that it encounters on the field. Coaches, in contrast, practice a mode of perception that compares the player to an imagined, fully autonomous, masculine ideal. When they read a player's health condition as psychosomatic, they are not merely questioning his attitude. They are refusing to acknowledge (or apprehend) the full complexity of the player's lived subjectivity.[16]

This chapter demonstrates that though the Bulls medical team was predominantly female and though its coaching staff was entirely male, there is no straightforward connection between a person's gendered experience and their capacity to perceive athletic precarity. That power of apprehension comes from experience, knowledge, and material proximity to rugby players and their bodies. The team doctor's perspective was, again, indicative. She identified as a black woman, and she highlighted her gendered identity in her framing of the challenges associated with providing medical care to players.[17] She told me that players regularly challenged her diagnoses. They would ask to speak with other doctors or ignore her assessments. She found these responses frustrating because they suggested that players thought her opinion less credible than that of a male doctor. Over time, though, she found it useful to speak to players at the register they knew best—their own experiential knowledge of their bodies. She realized that every additional doctor's confirmation of her diagnoses lent credence to her authority, and she once even referred a player to a specialist for a "second opinion" when she knew full well that he was actually able to play. She believed that his physical injury had damaged his confidence and that he needed to hear the good news from a specialist before he would believe it for himself. If players wanted to ignore her assessments, she tended to allow them to follow their inclination if the team was out of season. She would warn them of the risks, of course, but they would learn their own lesson if their decision set their recoveries back by several weeks. Far from feeling like her concern for players and their bodies came from her gendered identity, it was her position as a doctor that prepared her to realize that players need to be addressed in the embodied language they know best. "Experience is the best teacher," she explained.[18]

A fixed, binary model of gendered perception also cannot explain the subjective experience of players. Male professional rugby players in South Africa are by no means unrecognized bodies in that regard, but they are frequently misrecognized or recognized in ways that fail to account for the complexity of their subjective experiences. Even players who play the sports they love for cash are, as Butler puts it, "framed" by norms of recognition (2009, 6–7). As professional athletes, they are subject to the usual grounds on which personhood is acknowledged (beginning, first and foremost, with the recognition of their bodies as belonging to persons who live, can die, and are worthy of grief) as well as to the performative norms of rugby, which obligate them to try their best to act as autonomous beings that feel the "bites" of rugby's violence as painless "nips." Coaches may imagine rugby to unfold within a temporally and spatially bounded "play frame," but players know better. Like Adorno (2007a), who took artistic autonomy to be a socially powerful fiction, professional players understand that their bodies can never fully traverse the boundary between fight and play, everyday and sanctified, bound and apparently free. With that expertise in mind, they can claim to know what their bodies need in order to perform. Professional players are uniquely prepared, then, to appreciate how deeply damaging a coach is being when he dismisses an injury as fabricated, because their bodies experience the precarity firsthand, on the field.

When players who feel that they have been mistreated by their team cannot or will not give up on rugby, another option remains: they can join the increasing numbers of athletes who are using their bodies as resources to facilitate their migration (cf. Besnier 2012; Besnier and Brownell 2012). Because of the competitiveness of the labor pool (which I described in detail in chapter 2), players regularly move between teams. Some get better contract offers, and others fail to have their contracts renewed. Some get relegated to lesser teams, and others opt to leave South Africa and play abroad. In many instances, movements are involuntary, but in some cases, players who decide that their abilities have not been respected strike out on their own. One promising young player was told that he had a better chance of gaining a senior contract if he switched to a position that he had never played before. Though the player refused to comment about his situation, several of his teammates agreed with the interpretation that came immediately to my mind: the player was trapped in a difficult bind. Each position on the rugby field brings its own relatively distinct requirements. In switching positions, the player would have to learn a completely new set of skills, which meant also learning to use his body in new ways. He would be exposed to potential injuries for which the mechanics he had developed in his body could not prepare him. Those challenges and risks came with no certain reward, as the team might still decide not to renew his contract. Were the player to refuse to change positions, though, he would appear unwilling to improve himself. An ideal player would be able to switch effortlessly between positions, of course, but even a mortal player could show his "good attitude" by embracing the switch and embodying the ideal as best he could. After weighing his option for some time, the player ultimately decided to sign with a European team that was interested in his services at the position he knew best. That move allowed the player to reassert control over his body and its physical capabilities, but it also came at a cost. He was required to join a new team in a different country, which meant, in the conception of sporting subjectivity I have outlined here, that he was required to attenuate (if not completely sever) his familiar networks of support. While the player likely experienced that compromise on his body and in his relationships on an everyday basis, its manifestations were most visible to an outside observer at a symbolic level:

because of formal questions of player availability as well as informal anxieties about national loyalty, South African players who choose to play their rugby internationally are generally passed over for national team selection.

CONCLUSION

Rugby is governed and organized by its rules, which structure the sport's uncertainty and give it a degree of coherence and continuity over space and time. Even so, the official rules of rugby change more slowly than the sport's on-field performance. Burdened by bureaucracy, referee interpretation, and the vagaries of live play, rules become a relatively static constraint out of which the actual practice of rugby frequently explodes. In May 2011, just a few weeks after the Bulls match described in the opening of this chapter, *Die Beeld* (an Afrikaans daily newspaper distributed in South Africa's northern provinces) reported that a player had been found responsible for injuring an opposing player's neck during a match. Predicated on a clear definition of player inten- tion on the field, that verdict treated the player's injury as a violation of the contractual agreement of sports. Though the player's actions were permissi- ble within the boundaries of the informal "gamesmanship" that rugby refer- ees and coaches often permit in practice, the guilty player had played outside of the rules of the game (Nel 2011). He was therefore culpable for the harm he had caused, just as he would have been in other circumstances. His action may have been intended as a "nip" in the moment it was enacted, but the judge decided that it was actually a "bite" and treated it as such.

The transition of "nip" to "bite" points to a meaningful ideological tension concealed in Gregory Bateson's metacommunicative conception of play. On the one hand, to "play" is, for Bateson, to convey to fellow players that what one appears to be doing is not what one is in fact trying to do. Bateson argues that the only way one can definitively demonstrate one's intention to play (rather than fight) is actually to play—to "fight" without fighting. Bateson thus writes, "Both in dream and in mammalian interaction, the only way to achieve a proposition which contains its own negation ('I will not bite you,' or 'I am not afraid of him') is by an elaborate imagining or acting out of the proposition to be negated" (2000, 327). That acting out suggests that play- ers are fully in control of themselves, able to demonstrate their intention to play (rather than fight) through their performative forbearance. On the other hand, Bateson recognized elsewhere that subjectivity does not end at the limits of the body. As N. Katherine Hayles has noted, Bateson's question of "if a blind man's cane is part of the man" opens up the possibility (explored in detail by Donna Haraway [2004]) that the body extends outward—via the cane and the information that passes through it—into the world (Hayles 1999, 84). For Hayles, that approach to the body (furnished by cybernetics) challenges not just subjectivity but also intention and leads ultimately, after passing through several generations of scholars, to the conclusion that "conscious agency has never been 'in control.' In fact, the very illusion of control bespeaks a fundamental ignorance about the nature of the emergent processes through which consciousness, the organism, and the environment are constituted" (288).

If Bateson's analysis of the cane highlights the dissolution of the polished, finished, subject, it also indicates that his differentiation between "nip" and "bite" is not sufficiently attentive to the implication of the nip's author in the world. As the case of rugby shows, that authorship becomes less transparent and more difficult to parse when the playful activity becomes an actor in its own right. For Hayles, the key question is, "Where should the . . . dissolution of boundaries stop?" (1999, 85). Where, in other words, does the line between subject and world get drawn, on what grounds is that line drawn, and what complexity of experience is excluded as a result? For the present book, the goal is not to answer Hayles (and Bateson too) by establishing a definitive boundary for the rugby-playing subject. (Indeed, it is fitting that establishing the legal limits of sporting consent is, as Kevin Young's 1993 article has shown, an extremely thorny issue.) Rather, the goal is to assess where that boundary is set by various groups that are associated with South African rugby and to consider the consequences that extend therefrom.

Thus, in the court case, the line was drawn at the physical boundaries of the acting player's body and the player's intentional control over that body. The judge ascribed to him definitive agency and, therefore, definitive responsiblity. The player's action was a "bite," not a "nip," and the judgment was not influenced significantly by the tolerance of the action in rugby circles, the fact that the player certainly learned it from someone else (who might therefore be partially culpable), or the chance that he might have done it before without issue. That subject-oriented "cut" through the complexity of rugby's uncertain performance is not especially surprising. As Talal Asad has observed, "Agency today serves primarily to define a completed personal action from within an indefinite network of causality by attributing to an actor responsibility *to* power. Paradigmatically, this means *forcing* a person to be accountable, to answer to a judge in a court of law why things were done or left undone. . . . A world of apparent accidents is rendered into a world of essences by attributing to a person moral/legal responsibility on whose basis guilt and innocence . . . are determined" (2003, 73–74).

Interestingly, coaches I knew recognized that such a perspective was not indicative of the true complexity of rugby's performance. They believed that the court ruling set a dangerous precedent in rugby because it assumed that one could readily discern culpability, or parse "bite" and "nip," in the playing of the sport. One coach addressed concerns about the player's learned "gamesmanship" directly, during a managerial meeting. He asked the team's legal counsel, "What if I teach a player a tactic that's in a 'gray area' in terms of legality but everyone still uses? Rugby is an unpredictable thing. Nobody can control all its conditions. What if, God forbid, someone got hurt? Suddenly I might be liable for damages too." Another coach, equally concerned, noted that if players were now likely to be held to a definitive legal standard, that standard should better reflect the way the game is actually played. With the aim of clarifying that standard, the coach told me that he had contacted international rugby's governing body and urged them to use a player's intent to injure as a means to distinguish between what he called "foul plays" and run-of-the-mill "dangerous plays." He told me, "Rugby is a dangerous sport. You can't tackle and have it not be dangerous."

The perspectives that the aforementioned coaches offer with respect to injuries and culpability cut to the thematic heart of this chapter. As I have argued, the rules, conditions, and historical significances of rugby produce a "play frame" that allows the sport to take on a kind of life. It is a magical "unpredictable thing" with which all players must contend. That "thing" may seem like an artificial construct, produced by an anthropologist for the sake of argument. But players, coaches, and medical personnel regard it as real (and dangerous), partly because its material effects are real. As the coaches I talked with suggest, rugby is a dangerous sport, and no amount of rule-governed order and legalistic scrutiny can wish that danger away.

At the same time, much like the court, coaches read players' subjectivities and intentions through a mode of valuation inspired by a raced, classed, and gendered conception of political subjectivity. To be an autonomous body, acting creatively and authoritatively on the field, is to perform, momentarily, the illusory subject of a Western Enlightenment tradition. Unlike the court, coaches are motivated in their approach by conditions particular to sport. When a player or team succeeds, in the gym or on the field, in producing certainty where uncertainty ought to exist, he/they appear to operate momentarily and tantalizingly free of constraint. Not only does that freedom possess an aesthetic appeal (as discussed in chapter 1), but it is consistent with team success. Coaches want to manufacture ideal performances because doing so will lead to victories. Presented with a choice—either to abandon the dream of the masculine subject, the athletic prowess it promises, and the opportunity to use that promise to compel players to perform or instead to attempt to apprehend the precarious and materially injurable bodies of their players—it is hardly surprising that most coaches I knew opted most of the time for the promise of success. Systematically effaced in that perspective are injuries (the material residue of rugby's pretend violence) and the embodied vulnerability and contextual dependence on teammates, opposition, and environmental factors that players carry with them into and out of the process of play. Effaced too is the uncertainty of rugby itself and its role in shaping player actions.

In contrast to coaches and their most readily available viewpoints, players, medical personnel, and sometimes trainers can become so cognizant of the materiality of the player's body that they understand that even the strongest and fittest players cannot be as autonomous as their best performances make them seem. They are not supermen, and tackles accumulate over games and years until even the strongest bodies break down. When a body does crumble, whether as a result of time or malice or an unfortunate accident, its dependence on others must be taken seriously. That precarity opens the possibility that the player will apprehend his dependence on others, but as Benhabib and Butler show, precarity (fully apprehended) is not conducive to the masculinist connotations with which rugby is associated. Players therefore end up in conflict with their coaches over the health of their bodies. Support personnel sometimes find themselves occupying a similar position. Their capacity to apprehend players' bodies as vulnerable—to see with their eyes what they know in their mind—sometimes turns doctors and trainers into advocates for players.

That position explains the trainer's suspicion, mentioned earlier in this chapter, about a coach's proposal to rehabilitate a player with an overtraining injury by "inconveniencing" him back to the field. It also explains one trainer's response to a group of players when one of player asked him why a long-injured junior player was still using crutches. "Have any of you ever had a muscle come off your bone?" he demanded. Another player admitted that he hadn't. "Have you ever broken a bone?" the trainer continued. The player shook his head. "Well," he concluded, "let me tell you, if that ever happened to you, you'd be on crutches too."

Standing by, listening silently to the trainer, I decided to chime in. "Rugby is a dangerous sport," I observed. The player nodded. Then he—like so many coaches and players before him—performed a boundary-drawing action of his own. He tied my remark about the efficacy of rugby's environment and the vulnerability indicated by the seriousness of the player's injury together with the player's long rehabilitation and his teammates' skepticism about the player's slow recovery and, in a breath, explained it all in terms of rugby's masculine ideal. "It's a *man's* sport," he said.

CHAPTER 4

Searching for Certainty
Rugby and Male Identity in a Former Model C School

Not long into my fieldwork at a former Model C[1] school for boys in South Africa, I decided to practice with its top rugby team. I had 12 years of rugby experience myself, and having observed and documented their training sessions for several weeks from a nearby pavilion, I suspected I knew something of what I was trying to do. Predictably—or so it seems now—I was humbled and humbled again. Rugby, the folk knowledge goes, is a sport of confidence. The more confident one is in one's actions on the field, the more decisively, quickly, and violently one can perform them. I began with confidence. But after a few slips on the muddy turf, slimy jerseys sliding through my cold fingers, and hard shoulders striking my chest, I was soon playing as though I were on ice. I could not stand. The mud on my arms and face surprised me, and I felt unclean and discovered. Players seemed to be running to test me, rather than to perform the drill as effectively as possible, and I questioned my decision to participate.

My feelings of self-doubt and vulnerability echo the contradictions that Narayan (1993) describes in her critique of the notion of the "native anthropologist." I was "rugby player" enough to feel the attraction of the initial moment of observational intimacy, to participate in the drill and recognize its ultimate aim, but not enough to handle the moments of contact it required of me. Each impact further marked my inadequacy, making me increasingly aware of the gap between the player I had thought I was and the player the boys had exposed. Groups continued to run into me as I grew battered, weary, and embarrassed. I missed my tackles with greater regularity, until, mercifully, the coach ended the exercise. As I walked to the sideline, I confronted myself with questions. Had I lost credibility with my performance?

Should I try to recover credibility by resisting the urge to give up (when it felt so obvious that I should), or would I lose further credibility the longer I stayed and failed? "To put [these questions] in the clearest possible terms," I wrote at the end of that day's notes, "do I show up to tomorrow's practice in my dress shirt or my jersey?" I appeared in my dress shirt the following day, and I recalled my practice long after my bruises had healed. Why had it felt as though the players had learned something about me during our brief encounter—not me as rugby player, as one might expect from my inability to perform the comparatively specific (some would surely say meaningless) tasks the sport required, but me in a fuller and deeper sense? How was my exposure to the players' violence a necessary part of the learning process? As I will show in this chapter, the answer to those questions comes from a combination of rugby's form and the particular conditions of Model C schools in post-apartheid South Africa.[2]

With respect to rugby's formal qualities, this chapter builds on the previous one's central claim that far from undermining the social significance of player performances, rugby's meaningless tasks allowed coaches to monitor, measure, and test the masculinity of their players. A player entering a rugby field is required to act under conditions of uncertainty and violence. Players best able to "impose their will" on their opposition, on the match, and on the uncertainty of rugby itself were interpreted as more masculine, not because physical strength and athletic skill are inherently masculine qualities, but because their performances appeared to demonstrate that they had realized (on an aesthetic level) the dream of becoming disembodied sociopolitical actors. The autonomy of rugby therefore cleared space for representations of an autonomous, white, male, and European-derived subjectivity. When young professional players failed to embody that ideal—whether on the field or in the gym—they were expected, by their coaches, to do the next best thing: to demonstrate their devotion to that ideal by striving continually to achieve it. Players' failure to embody an ideal of autonomy occurred not, as many coaches assume, because of a lack of desire or physical durability but because autonomy is a social position that no really existing human body could ever hope to realize. Coaches who use autonomy as a lens through which to scrutinize their players hold them, implicitly, to an impossible standard. That lens, as I showed in the previous two chapters, is rooted deeply in rugby's history as a British colonial creation.

Autonomy is not the only interpretive lens that shapes how rugby players are conceptualized in South Africa. This chapter and the one that follows it address two other powerful lenses that originate in South Africa in particular: the judgment of players according to their complicity with apartheid and its legacies, discussed in the next chapter; and the judgment of players according to apartheid-era standards of white masculinity, discussed in this one. Taken together, the two chapters show how rugby performances became intertwined with socially situated modes of perception (cf. Seel 2005, 21) and, by extension, how those modes of perceiving bodies continue to inform the judgment of today's players (and, as discussed in chapter 5, coaches and referees). Even at the levels of perception and interpretation, South African rugby continues to bear the traces of the social and historical orders from which it came (cf. Feldman 1991).

Mainstream "white" rugby was closely associated with Afrikaner nationalism and the National Party during apartheid, a connection that I here argue was built through minute and everyday forms of social practice as much as state ideology. From the 1960s until the 1990s, adults in white South African schools linked the violence of rugby to the "productive" violence of corporal punishment and military training, and they used those disciplinary practices to dismantle and reconstruct young men. I trace the history of those connections in this chapter, and I demonstrate the consequences of that history for South Africa's contemporary moment. Now, after the democratic state has curtailed corporal punishment and ended white male conscription, some parents, teachers, and coaches seem to have placed additional emphasis on the disciplinary powers of rugby's violence.

Since rugby's speed, uncertainty, and violence give its players little time to reflect on their actions before they make them, it often appears that the choices a player makes on the field, under violence and at high speed, are reliable indicators of "who that player is." Invested adults who watch young men respond spontaneously to the ever-changing conditions of play judge them according to their ability to live up to the standards of past generations of men. Is a player throwing himself into contact confidently or recklessly? Is he responding to the threat of violence with clever actions or irresponsible ones? In the classroom or on the street, a boy can be polite but disingenuous. When he is on the rugby field, there is little time for deception. He can be only who he is, who he has been socially trained to be, because there is little time to be anything else. When that understanding of rugby's interpretive possibilities intersects with the uncertainty that many white South Africans feel about the future of their country and about the place they hold in that future, rugby performances can seem comfortingly familiar. They offer a tantalizingly stable source of certainty in what can feel like unpredictable times.[3]

That said, post-apartheid social conditions have complicated rugby's capacity to deliver certainty in new and unexpected ways. Rugby may, for some spectators, stand in for discredited disciplinary practices, but recent concerns about steroids in wealthy schools can transform a disciplined performance into an act of deception. Similarly, if a boy is suspected of harboring professional aspirations, a good showing on the field can render him ungrateful to his school. Those acts are not simply dangerous to players' bodies or disloyal to amateur institutions. Because judgments issue from a particular combination of rugby's social significance and the novel forms of youthful masculine agency that the schools produce, such acts expose something of the economic and social contradictions that sustain former Model C schools. Simply by playing rugby notably well, boys in South Africa can (inadvertently) turn rugby's capacity to deliver certainty into a critique of the schools they attend.

HIT US IN OUR BRUISES: RUGBY AND DISCIPLINARY VIOLENCE

As my post-practice reflections illustrate, the notion that rugby indicates something about the inner life of its players is not uniquely South African. The ideological roots of that idea can be traced, in part, to the doctrine of athleticism in 19th-century British education (cf. Mangan 1981, 1996). Though South Africans never perfectly duplicated the dominant perception of the sport in Great Britain, Grundlingh has shown that South African readings of rugby were generally similar to British ones until the expansion of Afrikaner nationalism in the 1930s and 1940s. At that point, Grundlingh writes, "whereas the British might have projected the game as a training ground for the inculcation and encouragement of values such as sportsmanship, gentlemanly conduct, and fair-mindedness, Afrikaners placed less emphasis on these and more on the game as an opportunity to demonstrate presumed Afrikaner qualities, such as ruggedness, endurance, forcefulness and determination" (1994, 414). Grundlingh attributes that refiguration of rugby to the triumphalism of Afrikaner nationalists and to a duality in rugby itself: namely, the fact that the sport prioritized moral development as well as the physical characteristics of strength, speed, and stamina. That reading may be persuasive, but it offers few details about the mechanics of the institutions that gave rugby that particular significance. Jaclyn Cock has highlighted the ideological importance of white schools to the apartheid state and some of the forms of coercion that occurred within such schools, not only a "cadet system" including over 250,000 students by 1987 (Evans 1989), but also a "Youth Preparedness Programme"—a school subject that emphasized "military preparedness, discipline and patriotism" (Cock 1991, 71), "*veld* [field] schools" that exposed young men to military and survival training, and formal and informal partnerships with Voortrekker youth groups.[4] That militarization of white, male education shaped the significance of the rugby within those institutions.

Consider one coach's story about his first rugby match in the early 1970s. He was six years old at the time, and his team won handily, 40–0. The following day, when the boys returned to school, the headmaster was waiting for them, cane in hand. "He made us strip down to our underwear," the coach recalled, "and line up facing the wall. Then he went down the line. He stopped at each of us, picked out the bruises and cuts that we'd gotten in the game, and whacked us all three times. He made sure to hit us on our bruises. When he finished, he told us that he'd done it because we were getting big heads. He didn't want us to be too proud of ourselves." Though my informant remembered his story with nothing more than a shake of his head, I was struck by the continuity of field and schoolyard violence in the punishment. While the headmaster may have intended simply to increase the pain of the lesson by hitting the boys in their most tender spots, his blows connected the impact of the cane to the moments of rugby violence that spawned the bruises in the first place. Such a punishment showed that rugby was much more than a metaphor for war, because bearing the brunt of the disciplinary lesson demanded that boys bear the echoes of rugby's pain as well. The ordeal of rugby became the ordeal of corporal punishment, meant to teach a lesson of humility, and the process of experiencing and reacting to violence in the match was transformed, by the headmaster's choice of target, into the process of responding to a violent lesson. Such occurrences made it possible to conceive of rugby as a productive space into which disciplinary practices could bleed.

Those ties, once tentatively established, were reinforced by wider patterns of rugby-related disciplinary action. Holdstock's study of educational discipline, for example, notes that boys received corporal punishment from teachers for missing rugby practices and losing matches (1990, 349), and disciplinary violence intersected with rugby not just off the field but on it as well.

Fig. 4. A panel from the South African underground comic *Bitterkomix*, drawn and written by Conrad Botes and Anton Kannemeyer, juxtaposing rugby and disciplinary violence. For a deep engagement with the particular politics of *Bitterkomix* and with the implications of those politics for Afrikaner belonging in post-apartheid South Africa, see Barnard's "*Bitterkomix*: Notes from the Post-apartheid Underground" (2004). (Panel reprinted with permission of Anton Kannemeyer; from Botes and Kannemeyer 1998, 15.)

While my older informants had their own stories of coaches and teachers hitting them with jump ropes or whistle straps if they made mistakes on the field during training sessions, Daniël ("Danie") Craven—a legendary figure in white South African rugby circles—describes several particularly vivid accounts of that type of violence. Composing a book in honor of his coaching mentor A. F. Markötter, Craven (an influential figure in South African rugby in his own right) devoted the first chapter to accounts of Markötter's renowned on-field disciplinary techniques. Two testimonials from that rich collection of memories suffice here.

> One afternoon at practice [Markötter] had his customary stick with him and he often used to use this on players who annoyed him. He did so again to a number 8 forward who displeased him with his scrum work. He lambasted him just as he got down into a set scrum.
>
> The player pulled his head out in such obvious anger that he was ordered off the field. The rest of us stood rooted. [Markötter] when roused was not an easy person to talk to. Afterwards we tried to persuade the player concerned to make

his peace with [Markötter]. We knew that he would not be considered again until he had been to apologise.

When eventually he did get so far as to apologise he received a proper dressing down.

"You fool," said [Markötter], "do you think I waste m[y] time hitting anyone unless I feel I can lift him up? I wouldn't waste my energies on pushing anyone down." (Craven 1959, 28)

I was always jealous of the hits that [a particular teammate] had gotten [from Markötter]—we [this player and his teammate] were of course always roommates.

When I came back from the Free State and the Karoo to Wellington, I had to take part in a [match] in Wellington. Just before we got on the field—we all stood under the pavilion—[Markötter] arrived. I was unsure if I should greet him or not, . . . but I just stepped forward in front of him. Before the whole pavilion with all eyes on [Markötter], I finally got the hit that I am still proud of to this day. (47)

As those stories show, players came both to identify a notion of commitment with violence and to understand that demonstrating commitment meant tolerating (and sometimes even longing for) physical punishment. Many came to understand, to paraphrase Markötter above, that they were only being hit because an adult believed that they could be better players-cum-men as a result.

Such narratives direct our attention to the spectacular dimension[5] of the violence of rugby and physical punishment as well. Of the days of corporal punishment, one teacher recalled, "Those shots would echo around the whole building and none of the other boys would misbehave for the rest of the day." Young men did not simply accept punishment; they encountered it in front of others. Both rugby matches and canings were meant to be witnessed and appreciated as much as viscerally experienced. For the authority figures who embraced those practices, then, each disbursement of disciplinary pain offered a double measure of certainty. It confirmed that performances on the rugby field and performances under corporal punishment were mutually intelligible while at the same time underwriting the disciplinary potential of pain itself. Whether a boy was receiving a caning from a well-meaning teacher, passing through an initiation, or tackling a boy from another school, his responses to pain and violence were continually scrutinized.

PUTTING PAIN TO USE: IMMEDIACY, VIOLENCE, AND
PERFORMATIVE AUTHENTICITY

If young men were scrutinized in terms of their responses to pain and violence, then rugby acquires a special significance. Not only do boys throw themselves willingly into contact and into pain, but they appear to do so "authentically." In a given 80-minute game, each player will be expected to perform actions and make decisions much more quickly, in much quicker succession, under many more sets of eyes, and within narrower parameters than most people generally encounter in their daily lived experience. That compression of human action is significant because it produces a proliferation of moments that can be judged and because the actions are assumed to be executed instinctively, in relation to stimuli spontaneously encountered (an opposing player, the bounce of the ball, the angle of a kick, etc.). Such actions, the logic follows, reveal more about a player's motivations and state of mind than do actions performed outside the sporting frame, because the on-field actions cannot be mediated and, it is therefore thought, cannot be performed disingenuously. Rugby, as this advertisement (fig. 5) argues explicitly, cannot therefore be "faked."

Interestingly, some art theorists have used a strikingly similar logic as a means to theorize a gap between sports and artistic forms. In his work on aesthetic vision and appearance, Martin Seel suggests that artworks are compelling because they are "presentations," or objects that not only engage us aesthetically but present themselves to us so that we "can find *something* presented by them" (2005, 108). As presentations, art gains an important distance from the world and, therefore, a measure of political potential. "When we play," he writes, "we engage fully in the present. When we play aesthetically, we engage fully in the intuition of a presence" (136). Because sporting play allows no room for reflection, it also permits no self-aware presentation. Play (and its uncertainty, we could add) is too immediately performed. Seel continues, "The public spectacle of modern sport is an aesthetic event that allows spectators to take a collective time-out from the continuities of their lives—a time-out that does not, like the time-out of art, lead them to imaginative projection and reflections about the game of their lives. This is not art and should not be art; *it does not have any meaning and should not have any.* It is an aesthetic spectacle of its own kind that finds fulfillment in the visible genesis and passing of spectacular events" (137, emphasis added; see

Fig. 5. Advertisement for Windhoek Lager, found in the program for a professional rugby game in 2011. Windhoek is a Namibian brewery, and its lager is widely available in South Africa. The fine print reads, "It takes courage and an unwavering commitment to play rugby. Give 100%, [sic] 100% of the time and you'll make the cut. Anything less is inconceivable. We brew Windhoek Lager in much the same way. A single-minded dedication and commitment to brewing only 100% pure beer is at the heart of everything we do—let's face it, you can't fake 100% pure beer."

also C. Young 2008, 14). Theorists like Seel suggest that when artists create, they reflect on the world and respond to it. When athletes play, they play so deeply in the moment that they lose the capacity to construct representations of reality; they simply are themselves (cf. Danto 2013, 51).

This chapter suggests a slightly different position, which finds more common ground between art and sport than allowed by Danto (at least in the work just referenced) and Seel. Rather than foregrounding the intentionality of the artist or the performer in the production of meaning, the connections between rugby, as a framed activity, and forms of disciplinary violence show that rugby is capable of mobilizing a broad array of discursive, material, and embodied constructions that lend significance to a player's actions whether that player intended to produce that meaning or not (cf. Foucault 1998; W. Mitchell 2005). Seen in that way, a rugby player's actions on the field acquire meaning and political significance irrespective of the player's engagement in a performative present or—as Coplan has observed in the case of popular South African music (2008, 336)—explicitly articulated sentiments. Spectators, coaches, other players, and, after the fact, even the player himself can call up meanings (informed by race, gender, class, history, and more) that, in the moment of play, he may or may not have sought to provoke intentionally. While athletes try to immerse themselves fully "in the moment" of play (Danto 2013, 51), even full immersion can produce "presentations" if spectators mobilize immersion in a way that calls those presentations into being.

Seen in that way, the "authenticity" that rugby appears to generate is no less an artifact of the social situation in which players play than was the autonomy of the previous chapter. Not every action will carry great interpretive significance, of course, but that is precisely the point. Over the course of their young careers, boys will be disciplined by violence into standardized behaviors. In time, the thudding of bodies will produce a situation that requires a player to make a crucial decision. In that moment, the player's body will either act appropriately or fail to do so. That line of thought is even more persuasive in schools than in high-level adult rugby, because school rugby caters to many more players, with a wider range of experience and ability, than does elite, senior rugby. Raw newcomers are still welcome to join school teams, and years of practices and technical coaching have not yet culled weaker players and polished talented ones. In Model C schools, rugby's violence and spontaneity allow the sport to compel players to expose their discipline and the depth of their commitment for the world to see. A player, especially an immersively engaged one, is always on the verge of being "caught out," because one poorly made decision can expose weaknesses he might prefer to conceal.[6]

One coach referred to the weaknesses and flaws that the sport exposed as "glitches," describing them much as one might a computer virus. A glitch might reveal itself at any moment in a game or a practice, and once revealed, it was bound to reemerge. It was, he told me, part of the player's nature. He clarified his point with a parable. A scorpion, he told me, wanted to cross a river, so it approached a frog and requested a ride on its back. The frog refused at first, telling the scorpion that it could not risk getting stung. The scorpion promised it would not sting the frog. "What is more," it pointed out, "if I sting you and you drown, I would drown as well. I certainly would not want to harm myself, so surely I would never sting you." The frog appreciated the scorpion's logic and agreed to carry the scorpion across the river. Yet, in the middle of the river, the scorpion stung the frog, and both began to sink. The frog begged the scorpion to explain its actions, and the scorpion was apologetic. "I tried my best," it answered, "but it was my nature." The truth of its mental glitch (revealed, we might also note, in the crucible of a dangerous river crossing) was irredeemable and inevitable.

Rugby's social significance, coupled with the routinized ways that the violence of the sport overlapped with that of corporal punishment, helps to explain the importance of rugby to the apartheid state. The sport was not simply an easy vehicle for nationalist sentiments; organized rugby[7] put pain to good use. It became a means to bind young white men into a broader disciplinary apparatus. Indeed, one of Cock's informants drew a direct comparison between the masculinity of rugby and military service, telling her, "You somehow become a man through military training. It's like playing in the first rugby team, in terms of manliness and also the way girls respond to you" (1991, 75). In this context, rugby and other disciplinary practices were used in tandem to marginalize alternative masculinities and cultivate, and systematically reward, an ideal one that was amenable to the state and its needs.[8] As one teacher well-versed in South African rugby and military history commented, "It seems like we [young white men] got all our lessons in a violent manner in South Africa."[9]

POST-APARTHEID SOUTH AFRICA AND RUGBY'S PLACE IN A NEW DISCIPLINARY REGIME

Chapter 3 traced numerous contemporary legacies of the systematic privileging of the invulnerable masculine ideal—from the preferential selection of *menere* (sirs) at the Bulls, to the "inconveniencing" of injured players back to the field, to my experiences in the gym as a comparatively frail male-coded body. The violent lessons themselves (and the certainty they appeared to provide) have come under intense scrutiny in the democratic era. Since the early 1990s, the African National Congress has systematically dismantled the legal supports for the apartheid-era disciplinary regime in all South African schools. The cadet system and its accompanying *veld* school have been culled from Model C curricula, harsh initiation practices have been curtailed, and the South African Schools Act (1996) made corporal punishment illegal and punishable as a form of assault.

Many of the teachers I spoke with disliked those changes. The new disciplinary system depended on a combination of detentions and demerits, and teachers detested the quantity of paperwork and increased hours of service the new regulations demanded. Others were adamant that the demise of cadets and school initiations had undermined school discipline. While some teachers found creative ways to adjust to the new regulations, others could not or would not change. Senior male teachers (many of whom had been so enmeshed in the structures of apartheid military service that they may have been unable to justify or even easily conceptualize alternative modes of discipline) appeared to have the greatest difficulty reconciling their disciplinary repertoires with the modes of classroom behavior the state now legitimizes. One teacher, for example, drew his teaching philosophy explicitly from his military experience. "South Africa used to have one of the best armies in the world," he said, "and it all began with order. We were drilled like a machine." Despite his best efforts to preserve that discipline in his classroom, students regularly ignored his shouted orders and parodied his discipline. "I just want to give class," he said, "but it always gets disrupted." Students played pranks on him behind his back, threatened him, and giggled at and questioned his demands. He regretted that he had to "act like a tyrant" in response to their behavior, shouting at his students and firing off demerits, but he still thought it was the most effective way to teach. He regarded his classroom as a bulwark of order, his duty as enforcing discipline even if students objected to it.

That teacher's story serves as a reminder that schoolboys are active agents in most (if not necessarily all) disciplinary relationships. Just as some respond to the authoritarian methods of old military men with scorn and mockery, others defend themselves with the morality of the post-apartheid nation. As one teacher put it, "[Students] have learned a language of rights from the new government, but only to get themselves out of trouble. They have rights now but no accountability." Some students expressed concerns about a "disciplinary problem" in their school as well. The student council's head of discipline made his dissatisfaction particularly explicit in a speech to the student body. Younger boys had to "learn their place," he told his peers, "but the old 'welcome procedures' have been made illegal." New practices were needed that would be "tough and still feared; Tough but sensible." As the desire for tough, feared, and sensible punishments suggests, senior schoolboys are busy refashioning the disciplinary language of their parents and teachers to suit present conditions. Corporal punishment or harsh initiation practices might still be justifiable in terms of toughness and fear, but the legal definition of "sensible" has changed dramatically.[10]

That students sometimes appreciate "tough" punishments means that teachers can find unlikely allies in their own classrooms. Boys and teachers have been known to resolve their classroom conflicts with covert acts of corporal punishment, and many school authorities are willing to overlook initiation violence if it occurs within the secret world of school hostels.[11] Although such agreements certainly do not account for the majority of the instances of disciplinary violence in former Model C schools, they exist nevertheless, and the sentiments of the students help explain why. Some boys may prefer physical punishments simply because they consider them brief and convenient,[12] but others continue to find important lessons in the disciplinary tests. One boy recalling his initiation to the school commented, "If you don't push yourself beyond your limits, you will never learn who you are. We would always do things like go out in the middle of the night, and it [would be] bitter cold, and then we would start [to learn] who were are and what we can do if we must."

Though anxious or overprotective parents were often cited as the major reason why disciplinary regulations had changed, I found that parents also struggled with the implications of educational reform. One parent walked a discursive tightrope when she tried to characterize her choice of school in language appropriate to the post-apartheid nation. She had sent her boys to a particular school, she explained, because of its tradition and its discipline. Upon my questioning, she added that corporal punishment had been prohibited, but the school had still managed to maintain the "culture of respect" that she lamented most Model C schools in South Africa had lost: "The country has changed. It hasn't been for the worse, but it has broken down the white camaraderie of the past." Her intimation was that white camaraderie, historically produced in such schools through mechanisms of discipline as well as apartheid legislation, had been dismantled by the post-apartheid state. She left me to connect the remaining dots: the school she chose had remained an attractive option because it had retained that discipline, its culture of respect, and the accompanying traces of white camaraderie. The school's headmaster, addressing the matter equally delicately and without reference to race, also acknowledged an ongoing struggle with post-apartheid reforms. In a speech to parents at the end of the academic year, he commented that one of the biggest challenges facing the school was the need to bring necessary change into the academic environment without undermining the school's "character and culture."[13]

Such comments could be explained in terms of a nostalgic longing for security and political power, but the precise character of those concerns suggests something more specific. The repeated references to discipline, to character, and to respect indicate a pointed search for certain and stable interpretations, albeit within the context of a political regime many white parents felt to be morally, fiscally, and culturally undisciplined, lacking proper character, and systematically dismantling "white camaraderie." Under such circumstances, rugby becomes an ideal way for parents to know that their boys have acquired "character and culture." Not only is the sport exempt from the stigma of corporal punishment or initiations, but it is regarded as a leisure activity and is therefore both fun and voluntary. A young boy can "choose"[14] to play rugby, and an interested parent can watch his development and study his performances with the knowledgeable eyes of a connoisseur.

As Price (2001) and Bourdieu (1984) have recognized, connoisseurship is as drawn from the social context of judgment as is the object of taste itself (Price 2001, 11). Observers become connoisseurs of rugby—in depth of knowledge and certainty, if not necessarily in cachet—through their intimate familiarity with the historical and social associations that the sport has formed with disciplinary violence. Often, like the coach who was beaten in his rugby bruises, they experienced those associations on their own bodies during their school rugby careers. That familiarity helps them efficiently interpret a boy's confidently executed tackle for what it can also signify: his discipline and reverence for the school for which he plays. Exposed to many moments of violence from years of watching and, in many cases, playing rugby, connoisseurs feel that they can easily differentiate between an assured tackle and a weak one, a clever play and a simpleminded one, a tactically wise decision and a thoughtless one. Secure in their authority and convinced of the power of rugby to recapture the certainty of corporal punishment, discriminating adults judge a student's spontaneous reactions against a storehouse of idealized and realized actions, to formulate definitive conclusions about who that boy is and who he will become.[15] One boy I spoke to speculated on just that relationship: "My dad enjoys coming and watching my rugby because, as a father, you like to see your son play. I think he takes pride in it, it tells him that he has brought me up right and well." Such a dynamic between a son and his father is hardly unique to post-apartheid South Africa.[16] At the same time, the broader parental concerns the boy spoke of are situated within a post-apartheid social context that appears to lack and even actively forbid other forms of "sensible" discipline.

Fig. 6. Five-year-old boys wrestle with each other and learn the basics of rugby under an adult's supervision. (Photograph by the author.)

Though connoisseurs may, explicitly or implicitly, celebrate the disciplinary mechanisms used in white schools during apartheid, evidence suggests that these mechanisms were not always as effective as some may remember. One teacher admitted, "The cadets were a bit of a joke at [this school]. We didn't have a very good band. They couldn't keep the beat and that made marching difficult." An alumnus from another school told me about realizing, as a student, that he could avoid attending military exercises if he joined the fire brigade: "So I gave the teacher a note that said I was in the fire brigade, and I went to the fire brigade and gave them a note that said I was at the exercise. Then I went to the library and read books by myself." Other boys used stories and poems in their yearbooks to lampoon cadet discipline and complain about *veld* camps. Those criticisms were explicit, as represented by a cartoon (fig. 7) that found its way into a student annual in 1968.

STEROIDS, "HIDING," AND INEQUALITY IN MODEL C SCHOOLS

In a social context characterized perhaps less by threatened tradition and an absence of discipline than by the perception of such threat and absence within the context of widespread social transformation, rugby fields carry great interpretive significance: they remain places where the facts about boys are still definitively laid bare. At the school at which I worked, for example, coaches and trainers blended conventional fitness tests (quantifying speed, strength, height, and weight, among other things) with more

Fig. 7. Cartoon from a 1968 student annual. The caption reads, "Oh, so you're not on parade?"

subjective forms of judgment. Boys were given psychological profiles early in the season; coaches and parents would stand to the side, whispering to each other and watching players practice; and gym managers monitored the boys, always on the lookout for ones who were not training hard enough. Over time, coaches used those tests to form judgments about the boys they watched. One coach (perhaps unsure of what to tell an inquiring anthropologist) talked me through his players in precisely those terms. Producing his team list, he offered me a thumbnail sketch of each player, pointing to names as he went along: "This one is a loose cannon. This one plays in a feisty style." Some months later, I recorded another coach introducing me to his players in a similar fashion.

(1) That guy would rather drink than work out. (2) He was just lazy. (3) He worked out so hard that he started crying one day. (4) He's a nice guy, quiet but really strong—he can squat 120 [kilograms] all the way down and all the way up! (5) He is a cardio freak—he's a bit crazy but the fittest guy I know. (6) Remember that guy we said was fat and lazy? That's him. (7) This guy is, like, insanely strong, the "2 to 1" next to his name means that he [can lift] twice as much [on his] back as [his] chest. (8) He just had a bad attitude. (9) He had

a good attitude; he was just too small. (10) He's just a genetic freak. (11) *He's a super strong little guy that everyone thinks is on steroids, but I just think he's very precise about his nutrition and supplements.*

The movement from a player's performance to a definitive interpretation of that performance in terms of the player's character is obvious here. Some players failed to meet expectations not because they were unprepared or had other priorities or were not quite strong enough, but because they were lazy or had a bad attitude. Rugby exposed these flaws. If most of the coach's judgments seem to ooze with reliable certainty, though, the italicized statement should give us pause. Why does the coach inject his viewpoint there and not before? What explains the difference between "he just had a bad attitude" and "everyone thinks [he] is on steroids, but I just think [otherwise]," and why does the certainty of a bad attitude fall apart when it encounters steroids[17] and supplements?

Considered in the terms of this chapter, I suggest that steroid-assisted performances undermine the certainty of judgment by destabilizing assumptions about the connection between a rugby player and his play on the field. The sport can demand spontaneous performance, to be sure, but when a player uses steroids, that performance will say little about the player himself. The more weight he lifts and the more effectively he plays, the less legitimate his performance becomes, because his actions only underline his "corruption." One coach, for example, lightly dismissed a boy's accomplishments in the gym with a wave of his hand. "I suspect the needle," he said once we had walked out of earshot. That statement had a jarring effect. His words turned what had been an impressive physical performance on its head, to say nothing of the player's prior accomplishments on the field. Rather than producing discipline, the player's physical prowess and ability to dole out and tolerate pain only marked his guilt. If a boy can perform actions with quantifiable success while concealing his underlying glitch, rugby appears to be less effective at extracting the truth from bodies than coaches and other adults might like to believe.[18]

Subjective statements like the one italicized above can help make sense of recent consternation, facilitated by the South African media, about steroid use in school rugby. Following a positive test from a promising young player from Free State Province in late 2010, a crisis was perpetuated by a number of subsequent tests at high schools across the country. On April 8, 2011, *Die Beeld* announced that four players had tested positive for illegal substances at

Craven Week, an invitation-only tournament for schoolboys and an important site for talent identification for professional scouts (Karstens 2011). By
May 29, the *Times of South Africa* proclaimed "Steroid Scourge Rages in
School Rugby," citing a study finding that nearly one in six (21 of 130) students
tested at 18 "top schools" had used one banned substance or another (Govender 2011). That report was quickly supported, on June 4, by an interview
in *Rapport* done by René-Jean van der Berg and Hanri Wondergem. Their
interviewee, "Rodney," was an admitted user and unapologetic distributor of
anabolic steroids to students. The article, titled "Derde van skoolseuns gebruik steroïde; hoofde tjoepstil" (A third of schoolboys use steroids; school
headmasters silent), referenced a study suggesting that 30 percent of students
at five unnamed Johannesburg schools had used illegal substances and that
upwards of 84 percent had felt pressure to do so (van der Berg and Wondergem 2011).

Although the initial positive test was surprising and potentially troubling
for competitive rugby schools (it was the topic of endless debate at the school
at which I worked), it would be a mistake to use the self-evident danger of
steroid use or a proliferation of materials and technical knowledge as the only
explanations for the crisis. Both the particular identification of the problem
with 18 "top schools" and the cost of steroids (estimated by "Rodney" as a
monthly expense of between R2,000 and R8,000, or roughly $290 and $1,150
at the time) give a class dimension to the hysteria. Steroid use is a specific
sort of national concern, one that plagues families with enough disposable
income to send their children to such schools and to overlook so expensive a
practice. More than this, the articles are not just concerned with the damage
done to young users. They also indict institutions that are suspected of sac-
rificing their "character and culture" by tolerating (and, in some cases, perhaps actively endorsing) the presence of steroids in their schoolyards, in their
quest for continuing rugby success.

The reported crisis demonstrates the elite schools' bind. Rugby is one of
the best ways for schools to demonstrate the strength of their "culture" in
the post-apartheid era (confirming it for their faculty, parents, students and
prospective students), but the threat of steroids undermine the certainty that
rugby provides. Though testing for steroids could definitively resolve that
ambiguity,[19] it would do so at the expense of the school's "culture," because
the need for such tests indicates that the school was unable to instill the sort
of "character" in its boys that would discourage steroid use in the first place.
In the wake of these reports, "top schools" proposed a solution that was just

as ambiguous as the problem they sought to solve. Committed administrators and headmasters floated the idea of forming "informal and nonbinding" associations with other schools to make known members' investment in steroid-free sport. The proposed structure of these associations is no surprise—while those lenient organizations would undoubtedly be useful for practical and financial reasons, their informality also allowed each member school to join the public condemnation of steroids while maintaining the fiction that its particular "culture" remained strong enough to dissuade students from such illicit and dangerous behavior.[20] By countering the ambiguity of steroids with ambiguous regulation, school administrators and parents could keep alive rugby's disciplinary possibilities and protect the reputations of their schools. At the same time, though, reluctance to embrace definitive testing weakens the certainty of rugby while also highlighting the inability of invested adults to reckon with the systemic and structural dimensions of steroid use in their schools. Moreover, the very use of steroids is itself ambiguous and problematic, because it inverts rugby's established social significance. Rather than adults using rugby to find certainty in boys, boys are using steroids to manipulate that same social importance for their own social (and eventually economic) benefit. Irrespective of its harmful effects, steroids allow boys to succeed in the physical trials their parents and teachers seem to value.

In addition to the official termination of apartheid-era disciplinary techniques, rugby's ability to deliver certainty has become a matter of importance in schools for another reason: the South African state has ended the legal segregation of the country's educational system. The transformation has been less dramatic than legislation might suggest because of a set of interlocking logistical and political concerns. As I was frequently and earnestly reminded, the demand to attend such prestigious and resource-rich schools far exceeds the available spots. "If the government had its way," one administrator grumbled, "we would have 5,000 students here instead of 1,200. And 1,200 is already more than we can handle; 800 would be better." As his statement suggests, school administrators seemed often to read the post-apartheid state's projects of racial integration and educational transformation as attempting to profit on already "successful" apartheid-era institutions. Perhaps in anticipation of integration or perhaps because schools were already shouldering a significant portion of their own expenses, Model C schools were permitted to increase their tuitions in 1992, during the final years of National Party rule (Nattrass and Seekings 2005). Those fees have had the long-term and demonstrable effect of limiting access, to those students who have the means to pay. Not every such student is white, but increased fees are part and parcel of a wider shift in South African society, from legislated racial exclusion to liberalized class (and still racialized) exclusion.

In another respect, though, school fees produce a dynamic that is unique to the formerly white schools: such fees serve as a financial bottleneck, allowing schools to identify and selectively sponsor "underprivileged" students who are deemed to be more valuable to the school than most of the 5,000 who might have plausible claims on the basis of a geographical proximity (cf. Besteman 2008; Brook 1996; Nkomo, Mkwanazi-Twala, and Carrim 1995; Sharp 1998). Because alumni pay for student scholarships on a case-by-case basis, alumni interests generally determine how that value is defined. Rugby players are therefore prioritized, because they are considered necessary to school prestige. Those scholarships are far fewer in number than the young players who are desperate for them and the opportunities they bring. One father, who identified as black, tried to lobby for a scholarship for his son, but school administrators were not familiar with his boy's rugby abilities and he was not admitted. Another parent, who identified as coloured and whose son was accepted, explained that he and his family "come from a small community, we are very disadvantaged people with low income, and we decided we wanted the best for [our son] and that meant a Model C school." "If you don't have a scholarship," he added, "a lot of parents in my community can't afford it. One or two can go there, but it's really about the money. It's too expensive."

Despite the inequality of the system that nourishes rugby in large, wealthy high schools, school administrators describe their scholarships as a service to the development of South African sport. Jurie Roux, chief executive officer of the South African Rugby Union, reported in 2015 that SARU had spent over R500 million on development since 1992 (Nel and Bester 2015), but the school administrators I interviewed in 2010 and 2011 were not impressed by SARU's expenditures. One said, "Some guy gets 30 balls and a bunch of t-shirts. He holds a 'sports day,' hands everything out, and it all goes missing." Arguing against investing unsustainable amounts of money in the pernicious problem of sporting resources in poorer areas, that same administrator suggested, "Why not give the money to me? We [at this wealthy school] already *have* the resources. We already *have* the facilities. Let us identify the talent and develop it. We're already doing it, but we could do it better with government support. If they support us, more talented black players will come through the ranks, and soon the national team will reflect the diversity of the country."

SARU has not, to my knowledge, seriously considered that administrator's solution, probably because it indicts SARU's past efforts and conceals, rather than resolves, the underlying problem of unequal resource distribution. Nevertheless, one can see why that solution appeals to elite schools. First, it allows white administrators to declare that they are aware that resources are unfairly distributed and that SARU has not adequately addressed the problem. Second, because the solution reaffirms wealthy schools' commitment to the country's sporting development, it protects those schools against the claim that they are perpetuating white control over South Africa's rugby. Finally and most important, the solution allows elite schools to maintain their exclusivity and intense talent saturation through their high fees and scouting of underprivileged players. The rugby teams at those schools would become even stronger with SARU support, and a school's alumni could continue feeling a paternalistic attachment toward the special players—or "rough gems," as one coach called them—whose talents the school identifies and cultivates.

With the satisfaction of paternalism, however, can come the nagging fear that your generosity could be exploited. As an unintended consequence of the scholarships, interested connoisseurs now find that they must be on the lookout for schoolboys who appear to be "playing for the wrong reasons"—that is, to further their own rugby careers rather than the greater glory of their school. Chapter 2 of this book located that problem's roots in the increasing integration of school rugby into the structures of professional rugby in South Africa. Knowing that high schoolers are signing contracts at younger and younger ages and moving to new schools that offer them bursaries, administrators in elite high schools worry that economic relationships are bypassing and even nullifying the bonds of loyalty on which amateur rugby allegedly relies. We cannot afford, though, to overlook the demands that coaches, alumni, and parents place on scholarship players: they want to draw value from the talents of underprivileged boys but also want those players to demonstrate an "authentic" commitment to the school. The more urgent a player's need to attend a prestigious school is, the less tenable the economic claim becomes. While this discourse can target any player, then, it is clearly racialized by the fact that the students who need scholarships are rarely white and, as such, find that they must continually perform their investment in the school to skeptical faculty and parents. Several of the players I knew who identified as black, coloured, or African were aware of that skepticism and responded in kind. One said simply, "I'm not attached to this school. I've never been embraced here."

The performance of rugby appears to offer a tantalizing solution to the problem of assessing player loyalty. By its violent and immediate nature, rugby is supposed to separate the committed from the lazy, the active from the passive, and the selfless from the selfish. Yet, for that to be true, connoisseurs must render actions meaningful, and there are far too many actions occurring on a field in a given moment for an observer to monitor them all. As such, the vast majority of actions go unobserved and hover at the edge of interpretation. Many coaches I knew, for example, were confident that one schoolboy was "just playing to look good for the scouts" rather than to meet the needs of his team. That boy, a coach explained, "hid" conspicuously on the field, deliberately placing himself in positions where he was not obligated to make difficult plays. As the reference to "hiding" suggests, judging the boy's disinterest was complicated by his apparent unwillingness to do the sort of small, often violent work (the same repetitive work that makes glitches visible) that would rarely get noticed in the first place. If this boy was not involved in a particular moment of action, the challenge then is determining, *ought* he have been? In schools already concerned about "culture" and "tradition," identifying a performance made disingenuous by steroids is difficult enough. Finding disingenuousness in the moments when a player should have availed himself of violent contact is even more challenging. Professional teams (which spare no expense and have no doubt that they are "using" players to further their goals and that players are similarly "using" them) have attempted to address that problem with sophisticated technology, drawing on multiple camera angles, trained statisticians, and state-of-the-art coding software to root out unsatisfactory performances. Connoisseurs of school rugby, however, have little choice but to monitor practices and matches, scrutinize player behavior, and hope that rugby will eventually force a hidden player to reveal himself.

CONCLUSION

Exactly three days after my own revelatory performance on the practice field, I watched the same boys who had pummeled me compete against a rival high school. The match was extremely competitive until just before halftime, when something wholly unexpected occurred. I was positioned at one end of the field with the team's coaches, when a player, known to the coaches for his "feisty style," found himself with the ball and opted to chip kick it over the opposing team. His action was unexpected for several reasons. First, it occurred at the end of the first half, a point of the match at which teams typically limit their losses or consolidate their advantages and choose to play conservatively. The player had taken it upon himself to try something adventurous instead. Second, he was in a strategically poor place to attempt such an action. As he reflected later on his decision, he admitted that he had thought about "playing it safe" but decided not to do so, because the defense had anticipated the safe option and prepared for it. Lastly, while the coaches might have considered him "feisty" in some respect, he was not a recognized kicker of the ball, so nobody among his teammates, his coaches, or the opposition was prepared for his action.

As a result and to the coaches' (and my) amazement, his little gamble worked perfectly. The kick went up and just over the opposing team, landing in a patch of empty grass behind them. Using the instant of recognition to his advantage, the player who kicked the ball rushed after it and reached it first. It bounced directly into his hands. He passed the ball to a teammate as the last defender tackled him, and in 30-odd meters, his teammate scored. The referee blew his whistle just a few moments later to mark the start of halftime, and the player who had kicked the ball so unexpectedly was mobbed by his jubilant teammates. The coaches were shaking their heads and smiling as they walked onto the field to join their players. They let everyone congratulate the player for a moment, and then one coach finally spoke. "Son," he told him in Afrikaans, "you can do that *one time a year*." Everyone laughed.

That player's action was much more complicated than common sporting narratives allow (they might describe it as "a dramatic act in an important match" or as a player "rising to the occasion and carrying the team on his shoulders"). It demonstrates the delicate unfolding of action and interpretation in South African rugby. A fraction of a second before the player decided to kick, possible actions presented themselves to him. He read those emergent possibilities and chose to chip. Connoisseurs in the audience, recognizing his movements moments after he started to make them, quickly reached awareness of the possibilities that inspired the action. Perhaps they felt, in that instant, a rush of excitement (as they remembered their own spontaneous chip kicks) or a sense of amazement (at the player's creativity). Or perhaps they felt nothing at all because they were distracted, speaking with a friend, or focusing too intently on their own son. At any rate, that instant of possibility opened a new opportunity for judgment. For those watching intently, the player's spontaneous decision confirmed the truth of his capacity to act in unexpected ways and thus underlined (or revealed for the first time) his "feistiness." As the ball hung in the air, the possibilities remained unresolved, but his feistiness had already been confirmed.

Once the ball bounced directly into the player's waiting hands, the kicker had completed the action. That gave his choice to act a permanence and, as such, a slightly different significance. The coach's scarcely delayed command ("you can do that *one time*") both expressed and confirmed that permanence. It acknowledged the player's ingenuity and his recognition of a flash of rare opportunity ("*one time a year*"), but it also framed the action in terms of its accomplished end and judged its repeatability (the unstated subtext was, "You executed that *once*, but it won't work again; any future attempts will be seen as foolhardy or rash"). The command's finality and transformation of a singular instant into one among many serve as an important reminder that rugby players have little control over how they are judged. They are not especially responsible for the context in which they play (nor the significance that adults put on rugby), and their spontaneous actions on the field can carry implications more far-reaching than most realize. The player's first chip kick was clever and feisty; a second attempt later in the season (let alone in the same game) would have been construed as irresponsible. Particularly for players of color, creative decisions that appear to be excessively individualistic or unduly confident can mark a boy as undisciplined or worse, and such judgments can produce damaging effects. It can mean lost opportunities for rugby success and can also influence how a player's everyday actions are interpreted. The glitch is stabler and more certain than life. If a boy shows disdain for his school on the field by "hiding," it becomes easier to code his more-ambiguous behavior in the classroom or the schoolyard as disdain as well.

But even the preceding account of a chip kick is incomplete, because it risks overlooking the violence that made the action possible. Gumbrecht has suggested that all competitive ball sports may contain some measure of ontological violence: "Violence is the act of occupying spaces or blocking their occupation by others through the resistance of one's body. Timing and violence are inseparably related because timing, at least in ballgames, presupposes that a specific place on the field is the one and only right place for an individual athlete to be, with his body, at a certain moment" (2006, 199). Even if violence is present in all sports to one extent or another, South African rugby remains a special case. By its very design, rugby continually presents situations that require boys to experience physical violence on their bodies. That violence and the pace at which players encounter it pull decisions out of them and produce opportunities for judgment. That aspect of rugby, combined with the context in which the game is played, raises the stakes of its performance significantly.

A white teacher at the former Model C school where I did my research succinctly summarized those stakes.

> We used to have cultural organizations when I was little, . . . but people are moving away from those organizations. It's not the "in thing." It's not politically correct to be part of an organization that teaches you about your culture and your background, an environment where you are proud to be an Afrikaans-speaking person. I won't say [this is true] always or everywhere, but that might be one of the reasons [why rugby is so important to many white South Africans]—rugby gives you a community, rugby gives identity.

One reading of that teacher's statement would suggest that white South Africans, especially Afrikaans-speaking ones, have used rugby to perpetuate and naturalize older, less "politically correct" notions of identity and community. From that perspective, organized rugby is appealing because, unlike school discipline and initiations, it is a practice that will not tolerate compromise. It requires violence and immediacy and refuses to operate without them. As long as rugby exists, then, it can continue to reliably produce identities for those who see its violence as productive. That reading may be true for some people, especially given the social and economic contradictions that sustain former Model C schools.

Another interpretation, however, would suggest that rugby's capacity to "give identity" might shed light on some of those hidden contradictions. Referring to "the scourge of steroids" and "hiding" highlights changing social and disciplinary conditions in South Africa, as well as the novel forms of agency that boys employ under those conditions. Those terms thus acknowledge the limits of rugby's certainty. Contrary to the beliefs of many of my informants, players who are suspected of using steroids or "hiding" cannot be easily dismissed. Rather than being a cynical cheater, a potential steroid user indicates as much about his school as he does about himself. He reflects its class bias, as well as its unwillingness to compromise rugby performance or "tradition" in the interest of controlling supplements and steroids. Similarly, a player who appears to "hide" on the field could be a heartless professional who is disinclined to commit himself to the greater glory of his school, but he is also a symptom of the fact that the greater glory is only possible because "top schools" want both to control the sort of students they admit and to serve as the primary conduit for talented players into professional teams. Seen in that more generous light, the violence and immediacy of rugby would lead to an unexpected result: the greater rugby's importance to former Model C schools is and the more rugby connoisseurs come to depend on the sport for certainty and stable interpretations, the starker and more troubling the social contradictions within those schools may become.

CHAPTER 5

Fractured Frames

Rugby, Imaginative Resistance, and the Legacies of the Struggle against Apartheid

In the conclusion of chapter 4, I argued that concerns about steroids or young players pretending to care about their high school teams tell us more about the history of rugby in former Model C schools and about the interpretive lens that white rugby connoisseurs employ than about young players themselves. Those concerns, I suggested, give lie to the apparent objectivity of rugby's violence and reveal, in the process, the political conditions that structure rugby's performances from the outside. Far from existing as set-apart spaces where boys can play unselfconsciously, the rugby fields of former Model C schools are encased by race, class, and gender politics. Whether those politics reveal themselves spontaneously on the practice field (as when the player in chapter 2 remarked to a nearby laborer that he and his teammates were "working") or during the live play of a match, their arrival can unsettle spectators, administrators, and even players, because politics demonstrate that rugby is not as autonomous as it initially appears to be. For some in South Africa, particularly the white South Africans who benefit most from rugby's present social and political formations, the absence of autonomy can be difficult to accept.

For many black, coloured, and African spectators, in contrast, rugby seems so intertwined with the politics of South African history that the two cannot be easily distinguished. Should one look past the unequal distribution of labor and education on the training field, one confronts disparate playing conditions, avenues to professionalism that are open only to the privileged, teams (at all levels) that appear to preference white players, and even styles of play that gesture back to apartheid and its violence. This chapter pays close attention to those observations. It connects them to their antecedents in the anti-apartheid struggle and analyzes how that history of protest continues to inform and shape how coloured, African, and black rugby participants conceptualize the sport in the post-apartheid era. Rather than unfolding under its own terms, with its own special laws, rugby's autonomy has been an ever-open and ever-debated question.

What happens when observers and participants question and even reject the autonomy of sport? I will show here that in the case of South African rugby, the result is a very specific kind of "frame violation" (Shore 1994, 359), in which a historically produced awareness of the structuring presence of politics can cause a fracture in the generally stable spatial and temporal frame separating performer and fan (the former frame made manifest by the field's flat topography and white lines, the latter by the game clock and the referee's whistle). When such a fracture occurs, the distinction between Gregory Bateson's (1972) playful "nips" and combative "bites"—articulated in chapter 3 of the present study—can collapse. Rather than referee decisions being the result of mistakes, incompetence, or an inexplicable dislike of a team or a player, they can become malicious and cynically political. Rather than violence existing in a magical space where it is disregarded as partial or unreal, it can become a show of "real" hatred and aggression. Peter Alegi has observed a similar phenomenon in his history of the politics of football in South Africa: "An unacceptable result or event on the pitch would suddenly break the magical spell of a joyous communal ritual channeling the emotions of the audience. Supporters transformed a disciplined, symbolic identification with their team into violent, *real* conflict at the grounds. As in the case of Caribbean cricket, the development of football into a mass phenomenon in South Africa in the 1960s coincided with an intensification of fans' emotional attachment to their particular clubs and beloved idols" (2004, 132).

While Alegi attributes that response to the "poor, aggressive, male-dominated street culture of South African townships" in which football took root (2004, 132), I seek to show here that the "magical spell of a joyous communal ritual" may never have been fully cast over South Africa's rugby.[1] The stable (or magical) frame surrounding sporting events was partial or nonexistent for many black spectators, who lived in a country in which political hegemony hardly supplemented colonial and apartheid forms of dominance and control (cf. Guha 1997). That absence of hegemony, I argue here, opened the possibility of what Gendler, elaborating on the work of David Hume, calls "imaginative resistance"—a phrase that describes "our comparative difficulty in imagining fictional worlds that we take to be morally deviant" (Gendler 2000, 56).[2] White South Africans may have been able to watch rugby performances unfold through the sport's autonomous frame and to see players pursuing glory by means of fair competition and violence, but many black, African, and coloured spectators understood (as, I showed in chapter 2 of the present book, Adorno might also understand) that those "autonomous" performances were inextricably bound to the social conditions that produced them. That being the case, it was not unreasonable for such spectators to respond to rugby's "fictional" (or playful) worlds with imaginative resistance. Celebrating athletic achievement could be, in many circumstances, tantamount to celebrating something morally reprehensible: apartheid and the myriad forms of racial inequality that comprised it.

As the present chapter shows, spectators did not arrive at imaginative resistance on their own. During the height of the anti-apartheid struggle, conditions of life in state-mandated "Coloured" communities in apartheid South Africa produced a wide range of social influences that called the autonomy of rugby into question. Students pressured each other to bring politics into rugby, teachers used after-school practice sessions to raise political issues that they could not discuss with their students in the classroom, national anti-apartheid organizations popularized and internationalized that position with the slogan "No normal sport in an abnormal society," and parents conscientized their children in the stands and as they sat by the radio. In other, more explicitly coercive moments, boys identified peers who refused to take sufficiently political positions and fought them in the streets or at parties, older students banned younger ones from school functions or sports because of their (generally nascent and naive) political allegiances, relatives stopped speaking to one another over national and local sporting attachments, and towns split down the middle.

Those apartheid-era lessons and the imaginative resistance they generated continue to shape South Africa's rugby present.[3] This chapter opens with an account that I observed directly during my fieldwork in South Africa. The vignette and the apparent irrationality on which it depends are unpacked in the pages that follow, as they were unpacked for me by my informants—through a historical explication of the experience of life under apartheid and the ways in which rugby became, in many black communities across the country, one of the primary practices through which men discovered and expressed their political affiliations. That lens came to be tinted by two filters

and one question: "Are you a SARU player/person/family/town or a Federation one?" I complicate that distinction by describing some of the myriad
ways that people came to rest on one or the other side of that stark dividing
line and sometimes on one and then the other (though never—as far as I
am aware—on both sides simultaneously). The chapter concludes back at the
present moment, as people struggle with the legacy of a lifetime of imaginative resistance. Can a "magical spell" ever be cast over South African rugby?
If repairing rugby's fractured frame involves overlooking or forgetting apartheid's lingering presence in the sport, is the casting of such a spell desirable?

THE SPORTING ICONOCLASM OF UNCLE VALIANT

While I read and heard about the fragility of rugby's temporal and spatial
frame many times during my fieldwork, I only saw that frame shatter one
time, in August 2012. I was watching a club rugby match in the town of Stellenbosch, played between two of the strongest teams in the Western Province Rugby Football Union: one from the predominantly white, Afrikaans-
speaking Stellenbosch University (colloquially referred to as "Maties") and
one from the more heterogeneous Cape Town suburb of Tygerberg. The
game was quite competitive, with little margin for error on either side, and
the Tygerberg fans grew increasingly delighted as it became clear to everyone
in attendance that their team had risen to the challenge of competing with
one of the largest rugby clubs (per capita) in the world. "Die Boere is moeg"
(The farmers—Afrikaners—are tired), shouted one fan over and over. Each
decision that the white referee made against Tygerberg was greeted by boos
and taunts. One man yelled, "We have white players on our team too. Don't
they count for something?"

The temperature in the stadium was already running high, then, when
a Tygerberg player pounced on an errant pass that one Maties player had
thrown to another. Kicking the ball forward, he chased after it, and Tygerberg
fans began to celebrate as the ball bounced up into his hands. Running away
from the last chasing Maties player, the Tygerberg player scored under the
posts, putting his team into the lead for the first time in the game. The crowd
around me danced and shouted for a moment, until the spectators realized
that the referee and one of his assistants were deep in conversation at the
middle of the field. Nobody was entirely clear what was happening at first, but
word spread through the stands that the assistant had apparently observed

an infraction and had reported it to the referee. The infraction, we soon discovered, prompted the referee to give the ball back to Maties and, worse, to nullify Tygerberg's score.

The reaction of the crowd around me was immediate. Supporters of Tygerberg stopped celebrating their team and turned their full vitriolic attention toward the referee's assistant. Although he stood with his back to them, he was no more than 20 meters from the nearest spectators, and it was apparent from his posture that he could hear the extreme language and threats that were raining down on him from above. My own section of the stands, which had begun as a fairly mixed group of Tygerberg and Maties supporters, slowly and silently emptied itself of Maties fans until there were none but my friend, who was still sitting next to me in her Maties jacket. She told me seriously, "Maybe we should sit with my dad. These people might kill us if we stay here." Realizing for the first time that her dad had not joined us, I asked her where he was sitting. Laughing, she said, "He's over with the *Boere* [Afrikaners]. Where it's safe."

The Tygerberg supporters were content to express themselves verbally and from a distance until the next stoppage of play. At that moment, one Tygerberg fan jumped down from the pavilion and ran over to the referee's assistant. The fan got right in the face of the assistant, pointing and shouting at him. The assistant was visibly disturbed, and as he went over to speak with the referee, the Tygerberg fan pranced and preened for the crowd before jumping back into the stand and returning to his seat. A brief discussion between the referee and his two assistants followed, and the targeted official was relocated to the far side of the field, where he might be beyond the reach of even the most passionate Tygerberg supporter. When the game ended and the teams exited the field, some of the Tygerberg supporters turned their fury on the Maties players, cursing and spitting on them from above. One Maties parent, enraged and disgusted by the behavior of the Tygerberg fans, approached the chairman of Tygerberg's club. "Why don't you do something?" he reportedly exclaimed. The chairman retorted, "What do you want me to do? If I try to get them to stop, they'll attack me and carry on anyway!"

I was intensely curious about the spectator's motivations. Why had he run onto the field? What had he said to the referee's assistant? I was lamenting having missed my chance to speak with him, when my friend pointed over my shoulder. "There he is!" she shouted excitedly. He responded proudly to my inquiry: "Yeah, I did it. I went right up to him and [cursed at him]. And then I told him that the next time he comes to our field [in Tygerberg], we're going to fucking kill him." The irate fan added, "We should have won that game. That guy took it all away from us." When I asked if I could include his story in my research, the man nodded gleefully: "You can tell anyone you like about me. My name is 'Uncle Dapper.'" As he and his friends walked away, I returned to my friend, who had been eagerly awaiting information. When I finished sharing with her, she laughed hard and said, "His name isn't Uncle Dapper," she said. "*Dapper* means, like, 'courageous' or 'valiant.'"

One can probably attribute some of Uncle Dapper's courage to the influence of alcohol and some to the "heat of the moment." Giving alcohol and excitement full credit for Uncle Dapper's actions, though, would overlook the significance of his chosen pseudonym. The moniker transformed the man's decision to charge onto the field from an impulsive disruption into a heroic act. Much like football fans in colonial Zanzibar (Fair 1997) and the Congo (Fabian 1996), who saw colonialism and prejudice in the allegedly impartial decisions of sporting referees, Uncle Dapper evidently viewed the referee's assistant as more than a formal functionary. He addressed the assistant as a man, face-to-face and on the field, as if the man (and his personal prejudices) had ruined the game. Uncle Dapper may have appeared to fracture the frame around the Maties/Tygerbeg match, but in his estimation, that frame was already rotten to the core. His actions had exposed that rot for what it was, and he had only done what any Tygerberg fan would have done if possessing the courage to do it.

Seen from that vantage point, Uncle Dapper's action looks like less a violation of the sanctity of sport or a burst of irrational exuberance than a deliberate act of iconoclasm. Throughout history, Freedberg notes, iconoclasts have not generally opted to grind statues to dust or set paintings on fire. Instead, they have tended to treat art objects as living beings and to afford them a perverse reverence while destroying them. They humiliate and mutilate them, distorting their figures for their own political ends (Freedberg 1977). For that reason, Mike McGovern (2013), elaborating on the work of W. J. T. Mitchell (2005), has argued that iconoclastic gestures are performances of a particular kind of belief. Both iconoclasts and iconodules (those who venerate icons) share a belief in the liveness of the object; the iconodule believes in the power of the object, and the iconoclast believes that someone else believes. Uncle Dapper's gesture follows the same logic. His action was premised on the idea that someone—be it the referee or the opposition or white fans in general—fervently believed that South African rugby unfolds autonomously, above and apart from existing social and economic conditions. He therefore sought to call attention to the framing conditions of the match's performance, to make the crowd and the players realize the historically constructed biases of the referee and the disparity in raced bodies between the two competing teams. In short, the fan wanted to show that what the audience took to be a playful celebration of rugby was more like a performance of history. Following Uncle Dapper's act, the game continued, but its sanctity had been thoroughly sabotaged.[4]

Both Uncle Dapper's iconoclastic gesture and his perception of rot have a social and political genealogy. Some inkling of the complexity of that genealogy can be found in the decision my friend's father made to sit, as she put it, "with the *Boere*." Whatever safety that seat might have offered, it was not an easy one for him to take. Her father, Leon, was coaching for Maties. He had been with the club for little more than a season and a half at that point, and the transition had proven difficult. Prior to joining Maties, one of the largest and most influential clubs in South Africa, Leon had coached a small community team in the Dwars River Valley, a predominantly coloured region located just outside Stellenbosch. Widely regarded in the coloured community as one of the legendary (if often overlooked) players of the apartheid years, Leon saw that earlier coaching work as an extension of his playing career. He had played highly competitive and highly political rugby in the face of apartheid oppression in the 1970s and 1980s, and his coaching position continued that struggle by supporting an underrepresented club that was comprised of coloured men who worked for the extravagantly wealthy and almost exclusively white farm owners of the Cape Winelands. His success with that relatively minor team brought him attention, and the Maties administration sought to bring him into their own club structure. After much agonizing, Leon left his small club so that he might further his own coaching career.

The implications of that decision—amounting, he well knew, to succumbing to the economic and political structures of the rugby establishment—weighed privately on Leon's mind, but those implications remained largely his own concern until they were exposed at a match played two weeks before the Tygerberg incident mentioned above. As Leon described it to me later, his Maties team had defeated a team from Belhar, a predominantly coloured Cape Town suburb, and he went onto the field to congratulate both teams. As it happened, he ended up shaking the hands of his own players before he reached most of the Belhar players. The Belhar players noticed that apparent favoritism, and one of them muttered, "Hy is in die Boere se gat" (which translates loosely, "He is in the Boers' asses"). Leon explained that he was already feeling frustrated about his team's performance and had no patience for such a remark. He rounded on the speaker and cursed at him. Everyone else was stunned as he and the player continued to exchange insults and expletives. In the days that followed, word of the argument found its way to the Maties club chairman, who told Leon that he had behaved rashly. Even though he offered his players and his "heavenly father" a heartfelt apology, Leon told me that he still felt justified. "Belhar wants to play [against] the whites, but I can't coach them?" he asked me rhetorically.

The offending player's statement had not just been ill timed, striking Leon as it did at a particularly sensitive moment in his coaching career. It also tapped into a deeper vein of historical rhetoric. The phrase "in die Boere se gat" was not arbitrarily chosen. Rather, it was a variation of an accusation frequently leveled at coloured South Africans who chose to play with or against white establishment teams during the apartheid regime. The term *gat kruipers*, or "ass crawlers," permitted no subtle distinctions. One was either a *gat kruiper* or not, a collaborator or an agitator, and those conclusions hinged on an individual's response to one particular question: Are you with SARU or the Federation?

SARU, THE FEDERATION, AND IMAGINATIVE RESISTANCE

I here relate the dominant narrative about the emergence of the SARU/Federation question as told to me many times during my fieldwork. Following the massacre in Sharpeville and the Rivonia trial in the early 1960s, South African daily life was more explicitly politicized than ever before. In that environment and as a result of personal disagreements within its executive committee, the South African Coloured Rugby Board (SACRB), the governing body of "Coloured" rugby since the 1890s, fractured into two new organizations: the South African Rugby Football Federation, which continued the SACRB's relationship with and therefore (it was argued) subservience to the ruling white rugby body, and the South African Rugby Union. SARU was a breakaway organization that operated under the aegis of the wider anti-apartheid South African Council of Sport (SACOS), which had devised the well-known and rhetorically powerful slogan "No normal sport in an abnormal society." Whereas the clubs of "the Federation," as it came to be called, were sanctioned by the apartheid state (its players eventually given the opportunity to compete against white teams and even to represent South Africa as part of a "Coloured" national team), the SACOS slogan demonstrated that SARU took an entirely different position. Rejecting as illegitimate both the apartheid state and its capacity to bestow legitimacy on clubs, the SARU unions fomented imaginative resistance. In response to the apartheid state's small cosmetic changes to its ideology, organizations like SARU and SACOS continually highlighted the underlying inequalities of South African daily life. Insisting on a brand of politics that might be called "more apartheid than apartheid," those organizations enforced apartheid (between themselves and the illegitimate state) and refused all compromises. Theirs was a rigorous and thoroughgoing form of politics, and SACOS and SARU dogmatically reflected the inequalities of apartheid back at the state and the world at large. Scholars of that era of South African sport have argued that those organizations thus endeavored to make the performance of sport unavoidably political.[5]

In some instances, activists did not content themselves with "calling attention" to rugby's frame but sought to break it. For example, when the South African national rugby team toured New Zealand in 1981, a personal aircraft flew over the stadium during one match and dropped bags of flour onto the field. The aircraft was deployed by a contingent of New Zealanders who objected to the capitulation with the apartheid regime that the tour represented (cf. Nixon 1992). Breaking into the field from the outside and disrupting the fiction of the match was a deliberately political gesture. More than interrupting the playing of the game, the "flour bombs" disrupted the idea of the game itself. The New Zealand government had not simply welcomed a random contingent of South Africans into the country; it had acknowledged acquiescence to the apartheid state at each stage of the process. It negotiated with South Africa to set up the tour, arranged the tour locations and sold tickets to the matches, welcomed the South African team at airports, and protected the team from protesting "troublemakers." Most important, players who stood in metonymically for the nation of New Zealand shared in rugby's fiction in matches against players who represented apartheid South Africa. With sacks of flour falling from the sky, though, the autonomy of sport was impossible to uphold.

The rigorous opposition to "apolitical" rugby extended even to the foreign teams SARU players chose to support. The New Zealand All Blacks were a particular favorite. SARU players appreciated the apparent racial diversity of New Zealand's team and the fact that the All Blacks continually embarrassed the apartheid regime with attempts to bring (merited) players of color into South Africa to play the white Springboks. More than one informant told me not to underestimate the importance of the All Blacks name to SARU support. Even seeing the word *black* on a jersey was significant to some SARU players.

SARU appreciation of the All Blacks was based not only in the comparatively stable dimensions of racial demographics or the team's moniker but also in the much more fluid politics of style (Grundlingh and Grundlingh 2019, 73). One All Black supporter explained to me his amazement the first time he saw that Maori players were both included on the team and supported by their white teammates in the course of a game: "Maori players, they are naturally faster and more elusive runners, but in New Zealand, the Maori players will carry the ball and a white player will be right there with them, protecting and defending them." Even if that statement naturalizes sporting style in race (as did many comments made by the South Africans with whom I spoke), it also makes an argument about the intimate connection between politics and style. Fans of the All Blacks in South Africa, like the football fans with whom Roger Magazine (2007) worked, appreciated their favorite team's style of play because it not only symbolized but appeared actually to demonstrate, in the liveness of play, that a better world was possible. That significance was made explicit in a narrative Leon shared with me about the origins of the All Blacks' free and creative (but still physically imposing) style. "Up until the 1960s," he told me, "the All Blacks played in exactly the same way as South Africa. Then the Maoris decided that they wanted to have a say in the structures of New Zealand rugby and so they took control. They changed how the team played, they replaced all the old administrators, and they made sure the team was representative." This narrative, whether true or apocryphal, provided Leon with a satisfactory historical justification for the All Black's style and affirmed the social significance of the team's on-field performance. The heroic rise of Maori players, so inconceivable for "Coloured" and "African" players under apartheid, gave the All Blacks an almost utopian quality in the eyes of many SARU players.

Slowly but surely, the SARU/Federation narrative continues, the coloured rugby community was split down the middle as men and boys were forced to make definitive decisions about where their political inclinations lay. André Odendaal writes that the financial support the Federation teams and players received from the apartheid regime "could not neutralize the strong disapproval expressed within black communities about the participation . . . in multi-national sport. They were branded as sell-outs and as the lines were drawn droves of players left to join SARU" (1995, 58). Kylemore, the town in which I did my research, went from having one club to two—one that played in the Federation and one that played in SARU. Other communities, like neighboring Pniël, switched entirely to SARU, while others, such as Stellenbosch and Paarl, remained largely antagonistic to SARU's incursions. Teams with predominantly African players made similar decisions, with some Eastern Cape teams jumping to the SARU-aligned KwaZakhele Rugby Union and with some opting to send players to the apartheid-sponsored Leopards representative team. The stark divisions remained through the 1970s and into the 1980s, even as some towns (like Kylemore), finding social antagonisms difficult to maintain, amalgamated their clubs in one direction or another. Generally, amalgamation occurred in the direction of SARU. International and domestic pressure (particularly the international sporting boycott), coupled with the radicalization of schools following the 1976 Soweto student uprising, produced a political climate that was increasingly hostile to collaboration. As apartheid sport weakened, so did the Federation. In the early 1990s, SARU was recognized internationally as a legitimate sporting body in its own right, and the white rugby establishment (still on the back foot as a result of the boycott, aware of the impending political transformation, and therefore more inclined to compromise) subsequently joined with it to form the South African Rugby Football Union.

By the 1995 World Cup, the preceding narrative of coloured rugby's history had nearly rejoined the dominant one of white South Africa but for one telling difference: "Coloured" players like Chester Williams and the retroactively sanctified Errol Tobias, lauded by white fans and administrators for their rugby merit and their contributions toward political transformation, remained controversial figures in the coloured community, as a result of their apartheid-era allegiances. Both Williams and Tobias became known quantities in the white community because they had made their names under the Federation banner. Their appearance on the world's stage was somewhat less thrilling for many coloured South Africans than for white spectators. After white South Africans and the international rugby public had "discovered" and anointed Williams and Tobias, they were no less *gat kruipers* (or "coconuts"—as they were also often called, because they were brown on the outside but white on the inside, one of my interlocutors explained) than they had been before. Even in that version of the story, rugby's frame is fractured. The now widely accepted narrative of the 1995 Rugby World Cup as marking South Africa's triumphant return to international sport and liberal politics is one that many black South Africans, for reasons of history, have been unwilling to embrace. If a SARU player could ever consider a rugby team featuring one black player (e.g., the team fielded by South Africa through the World Cup) as proof that South Africa's society and sport had normalized, the fact that the black player was Chester Williams could still inspire imaginative resistance.

LOCAL GRUDGES: A POLITICAL GENEALOGY OF THE SARU/FEDERATION DICHOTOMY

Though the conventional SARU/Federation narrative may be subaltern relative to the overwhelming prevalence of white teams and players in the historiography of South Africa's rugby, it nevertheless paints too stark a picture of coloured rugby's politics during the apartheid era. Players, teams, and towns took convoluted paths to reach their public political positions, and even positions made explicit were under review and subject to change. Any and all subterranean shifts came to be read, however, in terms of their implications for the public expression of the dichotomy between SARU and the Federation and, in turn, for a democratic South Africa. As is the case with many narratives within the anti-apartheid struggle (Magaziner 2010; Peffer 2009), the totalizing politics of apartheid risks effacing the complicated and contradictory ways that South Africans reached political consciousness. With that concern in mind, it is necessary to try to recover the openness of the historical moment and to recognize that the SARU/Federation dichotomy was less of a litmus test of political affiliation than so many wished it to be (and wish now that it had been). Indeed, the same openness has preserved the relevance of the SARU/Federation dichotomy into the post-apartheid era.

Some clubs do seem to have come to unilateral and deliberate decisions about their political orientation. A former executive at the community club in the town of Pniël, for example, described its decision to jump from the Federation to SARU as a politically practical one.

> I realized one day that it just didn't make any sense for us to be in the Federation. Everyone in Pniël was voting for the Labour Party [the official opposition party to the National Party at the time] and we all thought that the tricameral parliament was an utter sham. Why would we play rugby for the NP when none of us were voting for them? I put the idea of joining SARU to a general meeting of the team and everyone agreed, so we put the ball in motion.

That description is perhaps as ideal-typical an account of liberal-democratic political thought as South African rugby could have produced during the struggle against apartheid. The executive recognized the incongruity between his political commitments and his rugby affiliation. After an open deliberation, the team aligned itself with a sporting body that better represented its collective interest. Sporting politics and social politics were brought under one and the same banner. I was informed that nobody objected or protested to the new alignment and that no rebel factions broke away to form new teams. When I asked about the conditions that produced such unanimity, the administrator credited Pniël's economic and social structure. He explained that Pniël's origin as a mission station shaped its civic development. While neighboring towns had expanded and contracted with the economic tides, Pniël had remained relatively stable, centered around one church (whereas neighboring Kylemore, a town with only 1,000 more residents than Pniël, had eight) and a small number of families (Lucas 2006, 174; Randle 2014, 47–48). Access to land and housing in Pniël was so rigorously controlled that some Pniëlers had begun to settle in neighboring towns because the Pniël municipality had refused to allow them to build new homes in the area. In the executive's opinion, rigid administration paid dividends in the town in terms of education and, in turn, occupation. He described a definitively middle-class Pniël, constituted of white-collar workers, entrepreneurs, and skilled craftspeople. In his view, the town's united religious, social, and economic fronts explained its untroubled, wholesale conversion to SARU.

If Pniël's transition was as smooth and stable as that executive remembered,[6] it was perhaps the exception rather than the rule. One town over, in demographically more heterogeneous Kylemore (cf. van der Waal 2014, 9), the process of rugby's politicization was much more contentious and complex. Most important, I was repeatedly told that the SARU/Federation question struck a fault line of local politics that had little or nothing to do with national debates about the legitimacy of apartheid. Not only were the founders of Kylemore's SARU club not particularly galvanized by the political programs of SARU or SACOS, but their focus was definitively elsewhere—on running a club as they saw fit, on trumping the bosses of Kylemore's other team, on continuing competitive relationships with neighboring clubs that had also joined SARU, and so on. As has been documented in the case of other social clubs elsewhere (cf. Turino 2000), national political concerns seem to have been largely incidental to the reasons why the older generation of SARU players left the Federation team behind. Their primary concerns were local, everyday interactions with neighbors and families across town. That those concerns happened to break along national lines was initially less important than many people now believe. One former player told me, "I suspect that a lot of people in Kylemore have forgotten why they joined SARU. They say it was all about apartheid, but it really wasn't at all. It was local grudges."

POLITICS, PERFORMANCES, AND RUGBY'S FRACTURED FRAME

Even decisions that are not meant to be overtly political can carry large-scale implications if they land on hotly contested political terrain. Such is the case with Kylemore's SARU team. Even if it did not begin with a deep investment in SARU's national program, its position shifted quickly following the student protests in Soweto (and across the country) in 1976. Many of the second generation of SARU players with whom I spoke recalled Kylemore's high school as a crucible of conscientization. Older students educated younger ones about the nation's political conditions, putting pressure on them to adopt political positions of their own, and teachers with strong political leanings used the rugby field as an opportunity to educate their students about the political issues they were forbidden to teach. As I described in chapter 1, that dynamic was no less present in other regions of the country than in places like Kylemore. One of the most significant of the myriad effects such conscientization had on local politics in the town was that it pushed Kylemore's SARU team toward the sporting body's national position. That younger players began to seek out the team explicitly because of its political orientation, rather than for notable local reasons, placed apartheid politics at the center of the SARU team's program. A senior Kylemore player hoping to get a young Leon to play for the club's junior team approached him in high school. Leon told me, "The first question I asked him was, 'Are you with Spartans or Young Seven Rivers?' When he told me he was with Spartans, I said, 'Okay, I'll join.' There was no way I was going to play with the Federation team."

The SARU team continued to present itself as a big tent. Many senior players remained politically agnostic. Perhaps even more notably, players occasionally switched from the Federation team to the SARU one for reasons that had to do more with the style of play (not without its own politics, as I describe below) and with the team's accomplishments than with any profound political realization. Though the preceding examples demonstrate that national politics were never the only reasons for the SARU club's existence, the examples also speak to an important difference between the politics of SARU and the Federation. While the dominant narrative of that era considers SARU's politics to be more rigorous and uncompromising, the actual experiences of SARU players suggest a more complicated story. In every case I encountered, joining SARU was described to me as a single definitive choice, in which players opted to play their rugby outside of the available apartheid structures. From that decision forward, national politics became atmospheric. Because the existence of SARU was itself political, the rugby played under SARU was necessarily political as well. That relationship seems to have produced a paradoxical effect: SARU had so thoroughly fractured the frame around rugby that players were free, if they chose, to devote their full attention to their rugby performance.

Far from undermining the position of SARU, that comparatively free play underwrote it. As Limón argued persuasively with reference to disenfranchised Mexicano residents of Texas, playfulness itself can be theorized as political when it "negates[s] the alienating constraints of [a] historically given social order" (1994, 135). Indeed, it was SARU players, not Federation ones, who stressed to me in interviews that apartheid politics did not disrupt the rugby on match days. SARU players just came and did what they wanted to do—play rugby. Because SARU teams could play rugby as if apartheid legislation did not exist,[7] they could attract players without explicit political leanings as readily as players for whom playing political rugby was a moral necessity. That gave Spartans a wide appeal. It drew its players not only from Kylemore but from neighboring Lanquedoc—a settlement established by Cecil Rhodes in 1902 to serve primarily as a labor reserve for his wine and fruit farms (Cash and Swatuk 2011, 55; Lucas 2006, 161)—and from Pniël as well.

Former Federation players, in contrast, found themselves confronting apartheid politics quite explicitly. Players stayed with Kylemore's Federation club for a host of reasons as well: they felt that responsibility to the town's history required them to play with Kylemore's first club, their family was a Federation family, or they feared that they might lose their jobs if their white employers learned that they were affiliated with SARU. Some seem to have aligned with the Federation because they had fond feelings for the ambiguous social position they held as Afrikaans-speaking coloured people in the Western Cape. Others stayed with Federation teams because they recognized the political possibilities that lay in playing with and against white teams. For example, one player argued that he felt compelled to play Federation rugby because doing so was one of the few ways that a coloured man could challenge the hermetic world that the apartheid regime had sought to construct. He explained that white administrators were disinclined to pick coloured players: "A coloured player must be ten times as good and work ten times as hard as his white competition in order to get selected for a team."

The struggles for coloured players did not end with selection. Most interesting for the purposes of this chapter, the presence of coloured players on the field complicated the performance of rugby itself. The same player recalled, for example, that he quickly learned to recognize when his teammates would choose to kick or carry the ball rather than pass it to him. Their momentary hesitations, within the context of the spontaneity of play, led him to believe that they had no confidence in his abilities. Another Federation player remembered being part of the first "Coloured" team to play against the University of Stellenbosch. When the two teams came together to socialize after the match, which Stellenbosch had won handily, it quickly became clear that the Maties players had been required to attend. The awkwardness of such moments (compounded, he said, by the fact that some of his coloured teammates "did not know how to socialize properly") was difficult enough, but the real blow was struck when the player encountered and greeted one of his opponents in a university building in the course of work the following day. The opposing player, he said, "looked at me like I was *a horse*." The player extending the greeting admitted to me that he might have been "too forward" with the other player—an indictment of their social inequality in itself—but the slight hurt him badly, especially because they had previously shared the field together. The lesson he seemed to learn from the chance encounter was that he could never count on the sentiments produced during a rugby match to have real demonstrable social effects. Whites, he told himself in that moment, "can go to hell."

Such experiences transformed a Federation player into a sort of martyr: overlooked by his administrators, scorned by his teammates, and misunderstood by his coaches, a Federation player was beset on all sides but soldiered on, confronting apartheid in each and every athletic moment. Although such heroic narratives could be easily dismissed as disingenuous or revisionist (many SARU players would likely describe them as such), they point to a profound truth: the rugby life of Federation players was infused with politics. Unlike their SARU antagonists, they were forced to continually locate themselves politically, analyze the climate in a clubhouse, and adjust to the political inclinations of their teammates on the field. Federation players were "bodies out of place," and the full social stigma of their anomalousness descended on them.[8]

Accounts like the preceding therefore demand greater complexity than a phrase like "trying to beat whites at their own game" affords. (Indeed, none of my informants said anything to that effect—perhaps because the statement presents coloured rugby as derivative of and therefore structurally inferior to white rugby.) Such accounts likewise challenge those who argue (as people often do about Jackie Robinson and other athletes of color who first integrated university and professional sport in the United States) that the central accomplishments of the Federation athletes was to demonstrate what persons marginalized on the basis of race were capable of and should morally be permitted to do. That view overlooks the fact that Federation players—and perhaps Jackie Robinson as well—disturbed the existing structure of relations by their very presence. Any argument about their moral rights or physical and mental capabilities were secondary interpretations that tried to make sense of that presence. SARU and SACOS chose to dodge those everyday confrontations, opting instead to challenge the structural conditions of apartheid and leave the regime to hang itself. But Federation players engaged directly with white South African spectators, players, and administrators on fields and in clubhouses.[9]

While the martyrdom discourse is one that aficionados of American sport may know well (cf. Kelly 2005), the particular version I have presented here may be uniquely South African in one important respect: there existed a meaningful continuity between field and street in communities like Kylemore. Facilitated by the SACOS brand of politics, which continually highlighted the relationship between sport and society under apartheid, SARU players refused to let their allegiances end at the edge of the rugby field's frame. SARU therefore constituted the Federation as its political and social opposite. One could not commit oneself to play on a Federation team and then hope to interact with one's SARU peers in town as if nothing had changed. In towns that fractured as Kylemore did, SARU and Federation players (or families) sometimes refused to associate. In such instances, they would attend different gatherings, avoid the streets on which each other lived, and fight each other when their paths crossed. Because sport at Kylemore's high school was controlled by SARU teachers and SARU students, the children of Federation families were unilaterally forbidden to play. Here again, we find the ingredients for a fractured frame. In Kylemore, rugby was no ephemeral leisure activity. Which team you chose and whom you played against had widespread implications for your social existence in the town. Coloured rugby did not just reflect national politics. As Bob White has written of popular music in Mobutu's Zaire, rugby was a field of action that fixed politics in place (2008, 250).

Politics intervened at every moment. For example, a Federation player might have been eager to join a white team because he intended to show them his "true self," but he would find himself frustrated because his teammates did not appear to trust him or because his coach only grudgingly let him into the game. That frustration would have occurred even for those players who may have preferred, as one informant described it, "to be submissive to whites rather than the same as blacks," because their commitment to the Federation as a whole was already predicated on an awareness of their social marginality. Some may have favored their position in the Federation over other marginal positions, but they were aware of it nonetheless. SARU players, meanwhile, made each other constantly aware of the social and economic disparities between their communities and white ones, their rugby facilities and white ones. Players who now love to describe the camaraderie that resulted from playing SARU rugby on pitted fields lit only by car headlights (rather than the large floodlights that many wealthy white clubs could afford) were always aware of the structural inequalities that produced such conditions.

Once the experience of apartheid had fractured the frame around South African rugby, styles of play became explicitly politicized as well. Leon presented that phenomenon to me as a stark dichotomy. Spartans, his club and SARU affiliate, assigned importance to playing a free and running style, taking risks and using the strengths of individual players to its advantage. In contrast, he explained, Young Seven Rivers (Kylemore's Federation team) played *stampkar* rugby (the style considered in chapter 1 of this book). That team was unimaginative and conservative, relying on percentages and violent domination in order to compete.

As persuasive as that dichotomy might seem in the context of Kylemore's political polarization, it was almost certainly overdrawn. If Young Seven Rivers did play a *stampkar* style, doing so did not require them to be "brainwashed" (as Leon also claimed). If they existed, stylistic continuities between a white, apartheid style of play and the style employed by Federation clubs can be explained by other means. For example, many Federation players served under John Cupido in the South African army's "Coloured" "Cape Corps." Cupido was later president of the Federation, so it is entirely possible that Federation players developed their stylistic preferences in the same manner as many white young men—under the institutional influence of the military and its preference for controlled, disciplined, certain rugby. There may have been pragmatic reasons for the stylistic preferences of Young Seven Rivers as well. They might have had players who were better suited to a *stampkar* style (damningly for Leon's argument, SARU players from Pniël were adamant that they too had used a *stampkar* style, simply because they had the players to do it properly). They might also have realized that to compete within the upper echelons of white rugby, they would have to learn to play in a style that was "legible" to their white bosses. Even if evidence suggests that Leon and others may have overestimated the contrast between SARU and Federation styles, their claims nevertheless alert us to the transparency of the politics of style for players like him. When a style was described as *stampkar* rugby, it was tantamount to dismissing it as a white style, and its conservatism and violence marked it with the taint of apartheid. If one could ignore, even for a moment, the way that politics structured the makeup of the national team, the shockingly manicured fields on which white teams played, and the segregation in the pavilions, South Africa's social and historical politics might still be rendered visible in a player's stylistic flourishes.

LEGACIES OF IMAGINATIVE RESISTANCE
IN POST-APARTHEID SOUTH AFRICA

Given the depth to which rugby's frame was fractured by politics (not just down to the appearance of the field, but onto and into bodies), it is perhaps less than surprising that imaginative resistance has persisted into the post-apartheid era. As the instances that opened this chapter demonstrate, though, that resistance now lacks a clearly defined target. One SARU veteran, for example, had no trouble enumerating the causes and effects of coloured rugby's post-apartheid struggles articulated throughout this book: professional rugby has created avenues of success that bypassed clubs in poorer communities; sponsors and teams are still predominantly run by whites; elite teams select black players reluctantly, as political "window dressing"; the only way to become a successful player is to play in a white fashion; talented black players who succeed have their talents destroyed by their white coaches and are systematically underpaid; and so on. But he threw up his hands when he tried to make sense of where the blame for the situation lay. Was it the fault of administrators in towns like Kylemore, who squandered the success and talent of SARU teams during the early 1990s, because they did not invest their clubs' meager funds wisely enough? Or is it the fault of those who continue to undermine the confidence of potential investors by squandering the rare financial windfalls of today? Could he blame rugby's sponsors, who only followed their own immediate interests and invested in rugby's existing structures instead of developing rugby in South Africa's poorer areas? Did the blame lie in the structural oppression of the past or in new structures just taking shape? Had individuals failed (or, worse, maliciously subverted) coloured rugby, or were they simply protecting their own reasonable investments? Where did individual responsibility end and collective, social responsibility begin? Referencing the context of post-apartheid South Africa, he said, "What are you supposed to do? You can't be mad at any one individual, and you can't be mad at the whole world either."

At one level, his statement shows what is lacking in the post-apartheid era: SARU not only offered coloured South Africans a clear through line of politics, from town to region to nation, but also directed all critique toward the state. As with other forms of popular protest during apartheid (Wolpe 1988, 77), SARU turned local debates into national ones and brought national concerns home. Now, without an independent and politically committed SARU (and, one could add, without the totalizing logic of apartheid), that through line no longer exists. At a second level, though, the veteran's remark points to the inadequacy of SARU's brand of politics for the post-apartheid era. After all, its politics was one of negation. It was a way of saying "no" to apartheid in the language of apartheid itself. That mode of politics worked well in opposition to apartheid, because of the nature of apartheid ideology, but is not particularly suited to the sort of positive interventions post-apartheid rugby seems now to require.

Another veteran found himself in a similar bind. He told me that he longed to support South Africa but found that he could not. Something about the way the rugby unfolded on the field gave him pause. After some discussion, we located the issue: he found apartheid still buried in the style of rugby that South African teams play. "It's so damn harsh and aggressive," he told me. He had material concerns as well, but his stylistic concern showed the depth to which imaginative resistance had fractured his conception of rugby's frame. Even if he could find a way to look past the unequal distribution of resources and opportunities for high-level participation, he still saw the ghosts of apartheid politics in the liveness of play itself. Both veterans showed themselves quite adept at using imaginative resistance to identify the lingering inequalities built into South African rugby, but that iconoclastic technique only disrupts rugby's autonomy. It is not at all suited to repairing it.

A third player found what I consider to be an ingenious and ironic way around that problem. He wrote off supporting South Africa, but he also wrote off supporting New Zealand and Australia. His reason was simple: "I don't see any sense in supporting the team of another country that also exploited people. What the Australians have done to the aborigines is horrible." To the argument that, as he put it, "coloureds should support the All Blacks because they [coloureds] were oppressed," he said, "we were never exposed to township oppression. Our lives were difficult but they were never so difficult as that." Of the sort of person who flaunts their All Black support in the post-apartheid era, he said, "People want to make rugby an extension of their miserable lives. They should care about things like their families or religion—things that really matter."

Predictably, his critique (which deconstructed the social importance of rugby down to nothing) extended to style as well: "People who say they support the All Blacks because of their style are just making excuses. Rugby isn't just about [flashy play]. Real rugby purists wouldn't mind a scrappy [ugly, uncreative, and low-scoring] game." To underline his point, he recalled, with particular fondness, the superficially unappealing style of the English national team in the 2003 Rugby World Cup. As a connoisseur of rugby in his own right, he saw through the ugliness (manifesting in slow and methodical strategies rather than flashy ones) to the small details that the team did well: "You do what you're good at. Rugby is rugby. It's not what anybody wants it to be."

That player's statements could be read as simple realism, since they refuse to grant rugby any more importance than it "objectively" deserves. Yet they hint at something more interesting at work. His comments about the impossibility of supporting Australia or New Zealand, for example, point not to a lack of significance but to an excess of it. He joins some former SARU players in seeing it as sullying to support a Springbok team that carries on the country's legacy of exploitation, but he also used the violence of settler colonialism to extend the same imaginative resistance beyond South Africa's borders and into New Zealand's. That extension enabled him to critique the utopia that Leon and others imagine exists there. His position, then, appears to involve not less imaginative resistance but more, and his apparent realism is an extension of that perspective. He draws his critical eye even further, to a realistic (but ahistorical) judgment of rugby's ultimate meaninglessness, with the result that, at a time when many people continue to see politics permeating rugby's production, he is free to support his teams of choice as if it were all irrelevant. The irony of that position should be clear: partly due to SARU's critical perspective, that player is now able to dismiss the politics of rugby in South Africa's contemporary moment. In effect, he used imaginative resistance to undermine imaginative resistance itself.

CONCLUSION

If a person refuses to ignore the historical inequalities that continue to shape South Africa's rugby, either because they have experienced those inequalities firsthand or because a lifetime of imaginative resistance makes the inequalities impossible to ignore, that person is left with few options for positive action. Leon has discovered that limitation. In his effort to use his own critical awareness to contribute to the transformation of rugby at Stellenbosch University, he has found himself in the uncomfortable position of being the anomalous one who is disturbing the existing structures of rugby at the university. Yet he insisted to me that his anomalous position allows him to bring real change to the production of South African rugby. He can bring talented and overlooked black players into the team and influence the style the team plays. Rather than a harsh South African style, he has coached them to play fluidly, in the manner of a New Zealand team. At the same time, though, his efforts to change Stellenbosch University's rugby from within get read (via imaginative resistance) as a recognizable performance of history—as capitulation in a Federation mold. Hence his Belhar opponent's accusation. Leon was not bringing change, he was nothing but a *gat kruiper*.

One person highlighted in this chapter seems to have found an active way to disrupt rugby's post-apartheid politics without exposing himself to the accusation that he is "in die Boere se gat." Uncle Dapper's imaginative resistance led him to intervene in rugby's politics, but because he did so visibly, briefly, disruptively, and only at the moment when that politics was most apparent (when the referee's assistant "took the game away" from his team), his action became unequivocally valid. For the spectators around the field who were able to see the legacies of apartheid unfolding as clearly as he did, his action was a welcome sight.

While it would be easy to dismiss Uncle Dapper's actions as irrational, desperate, or drunken, we clearly do so at our own risk. Not only do such dismissals deny Uncle Dapper's knowledge of rugby and his capacity for critical thought, but they also deny us the opportunity to understand an important avenue of contemporary political expression. If post-apartheid rugby seems to resemble the rugby of the past, insofar as it perpetuates historical inequalities and remains controlled by white South Africans, critical observers of rugby need not resign themselves to ignoring those resemblances or becoming paralyzed by the absence of a stable political opponent. They can always do as Uncle Dapper did and call attention to those resemblances by addressing post-apartheid rugby in the name of its unequal and white-dominated predecessor. Like anti-apartheid activists dropping sacks of flour from the sky, they can demonstrate the politics of rugby's autonomy (and the artificiality of the frame that separates rugby from everyday life) by puncturing that autonomy themselves.

CHAPTER 6

In Apartheid's Image

Rugby and Nationalist Spectacle in South Africa

RUGBY AS PRESENTATION, RUGBY AS PERFORMANCE

In the previous chapter, I introduced a former SARU player who told me that he wished he could support South Africa's rugby teams but found that he was unable to do so. He considered their style of play to be harsh, aggressive, and reminiscent of the violence and brutality of the apartheid state. If other South Africans notice similar echoes of the past when they watch their country's teams, that uneasiness would seem to complicate narratives about the importance of rugby to the post-apartheid nation. While the state has gone to great lengths to rebrand and redeploy South Africa's rugby, its attempts have failed to persuade knowledgeable spectators like the fan just referenced. Why might that failure be? Where does the sport carry the image of apartheid, and can that image be transformed to depict a new, post-apartheid South Africa? With such questions in mind, I argue in this chapter that the South African state's attempt both to reckon with the contemporary significance that rugby holds for many of its citizens and to refashion the sport to represent the post-apartheid nation is complicated by rugby's *beeld*, or "image."

The arrival of television in the mid-1970s raised a number of important political questions in South Africa, but one seems to have concerned rugby's administrators more than the rest. If matches were televised live, those men observed, cameras would be able to superimpose their invisible frames—supplied by their lenses—over the frame produced by rugby itself. Television could then steal the content of the sport and take supporters with it. In response to that novel threat, one union found a creative solution: the administrators associated with the Northern Transvaal Rugby Union (NTRU) began to think of their sport in terms of its *beeld*.[1] Like its English equivalent, *beeld* carries multiple connotations. Two are particularly relevant for this chapter. The first concerns the presentation of rugby. The presented image includes the embodied appearance of the players on the field but also extends to the creation and maintenance of a team's "image" as a marketable brand. The second connotation describes the performance of rugby and references a team's play as well as the coaches and administrators who facilitate that play. Given this, the conception of image-as-performance also references rugby's structures of violence and uncertainty and a team's particular and historically contingent response to those conditions.

It might be tempting to assume that one or the other of those two connotations of *beeld* must ultimately determine its second. In one reading, performance would be taken as primary and presentation as derivative, because the live performance of rugby and its inherent uncertainty make it possible to continually produce new events from nearly identical initial conditions. But such an interpretation overlooks the ways that presentation structures performance. Presentation serves as an archive of available significance. It sets the terms of the event by means of the players selected, the symbols worn, and the meaning those symbols and players can carry. More generally, presentation lends an important shape to an unruly and unpredictable contest by producing the conditions of autonomy that bring performance into being in the first place. Privileging presentation over performance would fall similarly short, because it would reduce rugby to the situation of the event. As previous chapters of this book have shown, rugby's uncertainty ensures that a live performance will always produce unexpected encounters, with which spectators, performers, and coaches must invariably contend. Furthermore, an archive of presentations is itself constituted by a range of performances, insofar as sedimented past performances set meanings and forms of significance in place (and, as Rebecca Schneider [2011] might note, presentations must be performatively framed as presentations, independent of their performance, for them to be understood as such).

As that dialectical interaction and its binding into the single term *beeld* suggests, the two connotations clearly coexist and commingle. Lisa Bloom has observed a similar relationship on the pages of the magazine *National Geographic*. After differentiating between, on the one hand, the image of *National Geographic* as the kind of magazine it was fantasized or imagined to be and, on the other, the actual photographic representations that the magazine circulated in its pages, she observes that "the two [images] cannot be separated," because "the *National Geographic* is in the image itself, it is the image" (1993, 65). Photographs served an iterative function for the magazine's brand image, and the magazine's image structured and shaped the patriarchal and racist narratives that the magazine favored and that its photographs represented. The performance and the presentation emerged simultaneously. W. J. T. Mitchell argues, too, that theorists of images need favor neither of what he, borrowing from a Sprite commercial, calls "image" (the presentation of the product) and "thirst" (the desire for the product, into which the fantasy of the Sprite commercial seeks to play). Rejecting the "all-or-nothing choice of images and thirst," Mitchell opts for an "acknowledgement that images are not mere things, and thirst not everything" (2005, 81). He argues that because he preferences neither presentation nor performance, he can examine the ways in which images elude human attempts at determining their significance and, by extension, can identify the grounds on which someone comes to attribute value to performance and presentation in their consideration of a particular image.

Seen through Mitchell's lens, NTRU administrators apparently used rugby's *beeld* as a means to open, discursively and conceptually, a small and analytically significant space for themselves alongside television, their new antagonist. While television, to a much greater extent than radio and print media before it, could capture and disseminate rugby's presentation, it found rugby's performance much more difficult to access. When the NTRU provided television broadcasters with matches that were not particularly telegenic, those broadcasters had little choice but to complain about the product. The post-apartheid state, I argue here, has found itself in a somewhat similar position. While the state has manipulated rugby's presentation in myriad ways, both large and small, it has not yet demanded significant changes to rugby's performance, for several reasons. First, as I have shown in several previous chapters, rugby's performances are never easy to control. That they unfold on fields and within their own conditions and are protected from explicit political intervention by the autonomy of the sport makes them inaccessible to all but the most targeted efforts (Uncle Dapper's iconoclastic action discussed in the previous chapter being a powerful example). Second, rugby's performances are managed in South Africa by professional organizations, such as the NTRU's descendent—the Blue Bulls, which ostensibly represent "unions" that are comprised of the teams that are based within the country's provinces and regions. The state cannot intervene directly in the performance of rugby without assuming control of those mediating "unions" and dictating the conditions of the sport's production. The colonial and apartheid regimes embraced that controlling position, particularly by making rugby a fundamental part of their educational projects, but the post-apartheid state has—to date—been reluctant to take so heavy a hand with rugby. It has also encountered the unions in a very different historical moment, when South Africa's sporting landscape is long established and not so easily transformed.

Third, the dominant *beeld* of South African rugby, as a historically constituted "image," came of age during earlier historical moments. Of particular importance to the process of rugby's South African making was the consolidation of an Afrikaner identity and the rise of the National Party. The post-apartheid state has inherited from its predecessors that dominant *beeld*, not the idealized version of the All Blacks style described in chapter 5 or the thoroughgoing compliance with uncertainty described in chapter 1. For that reason, I suggest, rugby's performance continues to tell a different (harsher) story from its presentation, even as the state has sought to deploy the sport for its own political purposes. Although apartheid-era administrators seem to have recognized the existence of their rugby *beeld* during an especially perilous moment in the domestic history of their sport, that legacy suggests that the term is more broadly relevant than it might at first appear. It directs our attention not only to the challenges that the democratic government, led by the African National Congress, has faced in refashioning practices like rugby into reflections of its post-apartheid political agenda but also to the performative qualities inherent in all sports, which make them such powerful (and elusive) vehicles for national and regional sentiments.

AFRIKANER NATIONALISM, APARTHEID, AND THE CONSTRUCTION OF RUGBY'S IMAGE IN SOUTH AFRICA

Scholars of nationalism have long noted the persuasive power of performance in the cultivation of regional and national identities,[2] and early Afrikaner nationalism demonstrates that persuasion as well. Isabel Hofmeyr has noted, for example, that the process of defining what it meant to be an Afrikaner necessitated cultural fabrication and mobilization. Hofmeyr explains that by means of the burgeoning Afrikaans-language print industry (in which many members of the would-be Afrikaner middle class were invested),[3] as well as Afrikaans debating societies, drama associations, coffeehouses, and schools, "what had previously been furniture became 'Afrikaans' furniture and what had been a house became an 'Afrikaans' house built in an *Afri-kaanse bouwstijl* (Afrikaans architecture)" (1984, 111). That process was distinctly marked by perceptions of racial difference and anxieties about miscegenation, particularly in the wake of the Carnegie Commission's 1932 study of the "poor white problem," which found that poor whites were "mainly of Dutch-French-German extraction" (Albertyn and Rothmann 1932, viii) and attributed their condition to, among other things, "long-continued contact with inferior coloured races" (xix; cf. Stoler 2001, 859–60; Dubow 1995). Light-skinned Afrikaans-speaking South Africans were therefore particularly in need of social uplift and education and were thus encouraged to read Afrikaans-language newspapers, attend debates and plays in Afrikaans, and take part in Afrikaner cultural activities. In short, they were invited to disregard regional and class distinctions and to recognize that they participated in the performance of a shared collective ethnic identity.

Rugby played several roles in that process. First, Afrikaans-speaking teachers and ministers carried rugby from the Western Cape (particularly from Stellenbosch University, where many were educated) into South Africa's hinterlands (Grundlingh 1994, 410). Not only did those men build associations between rugby and other markers of Afrikaner identity, particularly Afrikaans and the Dutch Reformed Church, but they also circulated the performance of rugby itself. English-speaking and Afrikaans-speaking teams competed against one another, both redirecting Boer War antagonisms toward the field (Allen 2003) and embracing a shared white South African identity, and teams from disparate regions of the country were able to meet on the pitch, operate within identical constraints, and work together to bring rugby's autonomy into being. Moreover, the formation of regional and national rugby bodies channeled talented players from community teams, through newly constructed provincial unions, to a national team that, in theory, encompassed the white South African nation as a whole.

Second, rugby stadiums served as ready venues for national spectacles. Not only did stadiums host rugby matches, allowing spectators to watch the performance of a strong, exclusively white and male (cf. McClintock 1991) South Africa, but larger stadiums like Loftus Versfeld in Pretoria hosted other nationalist celebrations as well. In 1939, for example, the executive board of the NTRU debated the seemingly innocuous question of whether or not it should permit a community celebration to occur on its main rugby field. While all prior requests for field use (whether by youth teams, "nonwhite" teams, or nonrugby activities) had been flatly rejected, the board both acqui-

esced to that appeal and promised to relocate all previously scheduled fix-
tures to clear space. The requesting organization and event was the Afrikaans
Culture Council (Die Afrikaanse Kultuurraad), and it had sought access to
the field in order to commemorate the 250-year anniversary of the arrival of
Huguenots in South Africa. As that example suggests, rugby fields were made
available for the casting and celebration of a nationalist-inspired Afrikaner
"collective memory" (cf. Grundlingh and Huigen 2008).

Third, the value of rugby was justified on ideational as well as material
grounds. The conditions of rugby's performance—its violence, its uncertainty, and its (literal) grittiness—were judged to cultivate and exhibit distinctly Afrikaner characteristics. Compared to their English-speaking counterparts, who showed a strong attachment to the values of "sportsmanship,
gentlemanly conduct, and fair-mindedness" that were more closely associated with a British imperial ethos of athleticism (cf. Mangan 1981), Grundlingh argues that Afrikaners "placed less emphasis on these and more on
the game as an opportunity to demonstrate presumed Afrikaner qualities,
such as ruggedness, endurance, forcefulness and determination" (1994, 414).
Archer and Bouillon write that Afrikaners, "who considered themselves to
be a civilizing elite, pioneer people conquering barbarism, recognized an
image of their own ideology in [rugby's] symbols" (1982, 66). Even if the
latter authors homogenize and dehistoricize white Afrikaans-speaking identities in their efforts to link rugby with an ideology of settler colonialism,
several chapters of the present study have elaborated on (and nuanced) that
observation by showing how rugby became enmeshed in the production of
a white, particularly Afrikaner masculinity during the eras of British colonialism and apartheid.

Given those layers of historical significance and the institutions in which
that significance developed, it is unsurprising that rugby was an important
piece of the apartheid government's "cultural policy"—its intervention in
and manipulation of cultural forms for the purposes of generating a specific
national imaginary in its populations (cf. White 2008, 68). Booth has found,
for example, that the state allocated funds for school rugby in a way that made
it virtually impossible for teams in nonwhite areas to sustain themselves. In
Pietermaritzburg, a white school of 1,000 students had access to six rugby
fields, while an African school of a comparable size had none (Booth 1998,
68). That the only sporting field that the African school had access to was
three-fourths-size and designated for football indicates that the government's
sporting policies helped to confirm apartheid's untenable racial ideology (cf.

Breckenridge 2005; Posel 2001). Because rugby was seen by the state to be a "White" and "Coloured" practice, it was understood that "African" schools needed no resources for rugby. But a primary reason that rugby could be seen as something that distinguished "White" and "Coloured" South Africans from the rest of the country's population was the denial of resources to "African" (and "Indian") schools in the first place. While rugby fields were by no means the only place where subject categorizations of persons were made "real" through state policy in the apartheid era, rugby did come with the added benefit of producing the image of a homogenous white nation that could be readily disseminated to South Africans and the world at large (cf. Nauright 1997, 80).

If this was the case, then the apartheid state's rugby policy found a ready ally in the medium of radio. Scholars have long noted radio's capacity to produce common perceptions, experiences, and feelings (Hilmes 2012; Vaillant 2002).[4] In the case of South Africa, the South African Broadcasting Corporation (SABC) may have claimed some measure of independence from the National Party's projects of cultural control, but state radio lost most of its autonomy following the massacre in Sharpeville in 1960 and with the ascension of Piet Meyer, a member of the Afrikaner cultural organization Die Broederbond, to its head (Hamm 1991, 153). Under Meyer's watchful eye, the SABC could be depended on to minimize domestic conflicts, accentuate foreign ones (particularly those in newly independent African nations), and represent South Africa as a healthy and prosperous nation.[5]

Sporting broadcasts were not excluded from the nationalist and white supremacist project. Merrett writes, for example, that the SABC "cancelled all coverage of the Natal Open Golf tournament [in 1963] because it was won by a golfer from the Indian community" (1995, 70). One of my informants recalled growing up in the years prior to television and hanging on every word spoken by Gerhard Viviers, South Africa's preeminent radio sportscaster: "I remember one boxing match Viviers broadcasted. The South African boxer lost and it took me completely by surprise. Viviers described the whole fight as though he had been winning. When he was knocked out, we had no idea what had happened or why." Viviers, the man supposed, had found the pummeling of the South African boxer so difficult to describe to his audience that he constructed an alternate reality to soften the blow. When the fighter finally succumbed, however, Viviers was forced to admit the truth of the bout to his (apparently baffled) listeners.

Viviers, for his part, seems to have believed himself incapable of such a deliberate act of mediation. In his account of a Springbok tour to Britain and Ireland in 1969–70 that was marked by intense anti-apartheid protests, Viviers wrote, "There is a point that I have to say and it is this: When you commentate live, your eyes follow the ball and you cannot always see the play. This is the reason why I cannot remember anything of the match, the play and the players" (1971, 46). Even just that small peek into the perception Viviers had of his own broadcasting practice suggests that he regarded himself as an empty vessel through which sporting events passed. His eyes follow the ball so closely that the events of the match leave no trace on his memory. In keeping with the argument about certainty, posited in chapter 4 of this book, we could say that the task of observing and describing the unfolding uncertainty of a rugby match occupied the anticipatory time it would have taken for him to concoct an alternative narrative and substitute it for the "true" one. Such a broadcast would have emerged from him in something like an oracular trance, truthful because it was unmediated, and then quickly forgotten as a result. Even if the conception Viviers had of his own work would lend itself to a different interpretation of the boxing match than that of my informant, both would likely agree that the sportscaster's voice was the primary authoritative means by which the event reached distant audiences in real time (cf. Hayles 199, 200). Radio-induced passivity can be easily overstated, given that the structure of the listening arrangement never determines a listener's reception (or what listeners choose to do with the narratives they receive), but prior to the arrival of television, transmitted depictions of sporting events were influenced significantly by the disembodied voice that described them.

When television was finally made widely available in South Africa in 1976, the relationship between event, voice, and listening population became unsettled. That development helps explain why the SABC opted to pair the first televised footage of police violence in Soweto in 1976 with a disembodied voice explaining to viewers how dangerous the apparently unarmed young people really were. That radio-like televised account, argues Krabill (2010, 58), marked an important transitional moment for the apartheid regime, in that it was an attempt on the part of the state to use the established authority of radio to intervene in the visual content that television presented.[6]

From the perspective of South Africa's rugby unions, television posed a different problem. Radio had long sought to capture rugby's content, but the nature of its form made it a comparatively unthreatening "parasite" (R. Williams 2003, 23). In the words of Martin Jay, radio "could preserve the *nunc* or 'nowness' of a performance but not its *hic* or 'hereness.' In so doing, it destroyed one of the crucial features of what Benjamin had called the 'aura' of a work of art, its ritual, cultish nimbus. Instead of experiencing [the event] with its 'auratic' qualities intact, the radio listener heard it in a depersonalized, collective, objectivized form" (1996, 191). In the case of rugby, that quality of radio seems to have suited both the rugby establishment, which knew that those spectators who desired an "unmediated" sporting experience would be drawn to the stadium, and the South African government and its censors, who could count on the vocal monopoly of Viviers, with his nationalist sympathies, to present matches in a favorable light.[7] Radio was valuable precisely because it could lend an ideological shape to both the form and content of every event it presented.

TELEVISION AND THE STRUGGLE OVER RUGBY'S IMAGE

Television appeared much more capable than radio of capturing rugby matches,[8] and its arrival in South Africa seems therefore to have prompted rugby administrators to reflect, seriously and perhaps for the first time, on the ways that broadcast media might shape (and even repossess) the cultural objects they produced. "We provided the stadium, the fans, the field, and the players," one administrator told me, "and they showed up with their cameras and wanted it for free. We found this unacceptable." As far as the unions were concerned, rugby had little but its content to offer its supporters, and administrators were not at all sure that anything of rugby would be left if television stole that content away.[9] The possibility that television might lure spectators away from matches and thus undermine ticket sales made television's apparent parasitism seem even less desirable.

Those initial fears seem to have been confirmed. The unions found that many spectators, given the choice between paying to see rugby in a stadium and watching it on television in their homes, were perfectly willing to stay home. In an angry missive to the South African Rugby Board (SARB), the secretary of the NTRU at the time, Robert Denton, cited numbers from a pair of matches against an identical opponent (the first untelevised, in 1973, and the second televised, in 1976), which appeared to show that television had reduced stadium attendance by nearly 50 percent. That new information provoked both consternation and accusations. Denton had particularly harsh words for "supporters" who thought they could demonstrate loyalty to their team by following them on TV. "The man who supports sport in front of the television," he wrote, "is not a sports supporter and does nothing to improve sports" (Denton to Alex Kellermann, November 26, 1976, BBRU Archives).

As letters circulated between the SARB, the NTRU, and South Africa's other provincial unions, it became clear that condemning spectators[10] was not a sustainable strategy for a long-term engagement with television and its consequences. Other strategies were subsequently proposed. Some administrators, citing financial constraints, advocated broadcasting matches on tape delay. Others observed that tape delay might also benefit players. One argument, circulated in a press release by the SARB in 1977 and perhaps crafted by SARB head Daniël "Danie" Craven (cf. Gerber 1982, 195–96), opined, "For the player to see himself play, he can see his own shortcomings or weaknesses as also his strong points, to such an extent that the task of the coach not only becomes easier, but in many cases superfluous. Players who have to travel long distances after matches are deprived of the opportunity to share in these advantages if televising is allowed on the same afternoon" (November 5, 1977, BBRU Archives). Another idea involved showing twenty-minute live segments of matches so that watchers could experience a taste of the excitement without getting entire matches for free.

As the popularity of television grew, the tenor of the negotiation began to change. Denton, writing on behalf of the union, informed the SABC that it would have to move its TV trucks because they were unsightly (Denton to Koos Ludick, April 7, 1978, BBRU Archives), but the SABC pushed back. It objected strongly to this suggestion, on the grounds of practical considerations and cost (Ludick to Denton, March 16, 1978, BBRU Archives). The SABC brought its own complaints to the NTRU in return—it railed against spectators (especially children) who stood and tramped on microphone cables and made it impossible for the microphones to pick up the sounds from the field (JHG Snyman to Denton, August 7, 1980, BBRU Archives). The SABC also asked that the NTRU consider relocating newspaper photographers because they were intruding on the sightlines of television cameras (H.J. Human to Denton, July 25, 1977, BBRU Archives). In short, the "parasite" of broadcasting had become such an active participant in the making of South African rugby that it was beginning to dictate the terms of production for its "host." By the early 1980s, it was clear that the NTRU was going to have to find a way to thrive within the conditions established by the medium.

As anxieties about television broadcasts stealing rugby's content suggest, those conditions were formal as well as technological and material. Because newspapers had few illusions about their ability to preserve the immediacy of rugby in the first place, they could dispatch a sloppy game in a few short sentences.[11] Radio broadcasters knew themselves to be responsible for generating excitement in listeners who could not experience it themselves. Television had a different relationship with the event. It may have offered a "hereness," in Martin Jay's terms (1996, 191), that radio and print media could not, but that "hereness" was still "simulated" because it took shape in the gap between occurrence and depiction (Buck-Morss 1994, 52). As Buck-Morss notes of cinema, that "simulated present" made possible the depiction of entities that, arguably, could not be properly conceived without it—the film star of Hollywood and the mass collectivity of the Soviet Union (2002, 149). In South African rugby, the "simulated present" of television was undoubtedly generative as well—of star players, broadcasting rights, and opportunities for advertising revenue among other things. Particularly with the advent of the professional era, the economic value of players and teams has made rugby in South Africa and in other countries a faster and more polished product.

In the late 1970s and early 1980s, though, this simulated present manifested for administrators in the NTRU as fears about lost revenue and empty seats. As a result of these fears, as well as with concerns about popular perceptions of South Africa's rugby as unattractive and dangerous, administrators began to view their team and their sport in a somewhat different light. They began, it seems, to see rugby as both a product, a show in its own right, as well as something that needed to be marketed and publicized. These revised conceptions of product and brand can be clustered together around a single term—that of the team's *beeld*. First considered in depth with respect to NTRU rugby, so far as I can tell, in a private *dinkskrum* (brainstorming retreat) in 1981, the term *beeld* shares connotations with "image" in English and *bild* in German (cf. Belting 2014). It described Northern Transvaal rugby in particular, and rugby in general, as a marketable "brand" and also as a "picture" of a kind, a performance produced in the stadium by players and coaches.[12]

While some presenters at the *dinkskrum* placed more emphasis on the internal management of the team's product, and others on how the team might market itself better to viewers, these two conceptions of *beeld* often ran together. A speaker with a background in marketing, for example, began by discussing the team's *beeld* as a brand image, but he drifted quickly into the realm of performance and production. To prompt those present to begin defining the organization's *beeld* for themselves, he offered up a string of questions: Who, he asked, is your customer? Do you know what they want? And what was the organization's product? Was it the match alone or was the team also part of the product? Were the players the product? Once the administrators identified their product and figured out the tastes of their customers, they could then promote their team more effectively. "I do not know what the image is," he said. "I think all of us have an idea of what the image is but the market research will clarify this for us" (*Dinkskrum*, BBRU Archives, 47). This attendee also stressed the power of television in the propagation of the team's image. "We cannot say there is no television," he said. "We did not need it, we ignored television. Television is here and we will have to get to television in order to promulgate rugby" (37).

Unlike previous exchanges, these observations clearly accepted that television had changed the terms of the relationship between the rugby union and its supporters. Also unlike previous exchanges, this framing of television's relationship with rugby was met with broad approval and support. "We all feel rugby must be on television," another attendee said (*Dinkskrum*, BBRU Archives, 45). A third participant even remarked on the power of television to emphasize the expertise that he saw in rugby. He proposed "a series of television programs where the talents of [particularly skillful players] could be offered. You often see these small pieces in the newspapers about golf, Gary Player and Doug Watson's putting, tennis, etc. But what about rugby? Can't we spread a little of the skillfullness of rugby [with television]?" (38).

Even as they accepted that television had become a valuable tool in the propagation of their *beeld*, administrators also used *beeld* as a means to locate their team beyond television's reach. The marketing expert, for his part, observed, "The question of the *beeld* cannot be emphasized too much, and it is also part of the product. The image of the business, the business itself, is the source from which the product springs and I think this is something that we need to pay particular attention to" (*Dinkskrum*, BBRU Archives, 47). Television, he therefore implied, might be a resource for the company to use once its market research had determined the image they should cultivate and circulate, but it was the union, not television, who controlled that product. Others addressed the team's control over its performative *beeld* in more oblique ways. In addition to branding and television, for example, the *dinkskrum* also devoted significant time to the prosaic complexities of running a successful sporting organization—of identifying promising young players and making sure they stayed with the sport, of improving standards in coaching, and with having good relations and reliable communications with area clubs. Though those complexities might appear somewhat tangential to the issue of image-making, the men at the *dinkskrum* seem to have recognized in those complexities that it was they, rather than television, who were the stewards of the union's actual product, whether that product be matches, the live stadium atmosphere that surrounded them (including programs, traffic, and parking), the players who performed in them, or elements of all of those things together. Whatever the case might have been, administrators were confident that the key to taking care of the team's *beeld* lay not in struggling against television, but rather in responding to the issues that television had laid bare. They needed to study their product. They needed to make sure that they were finding talented players, setting those players up with the proper resources and systems, and putting them in a lively stadium. They needed to make live matches into high quality events. They needed, ultimately, to look inward and make sure their own house was in order. If they did those things well, the team's image, and rugby's image, would also be preserved. They might even be improved.

Put in the context of this book, we could therefore say that NTRU administrators had begun to accept—however implicitly—that broadcast television could only superimpose itself over the content of NTRU's rugby images, its live and uncertain performances, once those images were produced.[13] It was the players on the field, the administrators who selected those players, and the coaches who trained those players who made the Northern Transvaal's rugby images happen. Hence, perhaps, the newfound agreement on the part of administrators about the utility of television. In this framing, television looked less like a parasite overtaking its host than a mouthpiece that administrators could use to amplify their preferred *beeld*. Seen in this way, even conducting research on the team's image became a way for the team to assert control over that image. Television could propagate the NTRU's *beeld*, but only the NTRU could study it and develop it.[14]

A remark by Martin Locke, host of the English-language sports program *Sportsview*, further underlines that reading. On June 1, 1979, Locke introduced the highlights of a match between Western Province and the Northern Transvaal with the following statement: "Before 60 000 spectators yesterday's clash . . . must have been a huge disappointment with Northern Transvaal playing very dull diversive [*sic*] pressure rugby in spite of getting 90% of the ball. We have put together some clips of what action there was." Following the show of the game's limited highlights, Locke added, "The match was a great disappointment as a spectacle and if this is what winning rugby is all about I'd rather watch soccer." Word of Locke's televised complaint traveled swiftly to the head of the Northern Transvaal union, who demanded a transcript of the segment. The SABC dutifully sent the text (as cited here), accompanied by a note of apology (Jan Schutte to Fritz Eloff June 5, 1979, BBRU Archives).

Media scholars have argued that what television sacrifices in immediacy, it attempts to regain in intimacy, proximity, and detail. Maurice Roche, for example, has observed that television supplements its sporting broadcasts with "aesthetics of compensation" in order to redress the problem of distance (2000, 164). Television's compensatory forms, including instant replays, the display of statistics, and the use of slow motion, are designed to help viewers overcome the incompleteness of their explicitly mediated sporting experience. In a way that resembles Walter Benjamin's conception of the camera operator as a surgeon of reality (2003, 263), those compensatory techniques invite the television viewer to imagine being inside the performance and to fantasize about controlling and manipulating it from within. Martin Locke's presentation of highlights could be regarded as a form of compensation too, insofar as his program sought to provide viewers with an opportunity to trade the full experience of a live match for an abbreviated version that emphasized the most important moments. If viewers tuned in to catch up on the rugby that they missed from the previous weekend, though, they were unlikely to waste their time on a match that they did not find aesthetically pleasing. It was incumbent on broadcasters to encourage the country's rugby teams to play a style that would produce sufficient highlights to bring casual fans to their sets.

Seen from the perspective of that necessity, Locke's parting remark ("if this is what winning rugby is all about I'd rather watch soccer") reads as something of an attack on the control the NTRU held over their team's *beeld*.[15] That remark was a way for Locke to use television, as a medium, to exert pressure on rugby's live performance. Because television gave viewers access to a number of different sports, all within the comfort of their homes and all at equal remove from themselves (cf. Buck-Morss 1994, 54), the historically and politically constituted primacy of rugby in the sporting consciousness of white South Africans was implicitly called into question.[16] It was now the responsibility of rugby's administrators to convince casual spectators that they should invest their time, energy, and money in support of rugby teams. In response to that challenge, some administrators at the *dinkskrum* sought to bring fans to rugby with more matches and more publicity and others wanted better coaching and more resources for players. Irrespective of their position, though, television was no longer figured as the primary obstacle to the flourishing of rugby at the *dinkskrum*. Consistent with Locke's remarks, football had become that obstacle. Administrators even gave the allure of football its own special name, *sokker sindroom* (soccer syndrome).

In the minds of administrators, football had a number of things working in its favor to undermine the appeal of rugby. It was cheaper to play, for one thing, and it was popularly perceived to be less dangerous as well. More importantly, it was recognized at the *dinkskrum* that young potential rugby players might be drawn to football because of the prospect of a professional career. While many of the successful South African rugby players with whom these administrators were concerned (that is, white male players) were actually losing money to play the sport—due to the fact that they, like so many players before them, were not only unpaid but had to take time off work in order to play—young (again, white and male) South African boys could look to football and see economic opportunities and global stars.[17] Given these conditions, it is perhaps not unexpected that rugby administrators were concerned about young white players becoming infected with a passion for football.

This infection, however, was not just a story of the administrators of an amateur sport attempting to compete with a professional rival. Rugby was so deeply enmeshed in white institutions, particularly Afrikaner ones, that the abandonment of the sport for football—a sport that was as racially marked as "African" as rugby was coded "White"—could be perceived as a threat not just to the viability of South Africa's rugby, but to the rigorously segregationist logic of the apartheid state as well. One speaker at the *dinkskrum* addressed this significance directly. It was, he apparently felt, unlikely that rugby would lose many young white men to soccer. "It is in our white people's national character to play rugby," he said, "so I don't think soccer is a threat because we are the physically competitive sort, where your black man wants to have a thing stand at a distance" (*Dinkskrum*, BBRU Archives, 32–33). By using a notion of "national character" to link whiteness to physicality and rugby, and blackness to a lack of physicality and soccer, this man naturalized race in sport in a manner consistent with the apartheid state's cultural policy. His embrace of that cultural policy evidently led him to think white support of soccer impossible, but should that support actually manifest—should white South Africans find a passion for soccer by television or any other means—that support would, in his conception, amount to both an embrace of a soccer sensibility (coded as black) and a betrayal of their own designated white national character.[18] If other administrators understood football's pathological dimensions in a narrower sense—referring, instead, to the sport's popularity with viewing audiences and young players relative to that of rugby— even that narrow perspective spoke necessarily to larger political concerns. Rugby's popularity was no more inevitable, no more organic, than football's; it too was a product of political interventions, media representations, social institutions, and framings of race, gender, and nationalism. To express anxiety about the popularity of rugby, then, was to express anxiety about the social context in which the sport was played as well as about the social significance of the sport itself.

REIMAGING RUGBY FOR A POST-APARTHEID SOUTH AFRICA

A good measure of the significance of the 1995 Rugby World Cup, which South Africa famously hosted mere months after the country's first fully democratic election, can be traced to the historical and performative ties that bound rugby (and its popularity) to the apartheid state. The post-apartheid state sought to turn those connections to its advantage. Maingard (1997) notes that the World Cup's opening and closing ceremonies allowed the state to display a new narrative of national unity and to offer a new reading of the country's past. That reformulation took a particularly transparent form: one by one, delegates from South Africa's religious and ethnic groups entered Cape Town Stadium and formed a group together, populating a giant map of the country that lay on the field. Both Maingard and J. M. Coetzee have noted that those retellings were partial and problematic in specifically South African ways. Coetzee described the ceremony as follows:

> [It] presented a de-historicized vision of Tourist South Africa: contented tribesfolk and happy mineworkers, as in the old South Africa, but purified and sanctified, somehow, by the Rainbow. When it got to the paler end of the spectrum, however, it found that it could not proceed without becoming, intermittently, not only a pageant but an historical pageant as well. And so, to the procession of timeless Sotho in blankets and timeless Zulu in ostrich feathers it had to add what looked very much like happy eighteenth-century slaves and slaveowners in knee-breeches. . . . There were also, somewhere in the middle of the pageant, half a dozen lost-looking lads in khaki shirts and shorts whose presence seemed to be more symbolic than iconic. (1995, n.p.)

In the annals of nationalist spectacles, that event is hardly unique or uniquely flawed. As Apter (2005), Askew (2002), and many others have shown, such spectacles provide regimes with ample opportunities for the telling and retelling of history for political purposes. What arguably distinguished the World Cup spectacle from prior nationalist spectacles in South Africa was not its essentialized depictions of Zulus and Sotho (depictions perfectly consistent with the apartheid state's framing of cultural difference) or even its sanitized recasting of South Africa's history of slavery and white supremacy (which fit comfortably within narratives of settler colonialism). In light of the NTRU *dinkskrum* and its emphasis on rugby's image, it was most noteworthy that the World Cup happened on what one of my black informants termed a "white field" and in conjunction with what we might call a "white event"—a Springbok rugby match. The opening and closing ceremonies were spectacles of presentation, which the African National Congress (ANC) mobilized explicitly for its own political purposes.[19]

If those spectacles were presentations, it is fitting that they ended (in the case of the opening ceremonies) and began (in the case of the closing) only once the rugby itself had stopped. Despite the presence of Chester Williams on the Springbok roster (a problematic figure in coloured rugby circles, for reasons explained in chapter 5), the relevance of the actual play of the Springbok team to the national audience the ANC sought to cultivate was considered only in terms of the game's results. As far as I have been able to discern, the ANC expressed no strong opinions about style of play or tactics. From the perspective of the state, rugby was a tantalizing platform for the presentation of politics but was not a performance of politics itself.

Following the popular success of the Rugby World Cup, the post-apartheid state sought to expand its influence. While still invested in shaping rugby's presentation, the state began to move closer and closer to the field. Martin Locke and the SABC had little choice but to use television as a pulpit to promote their interest in exciting rugby, but the state was able to approach rugby's operations more directly, particularly through its department responsible for sport, Sport and Recreation South Africa. Some within that department may have dreamed of entirely repossessing rugby's production from the country's provincial unions, but the professionalization of rugby in 1995 complicated matters significantly. In 1998, for example, one of the country's newly professionalized provincial teams—as well as the post-apartheid successor to the SARB, the South African Rugby Football Union (SARFU)[20]—

took the South African state to court over the right of the president (Nelson Mandela) to organize a "presidential commission of inquiry" to investigate the team's financial records. The team and SARFU charged that the president had "abdicated" his decision to order such an investigation to his minister, potentially rendering the task force unconstitutional. The state argued that it was in the country's "national interest" to ascertain whether the team was making a good-faith effort to foster rugby development in poorer (and predominantly black) regions of the country. The case eventually found its way to the Constitutional Court, which decided in favor of the state.[21]

Rather than engaging in additional public court battles or enforcing full-scale nationalization of the country's rugby resources, the state chose to work on South Africa's rugby teams from afar, like the SABC before it, but wielding far greater influence. In its more explicit attempts to intervene in rugby, state representatives have made and continue to make strong public pronouncements about the possibility of crafting stringent affirmative action guidelines for the rugby establishment. In late 1997, Steve Tshwete (then the minister of sport and recreation) warned rugby administrators publicly that should rugby not choose to become more appropriately representative of a united South Africa, the state could legislate that representation into being with the aid of a formal "quota" system (Booth 1999).

Other governmental attempts to shape rugby's *beeld* have taken less public forms, an example of which I observed in 2008. As I sat transcribing old administrative minutes in the head office of one of South Africa's provincial teams, the secretary for the head coach of the club (in whose office I worked) received a fax from the offices of the Sport and Recreation South Africa, congratulating the coach on winning a significant match against a longtime rival. Following well wishes on the result, the writer concluded the note with an expression of hope to "see more players like [a particular black player] on the field in the future." The secretary whistled through her teeth when she first saw the fax, clearly recognizing the message's significance: the team had shown promise in its initial attempts to reform its player base, the writer implied, but the government was far from satisfied. That comment, which had the force of government legislation at its back and thus contrasted sharply with Martin Locke's warning, was no idle remark.

Another state intervention into rugby's content concerns the emblem on the national team's jersey, a leaping Springbok. As Booth observed, the ANC's initial decision to retain the emblem was "a bold move and one fraught with danger. For three-quarters of a century the Springbok signified Afrikaner nationalism, racial division, and white exclusiveness and superiority. Instead of abandoning the Springbok for a new unifying symbol and risk alienating traditional rugby supporters, the ANC has attempted to confer upon the emblem an alternative set of values" (1998, 210–11). Booth added that the ANC's course of action seemed to upset both conservative rugby supporters (who saw a symbol they admired being tarnished by bodies that were deemed not fit to wear it) and the more left-wing members of the ANC (who sought to cleanse all traces of apartheid symbolism from the post-apartheid nation).

In the years following the initial discussion about the future of the Springbok logo, the ANC has neither steadfastly resisted change to the emblem nor replaced it. Though juxtaposed in 2002 with an image of the king protea (South Africa's national flower and now the official emblem of all South African sports apart from rugby), the Springbok nevertheless remained, together with the protea, on the left breast of the jersey, where the Springbok had sat since 1906. In the 2009 edition of the jersey, however, the Protea holds the historically significant left position, having bumped the Springbok to the right. That process, which seems to be quite clearly undermining the Springbok's symbolic importance, has unfolded within the context of frequent statements by the ANC leadership that the Springbok will never be abandoned. In an article entitled "ANC Throws Weight behind Bok Emblem," for example, the *Mail and Guardian* quoted ANC spokesperson Jessie Duarte as saying, "The ANC would like to state categorically that it would not like to see any replacement or change of the Springbok emblem until sufficient debate and consultation of all stakeholders, including rugby supporters, has taken place" (*Mail and Guardian* 2008). Read at the level of the post-apartheid state's "cultural policy," Duarte's statement looks like a form of strategic disavowal. He bestowed the Springbok logo with the ANC's unconditional future support while the state strategically marginalized the emblem in the present. In doing so, he and the state have effectively placed all present resistance to revaluation of the Springbok emblem beyond the realm of political debate.

THE POST-APARTHEID AFTERLIVES OF APARTHEID'S RUGBY IMAGE

Read at the level of rugby's *beeld*, the post-apartheid state's "cultural policy" seems somewhat misdirected. Again, the case of the NTRU is indicative of the situation. When South Africa's provincial teams began to rebrand themselves for the professional era, the NTRU approached the process in a manner that differentiated it from its most influential rivals. The team from Natal Province had been known colloquially as "the Banana Boys," an administrator recalled, but the Natal bosses dismissed that name outright. They chose to hire a market research firm to determine the name that would give their team the widest possible appeal. The resulting name, "the Sharks," captured the brand image of KwaZulu-Natal Province (whose coastline has been long associated with sharks) but had no connection to the team's prior performances. Western Province followed a related trajectory. Its players, I was told, approached their management and announced to them that they had decided to call themselves "the Stormers." That name, too, may have had a regional connection (the Cape of Good Hope being notorious among mariners for its storms), but the team nearly torpedoed its *beeld* when it opted to replace its traditional colors (blue and white hoops) with an all-black jersey. The administrator told me, "They almost killed their brand. Black was Natal's color, not [Western] Province's."

In contrast, the NTRU decided to adopt the nickname that its supporters had used since the early 1960s, "the Blue Bulls" (Blou Bulle). As Quintus van Rooyen explained in the newspaper *Die Beeld* on the date of the team's formal rebranding (October 11, 1997), the name owed a piece of its significance to Louis Schmidt, a player known for the tremendous mustache he sported when he played in the light blue jersey of the NTRU. As important as that narrative may be to the contemporary significance of the Bulls, a coach in the Bulls system offered me a more provocative origin story.

> Why did we name ourselves the Bulls? Before that, it was the Northern Transvaal, but then why is our play literally reflecting the Bull or a bison or something resembling that? The moustache was drawn as sort of a horn in a cartoon character, they portrayed it as a Bull with a moustache, but I think there's maybe a more profound connection than [that]. In a subconscious sense. It is embedded in us. Can we change? Maybe not. Maybe this is actually what we are. It doesn't matter what the modern game is, maybe—certain characteristics of the Bulls will stay. We will always promote a physical game, and sometimes people think it is arrogant or robust, but it's important to go back to your strong points and dominate with that, and your strong points will be instinctively what you think you are.

The coach bound the presentation of the Bulls (the team's post-apartheid brand and its historical origins) to the organization's performance (the name chosen by spectators, reflecting the team's performance on the field and the manner in which the Bulls ought to play). Even if one prefers to locate that connection in history rather than the subconscious, the power of the Bulls' performance remains evident. The team's live performance continually draws the brand and the team's *beeld* back to familiar historical territory.[22]

With that evidence, we can perhaps confirm that the ANC's investment in the Springbok logo misses the mark. The ideological salience of South African rugby may be only partially located in the Springbok emblem and the distribution of raced bodies on the field. To focus on those features of rugby's presentation is to overlook the unfolding and uncertain performances that make the sport such an important and longstanding vehicle for nationalist sentiments in the country. The Springbok comes to life, as it were, only in and through the performance of rugby itself, an aspect of rugby that the debate about sporting symbols tends to occlude. The post-apartheid state's efforts to manipulate player requirements and transform the jersey do not reach into rugby's performance and are unable to posit a new, post-apartheid *beeld* for the country's rugby. Short of a wholesale annexation of the country's professional unions, the state, like television broadcasts and rebroadcasts before it, operates solely on the level of rugby's formal presentation.

The informant comments that began this chapter lend credence to that interpretation. He sees South African rugby teams as playing "harshly," in the style of the National Party, because he notices not just the presentation of rugby but also the qualities of its performance. Other black players and fans told me that they felt alienated and excluded by that physical and fairly brutal style of play. Notably, one person made reference to television broadcasts and the forms of "aesthetic compensation" that accompany them. He told me that he found it frustrating that televised broadcasts continually highlighted the height and weight of players: "Why emphasize those qualities? I don't care how big and strong you are, I want to know what you can do with the ball!" He linked that broadcast tendency explicitly to a preference in South Africa's (predominantly white) rugby establishment for larger players over those who exhibit creativity and individual flair.

Even marginalized players who thrive within the constraints of South Africa's *beeld* seem to feel the effects of that dominant image. The raced consequences of that performative style are particularly apparent in the case of one particular player, Tendai Mtawarira, a Zimbabwean national who emerged as a phenomenal young player in 2007, when he began his upper-level rugby career with KwaZulu-Natal Province. By 2008, Mtawarira had played his way to what many South African rugby fans considered to be a merit-based (i.e., nonquota and therefore, in their view, "nonpolitical") selection for the South African national team. Although Mtawarira was, by the time of my fieldwork, a regular starter on the national team and a player of some renown, he was perhaps best known for his nickname, "the Beast."

In an article appropriately titled "Unleash the 'Beast'" in the magazine *Finding Touch: Transformation and Development in SA Rugby*, Carl Potgieter credits the nickname to one of Mtawarira's childhood friends: "He says that the name was given to him because he thinks that he was a bit of a violent child. However, he has calmed down says the giant [player] referring to himself as a gentle beast." The origin of the nickname, though, can hardly explain its ubiquity in South African rugby circles. Potgieter notes, "The cult of the 'Beast' has made huge inroads into the South African rugby supporters' minds. Greeted with a reverberating roar of Beeeeeeeast every time he makes an appearance, Zimbabwean-born Tendai Mtawarira is making people sit up and take notice" (2008, 31).

In terms of the argument of this chapter, I suggest that we cannot understand the "cult of the 'Beast'" if we do not connect the nickname and its significance to the on-field performance of rugby in South Africa. Mtawarira's body was not simply presented to fans on a formerly "white (symbolic) field." It was, instead, a body in movement, as Potgieter recognizes when he writes that Mtawarira's perception of himself as gentle "is cold comfort for his opponents who are still feeling the brunt of the wild side of the 'Beast'" (2008, 31). In keeping with the present argument, Ben Carrington has also emphasized the importance of movement to theories of race and sporting performance. Notably, Carrington connects the motion and activity of boxing with that of cinema. In his analysis of the white interpretations of the boxer Jack Johnson, Carrington follows Pronger (2000) and proposes that sports provide opportunities "in which black bodies can be gazed upon, [with spectators] safe in the knowledge that the circumscribed arena of the sports field provides a legitimate modality for such racialized homosocial dreaming" (2010, 86–87). Carrington explains that sports, like cinema, tell "moving, visual, and contemporary" stories (85). As was the case with Johnson, Mtawarira's body was on display, living and in motion, and available for racialized interpretation.[23] Like Johnson's, Mtawarira's bodily motions intervened in an overdetermined symbolic situation. He harshly and aggressively subjugated uncertainty in a manner similar to his teammates, but the fact that he was a black player performing those actions drew the predominantly white base of South African rugby fandom toward particular understandings of him and his body (cf. Van

Der Riet 1995, 105). For example, Mtawarira could never occupy the position of Archer and Bouillon's "civilizing elite, pioneering people conquering barbarism." That possibility was effectively foreclosed by the classed and raced history of rugby, by South Africa's colonial and apartheid history, and by the formulation of the ideology of civilizing and pioneering elites in explicit contradistinction to bodies like his.[24] Each call of Mtawarira's childhood nickname speaks therefore to a reading of his performance that links his presence on the field (and his embodied responses to rugby's uncertainty) to the work of black men (in the past and the present), whose physically exhausting manual labor in South Africa's fields and mines undergirds the country's economy (Feldman 1999, 124; Comaroff and Comaroff 1997; Meintjes 2017). In this sense, the popularity of Mtawarira's nickname echoes the undertones in the young white player's "Sisebenza" of this book's second chapter. In the latter instance, the player claimed the labor of black groundskeepers as his own. In the former, labor is applied to Mtawarira's play. In both instances, the movements of black and male bodies are framed within structures of history, racism, and power and thereby made legible, ideologically accessible, and available for use.

The post-apartheid state, for its part, has found its own historically and politically framed ways of making sense of Mtawarira. In an article published in the *Mail and Guardian* on November 20, 2009, the South African minister of sport intimated that "the Beast" did not technically qualify for a "scarce skills" visa as a rugby player and ought to be deported. Speaking even more clearly on the matter, a spokesperson commented, "We want to send a strong message that the ministry takes development of local sportspersons very seriously and that only South Africans should represent their country" (*Mail and Guardian* 2009). If rugby spectators read Mtawarira's active body through the representations of African men that were produced under colonialism and apartheid, the spokesperson's statement suggests that some representatives of the ANC government read him in terms of his contribution to the post-apartheid nation. If Mtawarira's presence in the country were to be sanctioned by the state, he could be seen as properly indicative of the diversity of the nation and of rugby's capacity to represent that nation on the playing fields of the world. If it were not sanctioned by the state, he would be rendered comprehensible in a very different and more pernicious way: he would become, in the xenophobic rhetoric that emerges with some regularity in contemporary South Africa, another African foreign national looking for economic opportunities (Chance 2015b; Chiweshe 2016; Comaroff and Comaroff 2005; Hickel

2014). Mtawarira was eventually granted citizenship in 2010, but at the heart of the state's concern was the legitimacy of his identity (as a resident worker in South Africa), not the character of his on-field responses to uncertainty. That concern further confirmed that the state continues to interpret rugby's political significance as an extension of the sport's presentation (rather than its on-field performance) and to implement cultural policies accordingly.

Some interested spectators seem to be aware of the limitations of the post-apartheid state's rugby-related cultural policies. That awareness was made abundantly clear when I watched the Springboks on television in 2011 with Leon (the former SARU player who figured prominently in the previous chapter's discussion). As the broadcasters introduced South Africa's starting lineup for one match, Leon fairly bounced up and down on the couch with excitement. "Black! The last three guys are black!" he shouted to me and to his daughter. She was less sure there was cause for excitement. "Those two guys in the middle there are white though," she observed, pointing. "No, no!" Leon responded, explaining, "[One of them] is 'n swartman [a black man]! It's a blackline!" Leon was making a pun on "backline," the set of positions the players collectively played. "A blackline!" his daughter shouted in delight, before collapsing in gales of laughter. Over her laughing, Leon turned to me, nodding, and declared, "Tonight I'm going to break for South Africa. My black players are on the team." Although Leon and his daughter certainly approved of the racial distribution of the players on the field, the presentation of the team, not its performance, won his support. As Leon's final remark suggests (and as he himself would likely agree), his attachment to the team was ultimately conditional and temporary. If the team's distribution of raced bodies had been constituted differently on that day (e.g., with an entirely white roster), he would have been less invested in the team's performance. The Springboks and, by extension, the post-apartheid nation had his support in that particular moment, but there was no guarantee that it would have his support in the next one.

Leon's friends and coworkers occasionally called on him to answer for his fickle patriotism. When they did challenge him, Leon responded with an explanation that accounted for both of rugby's images. During a heated debate one day, he told a friend, "It's like this. Let's say I work for Distell [a large South African alcohol conglomerate based in the Western Cape]. I may prefer another company's wine. I'll buy from this one and that one, but that doesn't mean I'm disloyal to Distell, does it? I work hard for Distell, but I prefer another drink. I'm from South Africa, but I prefer a New Zealand product.

That's all." The man had no response. How, after all, could he disagree with a matter of personal taste?

Leon's expression of taste suggests, as does the other former SARU player's comment about harshness and aggressiveness, that South Africa's rugby struggles to be both democratic and professional. In the current arrangement, the South African state concerns itself with the presentation of rugby's product. That strategy may have been relatively groundbreaking in the early years of the post-apartheid era, when the mere presence of nonwhite players on white rugby fields could have been regarded as a destabilizing and potentially revolutionary event, but its shortcomings have become increasingly visible to people like Leon, who long to see South African rugby more thoroughly transformed. As long as the present relationship stands—with the state contenting itself to make demands about logos and bodies while professional teams still control the terms of rugby's live performance—Leon feels entitled to approach the sport as a free consumer. If the state treats rugby as a brand, he evidently reasons, he will also view it like a brand and choose to support the national team that best suits his taste. The state could decide to take rugby's performance seriously, either by explicitly dictating the way that South African teams confront uncertainty or (more likely) by clearing the way for coaches and players like Leon to exert their influence over rugby's performances from the inside, but such actions would pose an explicit threat to the independence of professional rugby teams as business interests. It would cut against the state's social and economic policies, which privilege liberalization over democracy, but it would also carry the possibility of bringing Leon and others like him permanently into the post-apartheid national fold.

CONCLUSION: CONSIDERING A POST-APARTHEID RUGBY

The post-apartheid state has plainly won some measure of control over South Africa's rugby. A sport that was once an important piece of the apartheid government's "cultural policy" now better depicts (in race, if not in gender) the nation that the post-apartheid state wishes to represent. The Springbok logo has become a source of ongoing public debate and political controversy, and politicized bodies, formerly excluded from the South African rugby's autonomous frame, have made their way onto fields and, welcome or not, into the perceptions of rugby fans. Whatever problematic interpretations some South Africans may use to make the sport meaningful in the post-apartheid era, the state possesses the capacity to dictate the conditions in which meanings of rugby are made. Even a push-and-pull process of interpretation marks a fundamental change in the relationship between rugby, its spectators, and the state. What television broadcasts describe, the state has begun to transform.

But rugby remains a troubling cultural phenomenon in the post-apartheid era. Sustained by many of the same institutions that sustained it in the past, the sport owes a debt to the ways those institutions imprinted themselves on rugby's live and uncertain performance. The words of Martin Locke are relevant here once again. In 1979, Northern Transvaal administrators learned that he had used the pulpit of his television show to condemn one of their matches. Later, as a sports commentator for SABC at the 1995 Rugby World Cup, he was tasked not with critiquing style but with the more intimidating responsibility of linking the sporting success of the Springboks to the post-apartheid nation. He told his audience, "The new nation, the proud new South Africa, they did everything a team needed to do to win a World Cup and it's with great pride that we watch them now . . . they behaved magnificently. President Mandela, South Africa's mascot surely . . . we love you Madiba, no question. This man has done more for South Africans than one can believe in the last few years" (cited in Steenveld and Strelitz 1998, 621). Rugby's performance appears in Locke's words as much in 1995 as it did in 1979. Whereas his 1979 critique highlights the inaccessibility of the performance to the cameras that captured it, his 1995 comments notably and awkwardly link the performance to the broader political significance of the Springbok's win. The nation is proud because the team "did everything a team needed to do." He describes the players not as having played but as having "behaved magnificently." In the 1995 context, even Mandela becomes a mascot—a presentation of a political figure, more than a substantive living being.

For Locke and, as I have argued in this chapter, for the ANC, rugby's political significance is understood to enter the sport from the outside. Transforming the sport is thus a matter of transforming the ceremonies that surround it, the symbols that teams use, and the bodies that play it. To find politics in the Rugby World Cup Final, then, is to find it in the interest of the nation and in the presence of the president of South Africa, more than in the actions of players on the field.[25] As this book has consistently observed, though, sports like rugby are not available for nationalist sentiments solely because they can be transformed into spectacles and laden with nationalist symbolism. Those sentiments can be built into the performance of the sport, depending on how a team opts to confront uncertainty. Rugby is more than a tableau of bodies and symbols. It is moving and active, and the ghostly presence of the apartheid state can still be seen in that motion and activity.

South Africans may have bound themselves to the state through their attachment to rugby and their willingness to interpret the bodies and symbols it carries, but this chapter shows that the state appears to be equally bound. Its decision to transform rugby rather than abandon it (a choice that was and remains, as I noted in the introduction, a theoretical possibility) means that it cannot easily escape or even necessarily reimagine that historically constituted performative style. As indicated by the observations of spectators like Leon and the other SARU player I referenced in this chapter, that situation amounts to a demonstration of the shortcomings of the post-apartheid state's political project. Against the wishes of many of the sport's supporters, rugby continues to perform fragments of South Africa's political history in the country's "new" post-apartheid present. To watch the Springboks play is, for some, to see bodies still animated by forces from the past.

The arguments documented in this chapter and throughout this book suggest that South African rugby might be dramatically transformed—in its *beeld*, not just in its presentation—if marginalized players, coaches, and fans were positioned in such a way as to remake the sport from the inside out and the bottom up. The increasing professionalization of rugby in South Africa—which, with its beginning in 1995, seems almost precisely timed to prevent such a radical transformation—makes such a reimaging unlikely. Even so, considering the transformative perspective brings the stakes for the post-apartheid nation clearly into view: South Africa can deploy rugby as it is, transforming its presentation even as the sport recapitulates apartheid in each uncertain moment, or it can approach the structural conditions of rugby from a fresh angle and encounter the sport's uncertainty in a novel, potentially liberating way. The former position might represent a kind of living "counter-monument" to the lingering traces of apartheid and its violence (cf. J. Young 1992), and the latter would delineate a position for the country's future. What the new *beeld* would look like, however, remains an open question. Considered in the terms of this book, that question necessitates another: If the apartheid state responded to uncertainty by crushing it out, and anti-apartheid activists responded by embracing it, how would the post-apartheid nation respond to uncertainty? If South Africa intends to construct an image of its future out of the fragments of its past, these are important questions to consider.

Conclusion

The chapters of this book present a social institution at an impasse. The post-apartheid state apparently desires to reframe rugby to reflect and perpetuate its own preferred representative image for the South African nation. As theorists of nationalism and sport have shown, great symbolic potential can be unlocked in sporting spectacles if states can control them. Unlike its predecessors, which buried themselves within the performance of rugby, the post-apartheid government has (to date) concerned itself with legislating transformations in the sport at the level of its presentation. The mere presence of Nelson Mandela and Chester Williams on formerly white-controlled rugby fields may have dramatically destabilized the norms of that presentation within some circles (Sourgen 2010), but the 1995 Rugby World Cup's potent symbolic moment passed quickly into history. The state's inability or unwillingness to intervene in rugby's live performance seems to have rendered its efforts partial at best and self-defeating at worst.

There does not appear to be much room for transformative grassroots interventions in South African rugby either. For example, as discussed in chapter 5, Leon tried actively to reconstruct his corner of the sport from the ground up, perhaps contributing in a small way to the modification of the country's dominant *beeld*. But like the play of Tendai "the Beast" Mtawarira (discussed in chapter 6), Leon's efforts are interpreted through lenses structured by history. He is recognized as being "in die Boere se gat," and some players (who we might expect, in other circumstances, to share his opinion of the present state of South African rugby) write him off as a traitor to the cause of promoting equal representation and participation in the sport. In contrast, Uncle Dapper's iconoclastic action described in chapter 5 was a powerful political statement because it tore through rugby's autonomy and disrupted both its presentation and its performance, but his gesture was neither constructive nor sustainable.

Broadcast media would seem to have effected more thorough shifts in rugby's presentation and performance than any activist or state initiative. Rugby has become a faster and more polished "product" as a result of professionalization. Teams recruit, train, control, and quantify players in ways never experienced by previous generations, and those processes have only occurred because of the resources provided by sponsorships and lucrative television contracts. At the same time, though "aesthetics of compensation" (Roche 2000) might be able to cultivate a fantasy of presence and participation, broadcast media can never actually reach inside rugby's live performances and act on them from within. As I showed in chapter 1, the Bulls *maak vas* style cannot be attributed to professionalism alone. Television contracts provided teams with more money than ever before, but how that money was deployed was left to the individual teams themselves. It was spent on players the teams valued, on coaches and administrators that shared in that team's vision, and on resources to help deliver their preferred (historically constituted) styles. Martin Locke may have given voice to the preferences of broadcast media when he complained (as mentioned in chapter 6) about boring rugby, but no television contract to date (as far as I am aware) has stipulated how teams should *play* their rugby.

The Bulls organization takes full responsibility for the performances of its teams. It molds them in the days, weeks, and months before matches (when it recruits players, hires them, and trains them), during matches (with changes in strategies and discussions at halftime), and after matches (when its trainers and doctors tend to players' injuries and its coaches teach them in post-match video sessions). Its marketers have managed to successfully link those performances to a team presentation that both underlines a dominant team style and reverberates across South Africa's history. In short, the team responds to rugby's uncertainty with a unified and persuasive *beeld*.

The strength of that *beeld* has also limited the scope of the team's market appeal. When my informant in chapter 5 spoke of the "harshness" of South Africa's rugby and commented that, as he watched games unfold, it reminded him of the National Party, he was describing a style that the Bulls, for the most part, typify. While the Bulls desperately and earnestly want to attract new fans, the team struggles to reposition itself for a post-apartheid national audience. The marketing manager of the Bulls, newly hired as of the end of my fieldwork, seemed to understand that point. "Rugby," he said, "has 10 million supporters in South Africa, out of 49 million people, and the Bulls have 3 million of that 10. They're a big brand, the Bulls, a huge brand, but they don't market themselves like they are. How do you grow that 3 million?" For the manager, the problem was obvious: "The Bulls don't communicate with the black market at all. They only focus on the status quo. If they don't take a visionary perspective, looking five or ten years into the future, the brand will die."

That prophecy of a slow demise brings us back around to *Invictus* and its dream of rugby's quick execution. Death is made possible, in the former case, or necessary, in the latter case, by the same set of structuring conditions. The marketing manager might be focusing his attention on the size of the Bulls' predominantly white fan base when he identifies the team's commitment to "the status quo," but this book suggests that the commitment extends far beyond fans and advertising. It also includes the other side of the team's *beeld*—the team's selection and valuation of players and its dedication to a particular performative image of rugby. In that sense, the reference to "the status quo" is a gloss on South Africa's deep ties to white supremacy and the ways in which those ties continue to structure the country's post-apartheid present. *Invictus* makes a similar claim. Although the film could be accused of stopping short of telling exactly that complicated post-apartheid story, of whitewashing the politics of South Africa's present in the interest of positioning the 1995 Rugby World Cup as an event of outsized transformative importance, the film's unwillingness to provide even the most cursory outline of a post-1995 narrative invited a more provocative reading. The surest way to escape rugby's structuring conditions would have been to dismantle the sport after the World Cup Final—to build a new rugby or even a brand-new sport, from scratch.

This book uses *Invictus* as a framing device because the film's narrative (like the prophecy offered by the Bulls' marketing manager) repositions rugby's post-apartheid significance. It encourages us to suspend any preconceptions we might hold about the place of the sport in South Africa's contemporary moment. Through the lens of *Invictus*, we see rugby not as a vital social institution or as an inherently meaningful activity but as a particular kind of performative practice, which pulls South African persons, institutions, discourses, and social relations into its orbit. Sometimes, as discussed in chapter 1, that practice causes players to fight with each other. At other times, as discussed in chapter 3, it damages bodies. At still other times, it causes tremendous joy and satisfaction. In every instance, South Africa's rugby shows itself to have history and politics baked into its formal autonomy and the very liveness of its performances. As such, it appears to stagger forward into the future, neither breaking definitively with the past nor consigned fully to it. If this book finds South African rugby at an impasse, then, it also argues that the sport's immobility is the source of its present analytical import.

If *Invictus* elevated the 1995 World Cup to an event of mythic proportions, a more recent event echoed that mythic occasion for Bulls fans in particular. Shortly before I arrived for my fieldwork in 2010, the Bulls completed one of their most successful seasons ever. They led the Super 14—a rugby league comprising teams from, at the time, Australia, New Zealand, and South Africa—at the end of the regular season, and they had therefore won the right to host a home semifinal in the playoffs for the league's championship. If they won that match, they would play host to the final as well. What made that event so locally momentous was not just the success of the team but the fact that the Bulls were forced to play their home playoff matches away from home. The team's stadium—called Loftus Versfeld—was already reserved for the 2010 FIFA World Cup, so the team, scrambling to find a viable alternative venue, chose to play their games in Orlando Stadium in Soweto. In my interviews with players, coaches, and administrators after the fact, the two Soweto matches were routinely described as "unbelievable" or "unreal" experiences. In the team's documentary that commemorates the 2010 season, *Road to Orlando*, those words appear again and again, in English and Afrikaans. For the remainder of this conclusion, I analyze the narratives surrounding those matches and consider them in light of the major themes of this book: performance and uncertainty, formal autonomy, the political significance of rugby, and the ways that rugby's present impasse calls South African history into view.

The first and perhaps most important thing to note about the Orlando matches was their sheer unlikeliness. As more than one of my informants assured me, the Bulls never would have gone to Soweto without some sort of external pressure; they would have much preferred to play those important matches in their home stadium, on their familiar field, in front of their local crowds, and in support of their local vendors.[1] The South African government, for its part, was in no position to apply that pressure. Had the government intervened in the Super 14 tournament and ordered the Bulls to play the matches elsewhere—let alone in Soweto—fans and administrators would have likely interpreted the order as an attempt by the state to meddle in rugby and create political conflicts and acrimony where none need exist. In that context, world football (institutionalized in FIFA) appeared as a kind of deus ex machina, insofar as it intervened in an established political field and created a novel situation that South African rugby—in its present impasse—was unable to generate on its own. Put slightly differently and in the terms of this book, the onetime incursion of world football interjected a moment of structural uncertainty into the politics of rugby. That uncertainty, like uncertainty on the rugby field, posed challenging questions to the Bulls team and its administration. In the responses to those questions, as in responses to uncertainty on the field, history and violence could be found.

The Bulls landed on Orlando Stadium as a viable alternative for reasons that had to do less with its political significance than with the quality of its facilities. The team's first debt was to the conditions that would ensure success—conditions that would allow the Bulls *beeld* to flourish. Immediately after they received word that their usual stadium would be unavailable to them for their Super 14 semifinal, members of the team's management began looking around for alternative "home" fields. Each prospect failed, in one respect or another, to replicate an appropriately homely atmosphere. They were, I was told, too small or too distant or too dilapidated to be viable. The options that were in better shape posed problems for the Bulls *beeld* in another way. There were well-appointed stadiums nearby, but they were the home fields of rival rugby teams. The possibility of playing on one of those fields was dismissed out of hand; each was too associated with the brand of its usual home team to be a viable temporary "home" field for the Bulls.

Against that backdrop of inadequate alternatives, Orlando Stadium stood out. It was home to a professional football team, the Orlando Pirates, which had a "presentation image" sufficiently distinct from that of the Bulls to allow the rugby team to conceptualize the Pirates' stadium as a second home field. When a team administrator took a tour of the stadium, he found the facilities new and the ground pristine. As he explained to me, he knew from the moment he first stepped on the field that the players were going to "have the best day of their lives playing on [it]," and he said as much to them. The players initially thought he was being overly optimistic, he added, but they were quickly convinced when they took the field to train. The stadium, they seem to have found, would not disrupt their performance.

The administrator's assessment of Orlando Stadium was significant. Politically speaking, it affirmed that the stadium was a viable alternative, thereby encouraging the Bulls staff to begin the project of transporting its team and fans to Soweto for the matches. Analytically speaking, the qualities of Orlando Stadium preserved both the Bulls' formal presentation and their performance, allowing the team to transport its *beeld* without any kind of disruption. The

Bulls would play as they usually played, on a high-quality field, with high-quality facilities, in a stadium that had no noteworthy connections to any rival teams. Their performance would unfold, in a word, autonomously.[2] Seen in that way, the selection of Orlando Stadium marked a change in the quality of the event's initial openness. What had once been an "open call" for a new stadium became, quickly, a call for a stadium that resembled the Bulls' home stadium experience and could house the team's *beeld* successfully.[3] From that point forward, we could say, only an observer like Leon—with a keen eye for the politics of performance—would have found anything noteworthy on the field during play. Leon and his former SARU peers would have found exactly the same noteworthy elements that they saw every time they watched the Bulls (or the Springboks) play: a team full of white players playing a style that evoked apartheid in its violent directness.

Once Orlando Stadium had been chosen, the initial openness of FIFA's intervention began to crystalize even further, into readily available political narratives. From the perspective of the Bulls organization, the stakes of the Orlando matches were outlined by Liz McGregor in an article for the *Leader*, notably entitled "Blue Bulls: The Great Trek to Soweto." McGregor (2010) predicted that the match would be no regular one: "I felt a Mandela Moment coming on as I listened to Barend van Graan, CEO of the Blue Bulls, describe how he was going to get 40,000 fans to Soweto. The Blue Bulls are throwing themselves into it heart and soul. They are organizing trains and buses from Centurion and a park 'n ride scheme from Nasrec [a suburb of Johannesburg], some 6k away from the stadium."

Although McGregor described the matches as potential "Mandela Moments," the Bulls' excursion to Soweto could hardly have looked less like Mandela's decision to appear on the field in 1995. While President Mandela took to a formerly "white field" as a solitary figure of international renown, the Bulls traveled to Soweto with trains, buses, and 40,000 mostly anonymous, mostly white fans. By calling the Bulls' trip to Soweto a "Great Trek," McGregor may have intended to evoke the scale of the undertaking and the depth of the team's commitment to it, but the reference also played meaningfully on South Africa's history of settler colonialism. In that depiction, the Bulls and their fans are figured as white pioneers replicating the original "Great Trek" of the Voortrekkers, Dutch-descended settlers who migrated northward and eastward from the Cape Colony in the mid-19th century. That image represented white Bulls fans as entering, like the Voortrekkers, a historically black space. Van Graan noted those resonances even more explicitly in the team's documentary: "When we announced [the decision], there was resistance. Especially from some of our supporters. The Blue Bulls company and myself were accused of being Piet Retief [a Voortrekker leader][4] taking whites into Soweto. But when the team arrived at Soweto with the media and when I saw the reaction of the team, I realized it's going to be a big win-win for us" (cited in Willemse 2010, 00:55:18).

This book explains those references to history. The "Great Trek" of the Voortrekkers is linked with the trip of the Bulls athletes and fans not just by scale and race but also by sport.[5] South Africa's political history has coded rugby as a predominantly white sport of colonialism and Afrikaner nationalism, and that coding manifests not just in the symbolic significance of the team and the team's logo but also in the style of rugby that the Bulls prefer to play. To take the *maak vas* style into Soweto, with nearly 40,000 predominantly white fans in tow, was to perform a symbolic subjugation of the township and to call up the ghosts of similar acts from the country's past. It is hardly surprising to see the "Great Trek" invoked to make sense of the occasion. It is also unsurprising that fans invoked another, more contextually specific act of subjugation. One coach told me that he overheard one fan say to another, "We haven't been to Soweto since June of '76," referring to the month and year when approximately 176 people were killed by the apartheid police during student protests in the township.[6] Whether the fan making that comment was a member of the apartheid police or not is, from the perspective of this book, largely immaterial. The "we" he mentions could be the fan and his friend or the fans of the Bulls in general or even the Bulls organization itself. When the team in question was, historically, the team of the apartheid police, military, and correctional services, metaphor collapsed easily into metonym.

That reading is further buttressed by the fact that the Bulls' "trek" to Soweto sent the team and their fans against the usual flow of bodies in South Africa. Formally, under apartheid legislation, and informally, in the post-apartheid era, Africans have traveled regularly (often daily) from townships and rural communities to work in white-dominated areas—white homes, white-controlled businesses, and predominantly or exclusively white neighborhoods. Put into this broader context, it becomes clear that the Bulls' trek to Soweto was not the first sporting excursion "offside." The supporters of another South African professional team—the fans of the football team Mamelodi Sundowns—had been making visits to Loftus for many years prior. In 1992, Bulls administrators entered into a contract giving the Sundowns long-term access to Loftus for the eminently reasonable rate of R100, between

$10 and $12 at the time of my research, per game. (The fee to use Loftus to host a concert, I was told, is upwards of R1 million, or $100,000–120,000.) An administrator readily admitted that forming the novel partnership with the Sundowns had to do more with common sense and political savvy than with unadulterated goodwill. The Bulls knew that the Pretoria City Council could cancel the team's lease of Loftus, and they entered into a partnership with the Sundowns to display their openness to reform. Although an administrator at the Bulls argued that football fans are now *more* welcome in Loftus's Clydesdale and Hatfield neighborhoods than rugby fans ("They [the fans] come late and leave early, and they drink at home, in the townships. Rugby fans come early, they drink and eat and piss in the street, and then they hang around next to the stadium until two in the morning, drinking and celebrating"), the first match that the Sundowns played at Loftus in 1993 was met with far less enthusiasm—fans were received not by flags, beer, and sausages, but rather by "men who were standing at their gates with guns."

When the Bulls and their fans traveled to Soweto for the first time, they found themselves greeted not with guns or suspicion but with celebration. The township seemed not just to tolerate the signifiers of whiteness but to welcome them actively. The area surrounding the stadium was full of Bulls memorabilia, symbols, and flags. The stadium itself played a role in the signifying experience, as administrators had hoped it would. While looking and even operating like Loftus Versfeld, Orlando Stadium was plainly not Loftus Versfeld and also neither the high-quality field of a rival nor an inferior field of a team with which the Bulls had no association. Because it was a high-quality field of a football team from Soweto, the conditions of the match struck spectators and participants as both oddly familiar and exceedingly, tantalizingly exotic. A spectator told me, "It was like a little Loftus. The biggest highlight was the *braaivleis* [barbecued meat] and everything being the same around the field, only in a township." One of my (white, Afrikaans-speaking) informants, who had not attended the matches but knew plenty of people who had, described the effect: "You can't underestimate the element of fear in that situation. Many whites are terrified of going to the townships; I think the experience really changed their perspectives because they saw that the people around them had families and lived just like them." He added, "The unfamiliar became familiar."

The discovery of familiar (white, Afrikaner-associated) signifiers in an unfamiliar (black) space, of "everything being the same" but "in a township," allowed players, fans, and administrators to view Soweto in a new and different light. The township ceased to be a territory to fear and consequently to subjugate in the interests of safety, instead becoming a long-sought locus of racial integration. Of course, that integration was more fantasy than reality. In the fantasy, integration was produced less by the mutual sharing of space and a deep interconnectivity of lives (never mind a reckoning with historically sedimented forms of inequality and violence) than by a celebration of whiteness.[7] The sort of integration that emerged in that context demanded no compromises from Bulls supporters; it merely asked them to occupy an unfamiliar place, to find (unexpectedly) some important indices of whiteness already present there, and to celebrate those indices together with township residents.[8]

From that perspective, it is more than notable that Bulls players and administrators reported that the experience felt "unreal" or "unbelievable." It was "unreal" and "unbelievable," we could say, not just because it was an enjoyable experience nor even because FIFA made possible an event that would otherwise never have occurred. It was also "unreal" because the experiences of unity and racial harmony in Soweto were perhaps, from the perspective of the Bulls' white fans, a bit too perfect; those experiences met too many of the fans' desires without any effort at all.[9] Whereas Liz McGregor highlighted the transformative potential of the Soweto matches, Barry Bearak (2010)—writing after the event, in an article for the *New York Times*—offered a poignant reminder of just how white the Bulls' vision of an integrated Soweto had actually been: "The 36,000 Bulls fans never got very far into Soweto, and in the joyous streets around the stadium the white visitors outnumbered the black residents by perhaps 50 to 1."

Among the players and staff interviewed in the Bulls' documentary, Gurthrö Steenkamp (a longtime Bulls player who is commonly characterized as coloured by fans and South Africa's sporting media) came closest to acknowledging the fantastical dimension of the event: "I'm getting goosebumps just thinking about it," he recalled. "Thinking about people from various backgrounds, various cultures uniting just for a single game, it was amazing. I think a lot of people as well would agree it was probably one of the most significant events in our country after the '95 World Cup, you know, and driving to the field and seeing people *braaing* together and just socializing, you know—for that one day everyone forgot about all the hassles and issues that they have, and it was just amazing." Steenkamp added, "The atmosphere, it was just something different. It's just so hard to put it into words" (cited in Willemse 2010, 1:28:49).

The common conception of sports as an "escape" acquires additional significance in the context of Steenkamp's characterization, in that the escape occurred not within the rhythms of a familiar sporting event in a familiar stadium but in a politically and historically potent moment of racial anxiety. In Steenkamp's view, the experience of the Soweto matches became an act of forgetting, even as he invokes the 1995 Rugby World Cup to reckon with their significance. Forgetting implicitly framed the games at Orlando Stadium as an exceptional moment, in which conditions allowed the fans of the Bulls to ignore the "hassles and issues" of life in contemporary South Africa and to imagine briefly that the country (represented by a whitened Soweto) had decided to embrace the signifiers of whiteness and celebrate them uncritically.

Within the confines of that highly structured fantasy of validated post-apartheid whiteness, spectators felt free to play. One of the most remarkable aspects of the matches was not the play of the team on the field (which, as I noted above, looked quite similar to the play of the team at the Bulls' home stadium) but the use of vuvuzelas in the stadium. The famously loud plastic trumpets that gained international notoriety during the 2010 Soccer World Cup (cf. Jethro 2014) have long been used by fans at football matches in South Africa, but the Orlando matches marked the first time they had ever been permitted at a Bulls rugby game. The result of their use is noteworthy from our perspective: players, coaches, and even broadcasters reported that they struggled to communicate during the match. At the very least, those reactions demonstrate that vuvuzelas altered the predictable sonic experience of the match and gave fans a new opportunity to intervene in the performance of their team. Equally noteworthy is the fact of the prohibition against vuvuzelas in the first place. A Bulls administrator I asked about the ban suggested that it stemmed not, as one might expect, from the distracting sound of massed vuvuzelas all buzzing together but from the symbolism of the vuvuzela itself. At least until the 2010 FIFA World Cup, the instrument was as racially marked as football and therefore (the administrator very carefully and artfully implied) unwelcome in Loftus Versfeld during Bulls matches.

The embrace of the vuvuzela among white Bulls fans at a match in Soweto might be understood best as a permissible act of racial transgression, as the white mobilization of a signifier of blackness within conditions established by the Bulls organization. In several respects, that act of transgression (and the fantasy of racial integration) bears an underlying structural similarity to the logic—discussed in chapter 2 of this book—that Simon Gikandi (2006) found in the co-optation of African artistic forms by European modernists.

Like those modernists, Bulls supporters advanced their narrative of progress by mobilizing an African-derived form of expression as a means to liberate themselves from established norms and standards of behavior.[10] Also like those modernists, Bulls supporters were more interested in advancing their own narrative of progress (in this case, not artistic progress, but social unification) than in engaging meaningfully with African forms of expression. They celebrated the temporary realization of their fantasy of integration by "reciprocating" the generosity they discovered in Soweto. Since residents appeared to embrace the signifiers of whiteness, the visitors were free to co-opt the signifiers of blackness in return. Rugby seemed, however briefly, to be an agent of social transformation rather than an indicator of transformation deferred.

Given all that the semifinal had meant to supporters of the Bulls—as a break in the established structure of social relations, an acknowledgment of history, a fantasy of integration, and a playful (and unapologetic) exploration of signifiers of blackness—it is hardly surprising that the return to Soweto one week later for the Super 14 Final was even more highly anticipated than the semifinal had been. As white player Flip van der Merwe put it in the Bulls' documentary, "And then the final, when everyone knew what Soweto was about and everyone came out and there was no more . . . no one was afraid to get into Soweto, *jis*, it was such a great feeling" (cited in Willemse 2010, 1:23:55). That match, we could say, was an opportunity for Bulls supporters to relive the excitement of the semifinal, not just with higher sporting stakes, but with minds happily unburdened from the uncertainty of the initial planning stages and the accompanying acknowledgment of history. By that time, any fears that white fans might have held about traveling to Soweto for a Bulls match were gone. Everyone knew what they had not known the first time— that there would be nothing in the township to subjugate. That being the case, there was no longer any need to remember any previous subjugations either. There was only the excitement of confirming what nearly 40,000 traveling Bulls fans were assuredly going to call into being: that the Soweto found in the semifinal, a Soweto that celebrated whiteness and its signifiers, was going to be just as present (and just as welcoming, if not more so) as it had been one week before.

The team won the final and, thereby, the Super 14 championship, completing their own Hollywood story. That rugby still lived on was hardly an issue from the team's perspective. The Bulls have successfully navigated South African rugby's impasse for several decades, and the matches in the Orlando Stadium promised to further that success by ameliorating the Bulls' one major post-apartheid concern: in keeping with the team's goals to expand their fan base beyond an established, predominantly white and Afrikaans-speaking audience, Soweto's embrace of the team was easily read as the discovery of a hitherto unknown market. One staffer told me that only after attending Soweto matches had she and others "realized just how many black fans the Bulls actually had."

In keeping with that exciting discovery, the Bulls organization decided to reach out to that new market. They began to open clothing outlets in the township, so that they could continue to build their brand in the area, and they decided to bring rugby back to Orlando Stadium a few years later, in 2013. Though undertaken intentionally, that visit implicitly confirmed the team's reluctance to travel to Soweto in 2010 for the Super 14 matches. In 2013, instead of a semifinal and a final of a major international tournament, the Bulls played a nearby rival in a nearly meaningless preseason game. If world football's miraculous involvement in 2010 produced a moment of uncertainty, the continuation of that moment's narrative into 2013 reestablished a kind of safe position—in the parlance of the Bulls, a "default"—that stabilized the "magical" possibilities entailed in that initial moment of uncertainty, disciplined them, and mobilized them in the directions deemed most productive for the team.

It would be easy to disregard the significance of rugby itself to this account of historical narrativization. One could, for example, say that Bulls rugby is a metaphor for or representation of politics happening elsewhere in South Africa. Or one might argue that the Orlando matches were an occasion for historical narratives or deep-seated political tensions to emerge. Such interpretations would necessarily overlook the concrete material effects of rugby. They would, for example, implicitly de-emphasize rugby's actual violence, rendering it a playful facsimile of true violence, a nip rather than a bite. As I showed in chapter 3, many players would push back hard against the view that their violence lacks a reality of its own. They might even observe that such an interpretation of rugby has much in common with the strategies that their coaches and bosses use to dismiss the legitimacy of their pain.

Such interpretations would also struggle to reckon with those moments when rugby appears to generate political tensions and historical narratives. When a difference in stylistic preference—which, in South Africa, can be equal parts learned disposition and political position—leads to a fight between teammates, should the difference be considered a representation of politics or a novel enactment of it? If a Federation player insists that his white teammates used to reveal their racial prejudices on the field in the tiny decisions they made, is he putting a name to his existing suspicions, or did he discover new proof of those suspicions in the liveness of play? Can we disregard either the SARU player who saw echoes of apartheid's violence in the dominating style of South Africa's national team or the Bulls fans who used the Orlando Stadium matches to recall past subjugations of black spaces? Is the nickname "Beast," in its contemporary significance to fans of South African rugby, entirely independent of the sport, the style, and the specific embodied actions that his team asks him to perform during matches?

This book has sought to account for those affective, discursive, and material complexities, as well as the political history that inheres in South Africa's rugby performances, by attending to the uncertainty that lies at the heart of the sport itself. When a referee blows a whistle or a coach starts a drill, players begin to move. From those moments onward, their movements are more reactions than actions. Players read and respond to each other, to the bounces of the ball, to the field conditions and weather. Rugby comes alive and, as it does, it participates actively in the conversations that South Africans have about the sport. If rugby players are supposed to be invulnerable supermen, rugby torques their bodies and causes injuries. If players are treated as commodities, rugby produces moments of unpredictability and asks its players to do something creative, even magical. If the South African state wants to mobilize rugby for its own political purposes, rugby shows that history and politics are not just present in the symbols teams use and the distribution of raced bodies that they deploy on the field. History and politics are also buried in the ways that South Africans respond, via sporting style, to rugby's own uncertainty.

Those responses are political performances, whether uncertainty is rejected or embraced. As such, this book has been as much a study of the processes by which the uncertainty of rugby is mobilized as it has been a study of rugby itself. The Bulls' *maak vas* style is one kind of mobilization of rugby's uncertainty, a mobilization that tries, for the most part, to forget that underlying uncertainty by dominating it out of existence with embodied violence and physical force. The framing of rugby as an autonomous social phenomenon, independent from the conditions of everyday life, is another mobilization of rugby's uncertainty, in that it turns rugby's violence into a form of gentlemanly play in which values can be learned. It is also a kind of forgetfulness, albeit of a different order from that of *maak vas*. While the latter sort of forgetting is concerned with the performance of the team on the field, the former is concerned with the category of sports as a whole. Even so, both are political and historically constituted.

The Bulls' trip to Soweto mobilized both of those types of forgetfulness. The Bulls worked assiduously to make sure that they selected a stadium that would accommodate their team's style of play, and the trip as a whole was—as Gurthrö Steenkamp reported—an opportunity for fans to forget their hassles and issues. Seen as a kind of forgetfulness, the condition of "default" that emerged at the end of the Bulls' trip to Soweto was not so much a return to an established conservative position as a novel inscription of racial identity, national belonging, and white supremacy within changed conditions. Those inscriptions emerged from history and were informed by established patterns of inequality, but to argue that history and inequality determined the trajectory of the trip would be to overlook the initial structural uncertainty produced by world football's (and FIFA's) intervention, the concrete decisions that transformed Orlando Stadium into a "little Loftus," and the contributions of the Bulls' style to the "thinkability" of the narratives of settler colonialism that surrounded the matches.

South African rugby's post-apartheid impasse can be understood in a similar way. Although, as *Invictus* helpfully reminds us, South Africa's approach to rugby could always be otherwise, the absence of a radical reimagining leaves the sport in a now-familiar position. Rugby can be counted on to offer up moments of uncertainty, and South Africans to respond to that uncertainty with performances that recall and reframe (in a present context) the country's deep entanglements with colonialism and apartheid. In South African rugby's present condition, we could therefore say, "magic" is never fully transformative, but neither is "default" ever truly final.

NOTES

1. If a player fails to attract the attention of a top high school, there are other avenues to professional success. A player can attend a school with less resources and still
draw the attention of scouts if his talent is undeniable. He might be selected to represent
his province at the country's annual provincial tournament, called "Craven Week" for
the under-18 and under-13 age-groups and "Grant Khomo Week" at the under-16 level.
If he goes to a university, he can potentially work his way through the university's team
structure. Finally, he and his family can pay for him to join a rugby academy. Academies
offer players the opportunity to develop their skills with accomplished coaches, to train
with other aspiring players, and to (hopefully) secure contracts from professional teams.
Each of the alternative paths brings obstacles of its own. A school with less resources
will be unable to provide players with quality coaching, gym facilities and trainers, and
interpersonal connections to scouts and selectors. The people who select the players
who participate in South Africa's provincial tournaments must watch many different
players at numerous schools and will hear more about the players at elite schools. It is
not uncommon for provincial teams to draw many more players from elite schools than
from smaller ones that have less funds or recognition. Players who want to play competitive rugby at the university level must balance their rugby training with their other
academic and social obligations. Although I am aware of a few instances of players moving from universities to professional teams, it is far more common for players to do the
reverse—to recognize that their professional careers are coming to an end and to turn
their attention to their studies. Academies are an alluring option for players because they
promise to provide the hothouse training environment of a professional team without
the exclusivity. At the time of my fieldwork, academies were a fairly recent development,
and they can be quite expensive. Academies were also comparatively unregulated, and
some of my informants with professional teams were extremely skeptical of their quality.
While alternative avenues to professional success exist, their shortcomings demonstrate
that the most reliable path—by far—is to enroll at an elite high school that can provide
its players with the resources and reputation to get them noticed.

2. In journalist Liz McGregor's book *Touch, Pause, Engage*, the author quotes Paul Anthony, then a coach at the Blue Bulls, about the challenges young players face in getting recognized by professional scouts. "It's not [the province's] fault," he said. "They select their [all-star] side from Paul Roos, Paarl Gim, Paarl Boys' High, Boland Landbou, Wynberg Boys' High, Bishops, SACS, Rondebosch. You pick 35 to 45 guys out of all these schools and the rest get lost. . . . That's not even counting the coloured schools" (2011, 104). Though Anthony does not explicitly acknowledge the whiteness of the litany of elite high schools he named, the fact that the "coloured schools" are dismissed en masse demonstrates the knotted associations of prestige, sport, wealth, and whiteness that center these elite schools and ensure that the talents of the vast majority of young black, coloured, and African rugby players go unrecognized.

3. The dynamics of this connection has recently undergone some dramatic changes. In late 2016, the general council of South African Rugby (SA Rugby) announced that it was raising the threshold for outside investment in South Africa's rugby unions from 50 to 74 percent. For the first time, a private equity investor could own a majority of the shares of a South African rugby team. Although the effects that the new regulation will have on state-driven transformation initiatives are not yet clear, it seems all but certain that ownership groups will come to play an active role in the implementation of state initiatives for racial transformation. The change seems (from the perspective of increasing racial diversity at the highest levels of South African rugby) to be a double-edged sword.

On the one hand, investment groups that wish to shape transformation in rugby will be able to do so much more easily than in years past. A productive example can be found in Robert Gumede and Ivor Ichikowitz's failed investment in the Golden Lions Rugby Union (GLRU) in 2011. Guma TAC (TransAfrica Capital), run by Gumede and Ichikowitz, was slated to buy 49.9 percent of the Johannesburg-based franchise, and the partnership was initially hailed as an important step in the direction of sporting transformation and as a productive strategic decision for all parties involved: Guma TAC would relieve the team of its accumulated financial burdens, and Gumede would become the first major African investor in a South African rugby union. But Guma TAC ultimately removed itself from the partnership, citing the GLRU's lack of institutional transparency and general unwillingness to embrace Guma TAC's full participation in its operations. Gumede, quoted in an article on the website Moneyweb that explored the situation surrounding the failed arrangement, did not mince words: "We wanted to buy into the future, not get stuck in the past. . . . But no business person can be expected to invest a lot of money, especially in a struggling business, without having a say in the operational decision-making. . . . We will not be party to putting a veneer on transformation. . . . The GLRU wanted our hard earned [*sic*] money, but wouldn't allow Guma and TransAfrica Capital to work with them in mapping out their future and direction" ("Gijima Billionaire Withdraws from Lions Deal" 2012). Under SA Rugby's new policy, Guma TAC would have been able to buy a controlling stake in the GLRU and therefore to insist on a much more active role in its operations. The GLRU would have been forced either to struggle on entirely on its own or to accept Guma TAC's life preserver and embrace its leadership.

On the other hand, ownership groups agnostic about sporting transformation or suspicious that quota-based transformation initiatives might undermine team performance and sabotage team profitability can stand more definitively as a barrier between rugby union and the state than ever before. Tellingly, the investors that seem most interested in increasing the scale of their involvement in rugby are those who already have significant ownership stakes in teams—that is, at present, white South African investors such as Johann Rupert (whose company Remgro and its subsidiary South African Investments Limited own shares of the Bulls and several additional unions) and Altmann Allers of Glasfit (who bought 49.9 percent of GLRU's shares when Gumede and Ichikowitz pulled out of their deal). The ambiguity of SA Rugby's new initiative is perfectly captured in a *Finweek* editorial by Lloyd Gedye (2017). "According to [one anonymous rugby administrator]," Gedye writes, "most investors do not see their investment as a business transaction: 'It's a feel-good thing in their lives—knowing they are supporting rugby in the country.' Another union official termed these investments as 'emotional old money' transactions." In Gedy's editorial, the age and source of the "old money" and the form that such "support" of rugby might take goes conspicuously unarticulated. SA Rugby's recent decision also detaches professional rugby teams from amateur adult rugby clubs. While the South African state concerns itself with representation and transformation and while SA Rugby manages the South African rugby system as a whole (from youth rugby to high school rugby to amateur and professional teams), corporate investors have no such obligations.

4. Bradd Shore (1994, 350–51) has considered sporting frames in some detail, via the work of Huizinga (1980) and Eliade (1959) and their conceptions of time, space, ritual, and play. While Shore's interest in frames and rules bears a strong similarity to the present project, his deference to Huizinga marks an important difference. For Huizinga, play may be socially constructed, but particular social constructions of play are emblematic of the form's significance as something close to an underlying organizing principle of human sociality; thus "the great archetypal activities of human society are all permeated with play *from the start*" (1980, 4; emphasis added). Because Huizinga is invested in studying the primacy of play, he is inclined both to valorize play over the moments when playful moments collapse and to embrace play as a fundamentally agentive practice. The present study intends to offer a corrective to that approach on both counts. Using Arthur Danto's conception of a historically specific "artworld" (1981) and Theodor Adorno's notion of artworks as politically constructed and historically contextual "monads" (1997), I argue here that rugby is neither inherently autonomous nor a discernible product of any fundamental tendency toward play. Instead, rugby is a product of a political history that rendered it autonomous, that prompted it to be seen as such (cf. McDevitt 2000, 4–5). As a consequence of that historically produced autonomy, rugby is capable of acting back on its participants and, in doing so, pulling meanings from them. That formulation, which positions this project alongside Vossen's (2018) and

Consalvo's (2009) reconsiderations of Huizinga's temporal and spatial "magic circle" of play, privileges neither play nor its breaking, for both extend from histories, politics, and perspectives. The present formulation also challenges the centrality of human agents in the performance of play, for if rugby is an activity that—conceptually, discursively, materially, and affectively—positions human agents through its historically produced autonomy and insists that they react to that autonomy, no human agent can be said to have definitively authored that autonomy or brought rugby into being. In keeping with that approach, I show throughout this book how rugby's autonomy pulls not only players into movements but also coaches into strategies and spectators into interpretations of history and conceptions of gender, race, and class.

5. Michael Oriard (1981, 34) has memorably described the particular playing conditions of American football: "The beauty [of football] lies not in physical punishment nor in the mere accomplishment of [preventing an opposing player from doing what he wants to do on the field]—a psychotic with a mace could manage this, and inflict much more pain on the ballcarrier. The beauty lies in the form and precision of the tackle. . . . And the violence of the tackle itself is meaningful because it is incidental to a higher purpose and is prescribed by the rules—it is not equivalent to mugging elderly women in dark corridors or napalming children in Southeast Asia."

6. The claim that rugby possesses a degree of autonomy from everyday life should not be read as an argument in favor of allocating rugby to its own category of being. Rugby is autonomous because of its historical production and political significance. (In chapter 5, I emphasize that rugby is not identically autonomous for all South Africans occupying all social positions.) That said, the social roots of rugby's autonomy in no way invalidate the power and efficacy of that autonomy. Rugby acts back on those who play it, and it generates meanings and bodily experiences, not despite its historical production and political significance, but precisely because of them. Through those processes, it is available to be lived as real, and its autonomy is available for critical deconstruction and reconsideration.

7. When applied to rugby in South Africa, that "naive" approach—starting one's analysis with what one sees or hears, without immediately reading beneath it, in search of signs of some deeper truth—bears a close resemblance to Adam Ashforth's consideration of witchcraft. For him and also for Robin Horton (1993), studies of witchcraft that consider it to be a "vehicle of sense-making" miss the fact that for South Africans at least, witchcraft is no metaphor but a real force in the world (Ashforth 2005, 114). To study witchcraft in its fullness, one must be willing to acknowledge that witchcraft is a phenomenon that shapes social worlds. Witchcraft generates anxieties, provokes gossip, and demands management and redress.

Rugby too is taken (in practice) to be a real force that acts in the world. My interest in Ashforth's analysis stems from his theoretical approach. I do not draw from his work in an effort to posit an underlying shared experience of disjuncture, which manifests in two different ways—with residents of Soweto turning to witchcraft and, say, parents and teachers at elite, predominantly white and wealthy high schools turning to rugby. Such a comparison would risk flattening profound inequalities in South Africa and, in doing so, erasing the political history that generated those inequalities. For Ashforth, as for me, post-apartheid South Africa may be generating new and challenging questions about power, identity, and belonging, but those questions are not making the phenomenon under consideration either more or less real. Witchcraft and rugby have long been real in South Africa, though the perceived nature of that reality changes with time. Witchcraft and rugby are almost certainly real elsewhere too, though the perceived nature of that reality will differ from place to place.

8. That approach also shares affinities with the work of an incredibly broad range of scholars who have problematized, in myriad ways, the assumption that the individual human body is a privileged site of creative and thoughtful action. Narratives of human exceptionalism contain conditions about how the human should see, think about, or act in the world. By imposing those conditions, such narratives set limits (whether inadvertently or intentionally) on the category of the human itself, invariably denying some bodies access to privileged position. Whether grounded in the necropolitics of slavery and colonialism (Mbembe 2003), the biopolitics of the scientific excavation of Sarah Bartmann and other nonwhite, nonmale, non-European bodies (Fausto-Sterling 1995; McClintock 1995), or the construction of a nonsubject like the *homo sacer* (Biehl 2001), humans have not thought or acted themselves spontaneously into being as much as they have found voice by means of laborious and ongoing processes of silencing and ventroloquizing, excluding and embracing, and erasing and inscribing the bodies and beings of marginal Others (Gilroy 1993). For this reason, among others, Donna Haraway (2004) offered up the cyborg as a radical and destabilizing source of feminist inspiration. The cyborg refuses to define the human in terms of limits. It rejects all origins—it neither longs for a return to an unadulterated Eden nor reveres its scientist "father"— and is free to theorize itself as an entity within which nature, technology, and humanity mingle. It is an irreverent, unrestricted, and therefore blasphemous assemblage.

Once the privileged position of the human has been called into question (if not fully dismantled), it becomes possible to recognize that the features of the living world that once appeared to structure and limit human creativity can themselves be productively theorized as participants within that world. Nature is not the material into which human agency etches itself. Rather, natural agencies and human agencies are coterminous and co-emergent, and human worlds come into being with those other worlds, inside and outside of them, and against them (Kirksey and Helmreich 2010; Kosek 2010; Livingston and Puar 2011). The built environment, which includes architecture, infrastructure, technology, and trash, is similarly alive (J. Bennett 2010; Chen 2012). So too are images and artworks, as W. J. T. Mitchell has persistently demonstrated (1994, 1996, 2005, 2011).

9. Bonnie Ruberg has made a strikingly similar argument in their monograph *Video Games Have Always Been Queer* (2019). In their chapter on *Pong*, Ruberg writes that "the ball is batted back and forth between paddles, yet to say that its movements lie entirely in the hands of the players is to overlook the drive and desires of the ball itself.

Within the world of the game, the ball is a force to be reckoned with. It is not served onto the table by one of the players, as in a traditional game of ping-pong. Instead, it enters the play space from off-screen, flying onto the table at an angle that the players have had no part in determining." Because I am less certain than Ruberg that the opening serve (or any subsequent hit) of the ball in a table tennis game is a determining act, I see a close parallel between Ruberg's analysis and my own. In rugby as in *Pong* (and, I suspect, table tennis too), the ball is, as Ruberg describes, not a "mere tool for the transmission of connection between paddles" but "a willful, dangerous, and at times chaotic entity that the players struggle to contain" (50–51).

10. This book's interest in rugby's own "life" should not be taken as a wholesale rejection of the agentive capacity of the rugby-playing subject. As Christopher Pinney and Webb Keane's contributions to the volume *Materiality* (2005) remind us, interactions between subject and object are invariably dialogical and reciprocal. The present book's project is premised on the notion that, as Pinney puts it, objects contain their own internal points of stability (which he calls "cataracts") that allow them to escape full determination by their contexts (269). Such objects, Pinney suggests, elaborating on the work of Bruno Latour and Michel Serres as well as Theodor Adorno, are best understood as "quasi-objects," which generate new meanings and new situations as they are encountered (268; see also Halsall 2016, 449). If Walter Benjamin's "Rastelli erzählt . . ." pulls the usual conception of the relationship between ball and player out from under our feet, Serres's description of the ball as a "quasi-object" and "quasi-subject" settles us on new and analytically fertile ground. "The ball," Serres writes (2007, 226), "isn't there for the body; the exact contrary is true: the body is the object of the ball; the subject moves around this sun. Skill with the ball is recognized in the player who follows the ball and serves it instead of making it follow him and using it. It is the subject of the body, subject of bodies, and like a subject of subjects. Playing is nothing else but making oneself the attribute of the ball as substance. The laws are written for it, defined relative to it, and we bend to these laws."

11. Rugby fields are certainly not the only locus in South African life where performances of history occur. Louise Meintjes (2017, 17) has recently showed how *ngoma* performances, for example, use bodily movement and vocal play to "draw from a repertoire of relationships near and far, contemporaneous and historical, imagined and remembered, material and elusive." The argument of the present book suggests that every sport will engender its own performances of history. If that is so, it is likely that other South African sports, most notably soccer, will offer narratives of history that differ wildly from the one that rugby presents. Nor can rugby tell even a rugby-specific version of South African history in its entirety. Theorists who study affect and memory caution strongly against the project of attempting to retrieve history and embodied experience in their fullness. Not only are experience and lived history always partially inaccessible, to oneself as well as to others, but they resist straightforward expression. Memories and affect can be documented only provisionally and contextually. To argue that rugby tells a unified story of South African history and that rugby tells that history in its fullness is to perform an act of theoretical violence—to deny the salience of other tellings and

to take as gospel those offered by rugby (with its unique ties to colonialism and the apartheid state, its mobilizations during the anti-apartheid struggle, and its processes of professionalization). If rugby is a performance of history, the narratives that emerge in the liveness of play will never be complete.

12. The autonomy of sport must also be learned. As Lucia Trimbur has persuasively shown in the case of boxing in New York, boxers must learn to construct frames that legitimize their acts of violence. Some female fighters, Trimbur argues, teach themselves to resist the temptation to apologize for their punches, others accept violence from their opponent before initiating it themselves, and still others shift responsibility for their violence onto the commands of their coaches and trainers. Those "practices of permission," explains Trimbur (2013, 100), are precisely the acts that create the spaces and durations in which punching is allowed. Frames could be particularly visible in fights between female boxers, who may tend to be less accustomed to the norms of sporting violence than their male counterparts, but Michael Messner has shown that even male American football players must be taught to embrace the use of violence on the sporting field. Jack Tatum, a former player for the Oakland Raiders and a famously aggressive tackler, seems to have disliked the violence of American football until it was celebrated by the people around him. He told Messner (1990, 207), "When I first started playing, if I would hit a guy hard and he wouldn't get up, it would bother me. [But] when I was a sophomore in high school, first game, I knocked out two quarterbacks, and people loved it. The coach loved it. Everybody loved it. . . . The more you play, the more you realize that it is just a part of the game—somebody's gonna get hurt."

13. To some theorists, art comes with similar stipulations. As I will show in chapter 2, for Adorno (2007a) the division between artwork and world turns artworks into social forms that operate like the figure of Cassandra in Greek mythology. In the dominant tradition of Western aesthetics, art's capacity to address the world makes it a powerful emissary of the beautiful and the politically salient. It can transmit the heights of exhilaration, the depths of sorrow and loss, and the complexity of a personal or group identity. It can hint at that which cannot be adequately or safely voiced, and it can contribute to the cultivation and development of a voice as well. At the same time, art's depictions remain mere hints of the real, and artworks that seek to access the real directly and even to mold it often slip over or under or around the real, calling it to mind but not into being (H. Foster 1996, 157; Ray 2005, 84). All experiences of the real may slip by in this way, but the very historical privileging of art as a space for calling attention to the real can make that persistent evasion all the more noticeable. Artists can use the autonomy of art to speak about political matters, but viewers can easily use that autonomy as a sign of art's independence from politics and, in doing so, render its statements insignificant.

CHAPTER 1

1. A number of other scholars have remarked on the structural importance of uncertainty to the sports and related forms of embodied practice they study. Writing in terms of the relationship between uncertainty and sporting participation, for exam-

ple, Heather Levi (2008) has noted of *lucha libre* that professional wrestling is generally regarded as more scripted than it actually is. The lingering presence of uncertainty makes wrestling both difficult and dangerous. Similarly, Rebecca Cassidy (2002, 166) has observed that the thoroughbred industry in Newmarket, England, "can be extrapolated from the basic uncertainty that governs which horse will finish first, second and third (and last!)." Greg Downey (2005, 123) has shown how "cunning" ("a combination of wariness, quick wit, savvy, unpredictability, playfulness, viciousness, aesthetic flare, and a talent for deception") takes shape within the performance of capoeira; and Eric Worby (2009) has directed our attention to the play of unpredictability in post-apartheid Johannesburg and on its football fields. Others have highlighted uncertainty's importance to sport spectatorship. In particular, Thomas Carter (2008) and Roger Magazine (2007) draw our attention to the ways that fan narratives about the teams they support emerge from conditions of social instability in Cuba and Mexico, respectively. In doing so, those authors' important works offer tantalizing hints about why sports draw spectators during unpredictable times.

2. That notion of magic resonates with other influential definitions as well. While E. E. Evans-Pritchard (1937, 439) characterized witchcraft as the social force that produces unfortunate events, for example, he also proposed that magic both prevents such situations and neutralizes their effects. Witchcraft, then, may name the cause of misfortune, but magic (for the Azande as well as the Bulls) allows its socially permissible redress. Michael Jackson, meanwhile, has carried this resonance to its logical conclusion. Elaborating on Michael Taussig's (1980) analysis of the figure of the devil in Colombian folk magic, Jackson (1998, 54) has suggested that magical medicines should be theorized as one of a broad range of strategies that human societies deploy in response to crises of "control and closure." In that regard, he, like Theodor Adorno and Max Horkheimer (2002), considers magical and scientific reason to address similar concerns about causality, certainty, and chance.

3. George Gmelch (1971) has made a similar point about the proliferation of "magical" rituals in baseball. He notes that pitching and hitting, aspects of the sport that are heavy with chance, seem to attract many more protective rituals than fielding, which is comparatively more reliable. Though I take my cue on the relationships among chance, sport, and magic from Gmelch's influential essay, I complicate his analysis in three specific ways in the coming pages. First, the present chapter suggests that activities like fielding—which, Gmelch observes, is performed successfully more than 90 percent of the time—can, on some occasions, be rendered all the more magically problematic for their apparent certainty. Second, while Gmelch notes that rituals of magic are common even among groups that regard themselves as scientifically rational, I examine some of the ways in which that rationality draws on magic to sustain itself. Third and finally, I take magic as an indicator of the structural necessity of uncertainty to rugby's live performance. That structural magic, which Gmelch acknowledges but does not examine in detail, constitutes sport's artistic aura.

4. As one anonymous reader of this argument rightfully noted, it would be an exag-

geration to claim that every player who passed through the NTRU (to say nothing of every player in South Africa) was equally committed to the *maak vas* philosophy. The inclusion of players from the University of Pretoria would seem to undermine the influence that the institutions of order held over the team's preferred strategy. One player who represented both the University of Pretoria and the NTRU, for example, stressed to me that the university played what he called open and creative "student rugby," influenced by their students' tastes and interests. Perhaps more significant than that observation, though, is the fact that the same student player, when invited to play for Buurman van Zyl and the NTRU, was told that the "games were over" and that he was going to play "proper" Northern Transvaal rugby or not play at all. Given that example, it seems appropriate to conclude that, despite important exceptions, *maak vas* gave (and still often gives) vivid and coercive expression to the preferred aesthetic of the apartheid regime.

5. If the NTRU did seek to quell uncertainty in that spectacular fashion, encounters with rugby's inherent unpredictability would seem to resist theorization as an emergent "structure of conjuncture" (see Sahlins 1981). Players and coaches within the Bulls' organization are well aware of the challenges that rugby's inherent conditions continually pose, and *maak vas*, magic, and default are specifically designed to address them. Only because the sport offers a structured encounter with uncertainty, then, can those historically and socially situated responses be arranged and, in the case of *maak vas* and default, practiced ad infinitum.

6. Lévi-Strauss may locate art squarely between the Bricoleur of mythmaking and the Engineer of scientific thought, but he suggests that games are explorations in a purely scientific mold (1966, 32). That analysis, however, may reflect the final result of a sporting contest better than the uncertain process of its unfolding. Indeed, as Karen Barad (2007) has persuasively argued with the aid of the writing of Niehls Bohr and his Copenhagen interpretation of quantum mechanics, even the scientific experiment may not be nearly as straightforward as Lévi-Strauss lets on. If the scientific experiment generates phenomena, it does so through a contingent process that requires the intra-action of numerous discursive and material agencies, of which the researching scientist is but one component. For Barad and Bohr, then, the scientific finding appears, in its superficial finality, to belie the complex and contingent process of its emergence. From that perspective, Lévi-Strauss's scientist looks more like an idealized representation of the scientist as dispassionate and apolitical discoverer of natural laws than like the intra-active artistic creators of reality they might well be, in practice.

7. All of the research collaborators that appear in this book have been given pseudonyms.

CHAPTER 2

1. If the content of those amateur anxieties replicates that of past generations, their form does as well. S. W. Pope (1996, 290) finds that American sportswriters expressed

concerns about the deleterious effects of professionalization in 1868, 1915, 1927, 1944, and 1995. Although Pope attributes those rearticulations to the instability of amateurism itself as an "invented athletic tradition," I suggest—on the basis of the argument of this chapter—that the continual "reinvention" of amateurism and professionalism in South African rugby is perhaps better understood as part of an ongoing process of framing and counterframing, in which discourses of amateurism and professionalism are mobilized to serve particular interests and used rhetorically to open and close particular political conversations about rugby's social existence.

2. For more information about the events that led to the International Rugby Board's decision to recognize and embrace the existence of professionalism in rugby, see Chandler and Nauright's *Making the Rugby World: Race, Gender, Commerce* (1999).

3. In my reading, Charl's revision of amateur ideology resonates, with surprising clarity, with an argument posited by Giulianotti and Walsh in *Ethics, Money, and Sport: This Sporting Mammon* (2007). While recognizing the historical production of amateurism and its systemic blindness toward the presence of money in sport, Giulianotti and Walsh observe that "it is not that [the essence of sport] is violated [by money] but that the values that emerge in and through sport are suppressed and the space for their expression limited" (62). Charl, like Giulianotti and Walsh, values the development of players as people and clearly believes that such development is abandoned when teams turn their attention to the unbridled pursuit of profit.

4. Danto's sentiment here fittingly bears a strong similarity to one articulated by Adorno and his collaborator Max Horkheimer in *The Dialectic of Enlightenment* (2002). "Art," they write, "has in common with magic the postulation of a special, self-contained sphere removed from the context of profane existence. Within it special laws prevail" (13–14).

5. Although Adorno doubted the efficacy of Arnold Schoenberg's explicitly political works, a remark that he once offered about Schoenberg's general approach to composition is notably relevant here. "Schoenberg," Adorno suggested, "worked so hard at leisure that he called the category of work into question" (1967, 150).

6. It is not surprising that the concept of slavery operates in this way, given that Buck-Morss (2009), Mbembe (2003), Gilroy (1993), Mehta (1999), Fausto-Sterling (1995), and numerous additional authors have shown that European conceptions of sovereignty, identity, and freedom have been produced in contradistinction to colonized and enslaved populations.

7. John Bale's *Imagined Olympians* (2002) is an invaluable contribution to the literature on sport, race, and autonomy, insofar as it documents that process in progress. In that work, Bale examines the archival and oral historical records of an indigenous Rwandan body culture—a ritual form of high jumping called *gusimbuka-urukiramende*. On page 69, Bale writes, "The Europeans consumed *gusimbuka* as a version of something known already to them; it also encouraged the use of Western models of recording athletic performance. These assumed 1) measurement of the Rwandan body itself . . . , 2)

quantified recording of the resulting athletic performances, and 3) measurement of incidental but related activities and artifacts." Though Bale does not focus explicitly on the ways in which interpretations of practices like *gusimbuka* contributed to the codification of a dominant conception of autonomous sport, his analysis shows how *gusimbuka* was framed as a sign of "raw athletic potential" and then incorporated into a European conception of sport, rather than understood on its own terms and in its own context.

8. While the player in question attended a high school that was so insignificant scouts never came to watch him play, he told me that he was fortunate. His parents were able to pay for him to attend a rugby academy (the cost of which was about R50,000—between $5,000 and $7,000, depending on the exchange rate at the time) so that he could build a profile for himself. He eventually signed a contract with a smaller province and parlayed his performance with that team into a bigger contract with a better one.

9. For example, Simon Gikandi finds this process replicated in William Rubin's account of Picasso's debt to African art, an account composed for the catalog for Museum of Modern Art's 1984 exhibition *Primitivism in 20th-Century Art*. Gikandi writes that "underneath his acknowledgement of the affinity between the tribal and modern, Rubin's project is also underwritten by a troubling surreptitious intention: the need to minimise the role of the Other in the emergence of modernism as a style and, in particular, the significance of Africa as an artistic model, even when acknowledging their overall affect" (2006, 47).

10. Those encounters, with their historical reverberations and close juxtapositions, have much in common with Walter Benjamin's conception of the "dialectical image." Benjamin's term, with its many interpretations, is too complicated to explore in depth in this chapter, but it underlines the fragility and the power of the moments here discussed. For Benjamin, a "dialectical image" is a political "constellation" that emerges when two conceptual images flash together, across space and time, and reveal their shared ideological underpinnings. Although that constellation breaks the linear flow of time, it is neither timeless nor universal, because it remains bound to the particular historical moment in which it appears (Benjamin 2005, 695–97; Buck-Morss 1989, 290; Taussig 1993, 245–46). That historical particularity not only makes the constellation disturbingly powerful in its instant of emergence but also necessitates that the constellation be brief and easily lost. The same qualities seem to be present in the rugby-related encounters discussed in this chapter. In each case, the proximity of exercise and work opened the possibility that the players and laborers might catch sight of the fragile boundary that kept those categories apart, but that proximity alone could never guarantee that the historical and economic conditions producing that boundary in South Africa would be universally recognized or called explicitly into question. Indeed, the boy's "Sisebenza," his professional colleague's threat to *bliksem*, and the laborer's dropping of the hammer brought the images to a close and left the encounters that produced them unredeemed (cf. Benjamin 1968).

CHAPTER 3

1. Brian Massumi's *What Animals Teach Us about Politics* (2014) demonstrates clear affinities between Edgar/Danto and Bateson on this particular point. In his reading of Bateson's essay, Massumi argues that play's performative gestures hold "in *suspense*" a bite's typical function. That suspension, he adds, "exerts its own force," which is "a force of induction" pulling the nipped into a play situation that "transports" the players into a "conditional reality" they occupy together (4–6).

2. Rebecca Farley makes a very similar claim in an article about theories of games. After remarking that players can be seriously injured in "sporting" activities, she writes, "True, you might forget yourself while playing, but what about afterwards? The embodiedness of players—the constancy of muscle memory, bruises and scars—imprints lasting effects on minds and flesh, inextricably binding the game world to the mundane." She adds, "To describe games as discrete, then, assumes that people are disembodied, completely rational and extremely forgetful: these are the only terms under which gameplay can be 'detached'" (Farley 2000; see also Newman 2013, 17). Elaborating on Farley's observation, this chapter demonstrates not only how injuries and player responses to them complicate conceptions of rugby's autonomy—it's "magic circle" (Huizinga 1980, 10), in the parlance of games studies—but also how the assumption of players as "disembodied, completely rational and extremely forgetful" can be used to discipline players and mobilize them in the direction of an idealized masculinity premised on flawless sporting performance.

3. One could observe that injuries are almost certainly less common on walks to school than in the violent crucible of the rugby field, but to make that observation would be to miss the important connection that the players and nonplaying adults are attempting to draw. What unites the field and the world is the uncertainty inherent to both. In the accounts cited in text, the unpredictability of the world was replicated, in miniature, in the unpredictability of the rugby field.

4. Although Starn does not make the point explicitly, the structure of his argument suggests a belief that the American public's response to Tiger Woods's marital indiscretions was informed not just by popular conceptions of race and gender but also by the nearly superhuman quality of Woods's golfing persona. Such a claim, though plainly difficult to make in a situation as contested and overdetermined as that one, would be consistent with the overarching argument of the present chapter.

5. Susan Buck-Morss (1992) and Anne McClintock (1995, 303) have considered that topic in depth. Elaborating directly on Eagleton's argument (1990, 64), Buck-Morss writes, "Doing one better than Virgin birth, modern man, *homo autotelus*, literally produces himself, generating himself, to cite Eagleton, 'miraculously out of [his] own substance'" (1992, 7–8).

6. In that respect, the present analysis bears a strong similarity to Harry Walker's consideration of soccer in Peru. As a spatially and temporally bound activity, regulated by rules and referee, organized soccer generates, he argues, a "functional interdepen-

dence within the team," as players assume responsibilities and roles on the field. Walker recognizes that the roles are undergirded by "a notion of the abstract individual—of the human being, equipped with a given set of needs and capacities, such as that invoked in the discourse of 'human rights'" (2013, 393). I share Walker's interest in that abstract individual, though I link the abstraction explicitly to sporting performance and the uncertainty of live play. In doing so, I suggest that the abstract subject who justifies soccer's division of roles might acquire an important measure of legitimacy by means of the fact that truly talented players can, in their occupation of a particular role, sometimes seem to actually perform that abstraction in their capacity to temporarily escape the contingency of the moment and dictate the flow of play. (Think here of the defender who always seems to be in the right place at the right time or of the "clinical" striker who makes shots from impossible angles seem routine.) That interpretation is paradoxical, of course, in that it requires the special talent of a player to reveal the abstract possibilities for all. But in this chapter, I show that the paradox does not trouble coaches (and other people of influence) in the least, because those rare talents establish a standard against which all other players can be measured.

7. "Meneer" is a respectful form of address that is frequently used with older men. I encountered it with regularity during my research when students, for example, communicated with their male teachers. Though I was never able to ask these officials about their preference for this term, it seems plausible that the term's appearance in this somewhat unexpected context (older men, discussing the physical forms and athletic prowess of much younger boys) speaks to a set of practices and discourses that serve to locate rugby's masculine ideal in South Africa in particular. I consider such practices and discourses—and their associations with race, power, and cultural history—in chapter 4 of this book.

8. No coach is ever happy about the injury of a player, but professional coaches have the luxury of being receptive to replacing players because that attitude aligns with the reality that, as I showed in chapter 2, there are always more—potentially superhuman—players who are waiting for an opportunity to play. One coach I knew who repeatedly demonstrated a deep fondness for his players outlined the situation quite clearly during a team video session. He dimmed the lights and, before launching into a conversation about the previous match, addressed his team about a player's recent injury. "Rugby," he began, "is a tough thing. It builds you up and cuts you down, and I'm only giving you this message now because you never know when you might have a career-ending injury." After a beat, he said, "[The injured player] has been crying his eyes out in my office because the team doctor just told him that he's out for six to eight months. I sympathize with him, but in the real world, what must I do?" One player asked, "Find someone else to play his position?" The coach nodded and said, "Exactly. I love the guy, but if [a second player at his position] gets hurt, we can't go to war with nobody."

9. That conception is consistent with the vision of the body valorized in dominant conceptions of exercise, and it too, like rugby, is structured by gendered conceptions of the body. Brian Pronger has noted that most conventional and scientific discourses

about physical fitness tend to be phallocentric, insofar as they privilege the hardness of the body over its permeability, its use over its being or becoming. "The phallic will to power [which the technology of physical fitness aims to realize]," he writes, "penetrates the otherness of decay, old age, and death to make it dis-appear. For this disappearing act to be successful, the sovereign self must remain impervious to otherness—i.e., it incorporates otherness without being altered by it—even though it lives perpetually in the shadow of the parergonal otherness of death." Referring to his 1999 article, Pronger adds, "I have written elsewhere about this other side of phallic desire, metaphorically, as anal closure—the tight anus that resists entry. It is misogynist desire—fearful of becoming open, of being penetrated by the other" (2002, 184–85).

10. As I show later in this chapter, players possess a deep understanding of their bodies and its limits. That understanding seemed to motivate their derisive invitations— because they knew that I would not be able to perform the exercises they chose for me— but it also gave them an appreciation for the satisfaction of collective experience and, as it happened, for anthropology's ethnographic methodology. The player who implied that I was an "American pussy" was especially eager to get me to exercise with him. One day, I wandered into the gym and over to him and his teammate. Both were hoisting heavy exercise balls over their heads and slamming them repeatedly against the floor. When it came time for a break, the player said, "When are you going to come and work out with us, eh? We'll show you that American pussies are weak." His remarks were often aggressive, but that one was cheerful. His teammate socked me playfully in the arm. I smiled and said, "Not today. I've got to do my research now." The player challenged me, "What are you going to learn out there? Come over here and do some in-depth research with us by lifting something." On another day, he said to me, "You're always fucking around with your notepad. Come and gym with us!"

11. When he thanked the company and emphasized the company's obligation to him, the player also implied that the company should be expected to treat the injuries that resulted from the rugby's violence with the attention such injuries would receive in many other professional contexts. In few other lines of work, he seemed to suggest, would the trauma of repeated blows to the body be regarded as psychosomatic and therefore as irrelevant to the job at hand (or, worse, as sign of a flawed character). In drawing those contextual connections, the player sought to erase any semblance of rugby's autonomy and to turn the "nips" of rugby into the "bites" of real suffering.

12. As the content of this chapter may suggest, trainers occupy an ambiguous position with respect to players and their bodies. Like medical personnel, trainers pay close attention to the health of players. Trainers manage players' rehabilitation and gym sessions and follow their performances closely. When the Bulls sought to monitor the body weights of their players on a daily basis, a trainer supervised the process. Like coaches, though, trainers are tasked with pushing players toward a position of full agency. Trainers manage the exhausting rehabilitation sessions and are generally willing to notify coaches if players do not appear to be approaching their fitness sessions with the appropriate intensity.

13. The doctor interacted with the materiality of her players' bodies numerous times almost every day. Although the frequency of the interactions could, in time, blur together into a string of diagnoses that might distance a doctor from the vulnerability of the players with whom the doctor worked, the paragraphs to come will demonstrate that the doctor I observed felt a strong commitment to understanding her players' experiences and, if necessary, advocating on their behalf in meetings with coaches.

14. Suffering, anguish, frustration, and tears form a crucial dimension of the support relationship. While players occasionally cry in front of their coaches, support staff members almost certainly see players cry with greater regularity. Support personnel are the first people to attend to a player in the moments after an injury. They motivate players frustrated over struggles with their bodies and provide counsel to players who discover that their careers are over. One trainer I knew acknowledged the inevitability of tears directly during his first meeting with a new crop of players. Standing in front of them, he told them about the rehabilitation schedules they might expect if they were to hurt themselves during the season: "If you suffer a long-term injury, say a torn ACL [anterior cruciate ligament], you'll be out six to nine months." He paused before continuing, "Go and cry a bit, because, shit, that's what you do. Then come in to work, because that's what we do. We'll get you back to your best."

15. Trainers and doctors can, of course, prove themselves to be just as neglectful, exploitative, and predatory towards players as any coach. Because accusations (whether made publicly or not) of malpractice and sexual violence did not feature in my fieldwork, though, I am not prepared to argue at length about either the possible differences in motivations that might exist between predatory coaches, trainers, and athletic doctors or the possible subject positions from which those motivations might emerge. Suffice it here, then, to note that it is possible that acts of malpractice and sexual violence that doctors and athletic trainers commit might be linked, in deeply complicated and damaging ways, to their intimate knowledge of materially vulnerable athletes and their precarious bodies.

16. Trainers and medical personnel, who appeared during my fieldwork to be more sympathetic to the experiences of players, often found themselves managing coaches' expectations. For example, trainers kept coaches informed about the status of rehabilitating players, giving trainers opportunities to defend players whose rehabilitations were taking longer than expected. Trainers would also suggest when coaches might consider giving players a chance to rest. In one management meeting I witnessed, a coach announced that he wanted the training staff to tell him the availability of injured players one week before an important match. The coach's intentions were good—he hoped to have his team organized and training together well in advance of the game, and he did not want injured players to push themselves beyond their limits in the interests of trying to play—but a trainer observed that the strategy was bound to fail. "From a coaching standpoint it makes sense," the trainer said, "but we can't tell them this. Guys will lie and hurt themselves worse." The coach appreciated the advice and agreed to follow the standard protocol.

Unsurprisingly, the team doctor was often front and center in such negotiations. She told me that though she generally preferred to inform both player and coach of the risks associated with a player's condition and let them come to a conclusion together, she understood that other interests made final decisions more complicated. Like the trainer referenced just above, she recognized that players want desperately to be selected. Also, coaches wanted to choose the players that the coaches liked best. Those interests meant that her advice regularly frustrated one group or the other. If players ignored her advice and tried to play before they were healthy, coaches were often surprised to find that a vital player had been judged unfit. During one medical update, for example, the doctor reported that a particular player's shoulder injury was worse than she had anticipated and that she did not feel comfortable approving him to play. The player's coach looked up in surprise. He moaned, saying, "But I need that player. [Another player] just got hurt again so I've got nobody left at his position."

17. This is not to suggest that black and African staff members did not feel marked out in the workplace on the basis of race. Perceptions of racial difference, history, and social hierarchy, even if not explicitly named or acknowledged, regularly infused social interactions. Once, for example, I was chatting with a group of team staff after hours and the topic of nicknames came up. One black staff person's name had been recently rendered playfully in Afrikaans by a white Afrikaans-speaking person, and when the staff person shared the news with the group, one of their peers shuddered in alarm: "You've gotta nip that in the bud right away. Otherwise, before you know it, you'll end up with something ridiculous, some African name that is nothing like yours." Another person nodded ruefully and said that when players want to make him mad, all they have to do is call him by the wrong name.

18. As the doctor's observations suggest, her hard-earned appreciation for the vulnerability of the player's body made her far less willing than coaches to dismiss a player's subjective experience of his injury as a sign of mental or physical failure. She explained to me that while she knew of coaches who would say that "some guys have injuries in their brains rather than their bodies," that kind of language made her uncomfortable. She knew from personal experience how long old injuries could linger, and the pain from those old injuries could reemerge unexpectedly on cold days or during tiring workouts. She explained to me that a bad ankle sprain she had experienced herself some 12 years previous still hurt her when the weather turned cold. She would exercise through the pain if she felt especially motivated, but she noticed that she would focus more and more on the ankle when she felt less motivated. The ankle became an excuse. The doctor believed that the same thing happened with some players. The little injuries are always there, she told me, but when the players are feeling good and going strong, they do not notice them. Only when it is cold, they are tired, and things are going badly do they remember their injuries, which turn into crutches. That perspective, which differs so drastically from the coach who questioned his player's request for an MRI, further underlines the doctor's awareness of the workings of the injurable body and explains her willingness (described above) to send a healthy player to an unnecessary appointment with a specialist to restore his confidence.

CHAPTER 4

1. The designation "Model C," to which I return later in this chapter, refers to those formerly whites-only schools that became semiprivate in the final years of apartheid.

2. Because this chapter examines the relationship between rugby and judgments, rather than rugby as a set of internalized practices, it will not speculate about the implications of those judgments, pace Bourdieu (2007), on a South African rugby habitus or "body culture" (Brownell 1995). Readers interested in pursuing that line of argumentation might consider Loïc Wacquant's work on the intersubjective and pedagogical violence of boxing (1995, 2004, 2007), as well as Greg Downey's ethnography about the experience of learning capoeira (2005) and his provocative critique of habitus from a neuroanthropological perspective (2010).

3. While a number of scholars have observed the implications of those perceptions for masculinity in South Africa (cf. Reid and Walker 2005; Morrell 2001a), comparatively less attention has been devoted to the dynamics of the moments and places in which white South Africans seek (and sometimes find) stable and familiar male performances. This chapter examines one such place: the rugby fields at former Model C schools.

4. Like Grundlingh, Booth notes that rugby was a major point of interest for the Federasie van Afrikaanse Kultuurverenigings (Federation of Afrikaans Cultural Associations), an organization at least partially responsible for the formation of the Voortrekker movement as a white, Afrikaans-speaking alternative to the English Boy Scouts (1998, 37). For an overview about the founding of the Voortrekkers and its connection with apartheid ideology, see Moodie 1975. For the specific politics of scouting and the relationship between the Voortrekkers and the Boy Scouts, see also Parsons 2004.

5. Making a similar observation about one of Morrell's (1994) accounts of corporal punishment, Debbie Epstein writes, "The ability to stand up to a beating, to 'take [it] very well' defined one's manliness. . . . The ritualised spectacle of the beating appears to have been titillating and the clear pleasure taken by [the teacher] in delivering it, 'trying out his canes' to gain the maximum impact from the fear of being beaten and then from the beating itself is obvious" (1996, 56).

6. Because rugby does not simply use violence and spontaneity but actually cannot exist without them, the sport can be usefully distinguished from other artistic forms that attempt to incorporate and control violence for the purposes of representation. Nehamas (1999) and Danto (2005) examine the case of artworks that try to use violence to reintroduce reality into art. They argue that such "arts of disturbation" generally appear hopeless and sad because they utilize artistic forms that have become so fully autonomous that not even pain and violence can awaken their audience to the substance of their political content.

The well-documented case of Dada is instructive in that regard. As the movement tried to attack seriousness through their nonsensical performances, the perception of the attempts as theatrical performances made Dada tend irresistibly toward comprehensibility despite itself. Goldberg writes, "The final Dada soirée in Zurich took place on 9

April 1919 at the Saal zur Kaufleuten. . . . The performance itself began on a sombre note: the Swedish film maker Viking Eggeling delivered a serious speech about elementary 'Gestaltung' and abstract art. This only irritated the audience primed for the *usual* combative confrontation with the Dadaists" (2001, 73–74; emphasis added). On the occasion Goldberg describes, the audience's anticipation of a confrontation signaled the end of any possibility of an "authentic" confrontation, forcing Eggeling back to seriousness in order to escape (Bürger 2002, 81). Dada was meant to catch its audience unawares, but the autonomy of the dramatic form destroyed that possibility as audiences enfolded that confrontation into their own theatrical expectation. Thus, concludes Gay's analysis of the movement, "Short of burning down the Cabaret Voltaire as a demonstration, the founding Dadaists took their critique of contemporary culture and of its art to the outermost point" (Gay 2008, 341).

7. Sociologist Jay Coakley (2004) makes the useful distinction between "informal, player-controlled sports" and "organized, adult-controlled sports." Although Coakley uses that contrast to capture something of the perniciousness of the increasing rationalization of high-level youth sports in the United States, the categories are equally important to acknowledge here. During my 17 months of fieldwork in South Africa, I saw disaggregated elements of rugby performed in all manner of places. Boys tossed balls back and forth as they walked down the street; they worked on their sidestep while waiting in line at the grocery store checkout line; they played casual games in parks, on parking lots, and on fields as well; I even observed two boys (who could not have been older than eight) stand side by side, arms locked, and tentatively try to push against the high school's massive "scrum sled." All of those practices constitute "rugby," and all of them create opportunities for judgment. That said, the uniform parameters of time and space, the strict adherence to formal rules, and the arcane details of strategy and preparation, all of which mark Coakley's "organized, adult-controlled sports," create the conditions for rapid, repeated, and (it is widely believed) reliable judgment. Under such circumstances, to borrow from Roland Barthes's observation about French toys, adults prefigure a particular understanding of the world for their children through rugby, monitoring how their children respond to the violence, speed, and possibility inherent to that world (1974, 53).

8. Rugby was also used as negative reinforcement. Cock quotes another of her informants as saying, "If I [refused] to go to [the *veld*] camps I'd loose [sic] my girlfriend, I'd be dropped from the first rugby team and I'd be chucked out of hostel" (1991, 74).

9. As Robert Morrell (2001b) notes, white male students were far from the only youth demographic in South Africa that "got their lessons in a violent manner." Unique about the experience of that group, I argue, is the extension of that disciplinary violence into cadets, *veld* camps, rugby, and, ultimately, the military and the police.

10. The student leader proposed multiple ways forward. One was to "reorient" the apparently insufficiently "oriented" grade 9 students. Another was to emphasize and exaggerate recognized and still legal performances of discipline: "You should always remember to stand up for [alumni], teachers, and parents. When you do, you stand

up *all the way*, straighten your back and greet them if you can. Boys of grade 8 and 9 [12- and 13-year-old], stand up for grade 12 students. Boys of grades 8 to 11 stand up for the student council." While those two policies received warm responses from his fellow students, the third met huge applause: he proposed preserving the spectacle of physical punishment by displacing it spatially, onto the grounds of the school itself. Projecting a map of the school onto a screen, he began to demarcate various areas with a finger: "This whole area is just for grade 12 boys, and this pathway next to it is reserved for grade 10s and grade 11s. Next to *that* pathway is another, and this one is for grades 9, 10, and 11. Grade 8s cannot touch that path either. They have their own little strip, off to the side." Similarly specific rules applied for walking through buildings or around them, and the student narrated those ultrafine gradations of privilege with great seriousness.

11. While the South African press regularly reports instances of disciplinary violence and physical initiation practices in the hostels of many large schools, the language and practices of official school orientations explicitly condemn such actions. At an orientation that I witnessed, a teacher explained to the incoming class of students what they should expect to encounter during the process: "We don't initiate anyone here," he began. "That's *common* [i.e., low class]."

12. More than one student told me, "We know what we did wrong. We get punished, and everyone moves on." Robert Morrell heard similar justifications from white students in his own study of disciplinary violence in South Africa in the late 1990s. He attributed those responses to the notion that such punishments build character and to a sense of "resentment about education and social transformation and the romanticization of a lost era as schools formerly reserved for whites have been opened to other races and in the process changed" (Morrell 2001b, 146). Unlike many journalistic accounts, Morrell's refuses to explain the lingering presence of corporal punishment in terms of teacher exhaustion, aggression, and laziness. Even so, there would seem to be little need to link the brevity of corporal punishment directly (as Morrell does) to apartheid nostalgia. Considered alongside practices like initiations and rugby, however, the association becomes more apparent: the apartheid state's militarization of education bound together a host of violent practices that were meant, in their immediacy, to inculcate a rugged and martial masculinity in boys and test them for "glitches."

13. Applicants to the school were clearly aware of its cultural language and did their best to use it to their advantage. One supporting letter read, "It is my privilege to recommend [this boy]. He is a young man with excellent characteristics and stands out as a dynamic leader. He joined [our community rugby club, and] he has . . . clearly stood out among the rest of his teammates. Because of his quiet personality, he inspired respect and esteem in the rest of his teammates." Another letter spoke of an applicant's dream to "be associate[d] with the [school's] tradition." In a third, parents mentioned that "the school's values, principles and aims are aligned with what we have taught, installed and cultivated in [our son]."

14. The notion that sports are voluntary activities demands further questioning in any context but especially when it is freighted with as much significance as rugby

appears to be in Model C schools. Though even young children are certainly capable of intervening and manipulating their sporting options, familial pressures should not be underestimated. In a semiformal survey that I conducted with 88 players at the high school at which I worked, roughly 17 percent (15 of 88) told me that their mother or father made them start playing rugby, explicitly against the students' own wishes. The notion of "choice" becomes more ambiguous still with a further 35 percent of students (31 of 88) saying some variation of "I played before I knew what it was," "I always loved rugby—it runs in my family," or even "My brother played and he got more attention from my dad so I wanted to play too."

15. Sharon Mazer has argued that fans of professional wrestling perform their spectatorship in a similar way. Far from being naive dupes who take "fake" wrestling to be "real," Mazer argues, fans mobilize their deep understanding of wrestling narratives and moves both to appreciate a story well told and to seek out those moments when "the real" breaks into the script (2005, 68). As a genre of performance, rugby may foreground uncertainty to a much greater extent than professional wrestling, but that reliance on uncertainty does not eliminate the possibility of spectators conceptualizing some moments of play as "more revelatory" than others and using such moments as opportunities to analyze and interpret the character of players. Indeed, the analysis in the present chapter suggests the contrary—that it is precisely rugby's uncertainty that makes those revelatory moments seem so alluring and, once found, incontrovertible.

16. Noel Dyck has observed that many parents use sports to confirm that they have raised their children properly (2012, 54), with parents of children involved in Canadian youth sports finding that confirmation by managing their children's sporting teams and leagues (75). At the South African school I examined, not only did parents enroll their boys at schools they thought would train them properly for sport, but parents also called coaches and administrators with suggestions and even reviewed matches with their boys to show them how they might improve their play. Despite those initial similarities, though, Dyck's analysis focuses on the social relations that shape the operation of community sports rather than the performance of sports themselves. As a result, his ethnography does not easily account for the disciplinary ramifications of parental "connoisseurship."

17. There are important distinctions, worthy of deeper consideration, between the medical definition of a true "steroid" and the much broader and rugby-specific category of "banned substance." For the purposes of this chapter, I have adopted the terminology that my informants of all ages employed in their own daily use. In my observation, I found that the term *steroid* was generally applied to all banned substances in rugby unless the speaker had particular reasons to refer to the substance by name (two professional South African players, for example, were briefly banned from rugby because they tested positive for "methylhexaneamine" during the time of my fieldwork). As such, I use the classifications "steroid" and "banned substance" interchangeably, despite the dangers present in conflating those categories.

18. Another way to characterize the issue would be to say that steroids problematize

a contextually specific definition of the "sports ethic." First posited by Hughes and Coakley, the notion of the "sports ethic" is an attempt to delineate the dominant norms to which competitive athletes are often expected to adhere. Hughes and Coakley identified four core beliefs involved in being an athlete: (1) making sacrifices for "the Game," (2) striving for distinction, (3) accepting risks and playing through pain, and (4) refusing to accept limits in the pursuit of possibilities (1991, 309–10). For Hughes and Coakley, steroid usage shows that that players are willing to endanger their bodies in pursuit of those norms (321). If we take the "sports ethic" as an interpretive framework used to assess athletes, though, it becomes clear that steroid use also undermines the stability of that framework. A player might appear to be making sacrifices for "the Game," striving for distinction, playing through pain, and refusing to accept limits, but the specter of steroids reminds us that one can never be certain that these sacrifices are legitimate.

Seen in that way, perceptions of steroids in South Africa bear a similarity (perhaps unexpected) to conceptions of diving in football that are held in other parts of the world. As both Alvarez (2016) and Healey (2017) argue, diving seems to frustrate some football fans more than other forms of "gamesmanship" because, as a form of recognized "theatricality" (Alvarez 2016, 18), it calls attention to the theatricality of all football performances and thus gives lie to any straightforward interpretation of a player and their actions on the field.

19. Mandatory steroid testing ought to make the ambiguity irrelevant, but the implementation of such a policy in South Africa is fraught with difficulties. The first problem, noted by *Sports Illustrated South Africa* and confirmed by my informants, is that players who seek out and use steroids often dodge positive tests by using steroids only during their off-season training. That practice makes "suspecting the needle" a default position for all but the most relentless coaches. A second problem, even more far-reaching than the first, is the prohibitive cost of a comprehensive testing program. One company, Drug Detection International, reportedly charged R1,500 for the processing of a single test in 2011, and while some schools have managed to allocate the funds necessary to test all of their players, most cannot or will not do so (Borchardt 2011).

20. In a previous year, the school at which I did my research contracted with a supplement company in an effort to regulate the products its senior students used. That arrangement lasted just a year. The school terminated it partly because it was ineffective, as the school could not ensure that boys actually used the free supplements they were given. (Many boys had not, choosing to sell them to eager younger boys and use that money to buy from supplement companies that the seniors felt sold a better product.) The arrangement was also concluded because school administrators refused to allow the school to associate its name with products that might prove harmful to its students. The refusal was justified in terms of liability, but one could not help but notice that by opting for less regulation rather than more, the school had distanced itself from any future positive tests. The school would welcome the benefits of supplements (in the form of rugby victories) and accept none of the risks. With the school severing its official attachment to supplements, students were required to find alternative modes of procurement. While

some families hire trained nutritionists to guide their boys through the overwhelmingly wide range of available products, most boys get their information from less reliable sources, such as their classmates or the internet.

CHAPTER 5

1. An important qualification is necessary before I go too far: the sort of violence I am describing here is of a qualitatively different sort from the violence produced by persons categorized as "football hooligans" and subsequently analyzed by sociologists and criminologists in Britain during the 1980s and 1990s. That particular sort of violence and debates about its origins have produced an incredible volume of scholarship and much contentious discussion, particularly associated with the 1988 book *The Roots of Football Hooliganism*, by Eric Dunning and Patrick Murphy (who may or may not constitute a school of thought at the University of Leicester; see Dunning 1994) and John M. Williams. Though Williams subsequently revised his position, with Stephen Wagg, in *British Football and Social Change* (1991), the 1988 text came under attack because it was judged to have been uncritical in its dependence on newspaper and police reports (Clarke 1992) and because it appeared to create discourses about the same working-class male "hooligans" it purported to examine (Armstrong 2003). Whatever opinion one holds about the legitimacy or the social origins of what has come to be defined as "hooliganism" in Britain, however, that sort of sporting violence appears to hold a very different relationship to the "sporting frame" than the violence I describe here. Violence in the stands, among partisan supporters, or violence in the streets after a match, though certainly animated by sport and its associations with the social conditions in which it is played, does not necessarily disrupt the frame of sport itself. It need not shatter football's frame by bringing violence into it. On the occasions when it does, scholars who analyze hooligan violence might find it profitable to explore the reasons why.

2. Gendler's work asks aesthetic philosophers why it is easier to imagine a fictional world where the earth is flat than a world where murder is right (2000, 58). Her notion of imaginative resistance emerges—in my reading—from her observation that imaginative beliefs, unlike beliefs about reality, necessitate an act of willful decision-making on the part of the believer. Believers are making themselves voluntarily complicit in the fictional world in which they participate, and that voluntary complicity can prompt a believer to resist. Though other aesthetic philosophers have contested Gendler's approach (Matravers 2003; Walton 2006) and though Gendler herself has refined it (2006), that voluntary complicity seems empirically valid in the context analyzed in the present study. In this chapter, I show that marginalized players were widely aware of both the discourses about the immorality of apartheid—even if they themselves may not have always regarded apartheid itself as immoral—and the discourses that linked the fictional worlds of rugby to the apartheid regime. To play rugby as an "African" or "Coloured" man in South Africa was to take a position in relation to the larger anti-apartheid struggle, even if one did not necessarily think that positioning valid or fair.

In this chapter, then, I am invested less in the philosophical debates about imaginative resistance than in the practices that generated and the social consequences that emerged from imaginative resistance in apartheid (and post-apartheid) South Africa.

3. Besteman has argued, for example, that coloured people whose neighborhoods were demolished and whose history was obliterated by the Group Areas Act "have an excruciating awareness of the old border and can recite exactly where the borders were drawn in their old neighborhoods" (2008, 68). A similar understanding was conveyed by one of my informants. When I asked him, at our first meeting, to tell me the names of the players who most inspired him when he was young, he initially refused. "You wouldn't have heard of any of them," he told me simply. The title of the most exhaustive history of politicized coloured rugby during apartheid, *Forgotten Heroes* (Booley 1998), memorializes the same structured invisibility. If we consider acts of sporting and spectator violence to emerge from systemic erasure and historically cultivated experiences of imaginative resistance, I suggest that we are also able to regard the perpetrators of such acts as thoughtful and knowledgeable analysts of sporting performance. For, as Besteman observes, "When different understandings of the past collide, the result can be dramatic" (69).

4. The act has ties to other forms of political iconoclasm in South Africa. Peffer has analyzed cases of artistic iconoclasm, in which the shibboleths of Afrikaner identity and apartheid were repossessed, manipulated, and defaced for political purposes. Artist Wayne Barker, for example, copied Jacob Hendrik Pierneef's *Apies River* and painted over it to "[bring] to the surface that which the [original] repressed: all the horrors censored behind a screen of white purity, the empty land presided over by God, and the political ideology of apartheid that was their bolster" (Peffer 2005, 49). The 1984 call of the African National Congress to make South Africa's townships "ungovernable" could similarly be regarded as an iconoclastic gesture, insofar as it deliberately targeted the image of the order that the apartheid state sought to cultivate amid its machinery of repression.

5. Farred (1997, 14–15) has argued that the SACOS brand of politics transformed sporting fields into venues of resistance, and other scholars have expressed similar opinions. Douglas Booth, one of the preeminent historians of the South African sporting boycott, writes, "SACOS showed that every aspect of apartheid adversely touched sport. For most people this was a revelation given sport's status as a sacrosanct practice and it helped clarify the objectives of the sports boycott" (1998, 110). Elsewhere, Booth explains that while the SACOS stance was not necessarily original in South Africa, "it was SACOS, through its (clandestine) links with [the South African Non-Racial Olympic Committee], that challenged the peculiar apartheid ideology of sport and reminded the international sporting community that it could not ignore the broader conditions under which sport is played" (2003, 484).

6. Bracketing, of course, the structural violence of apartheid and settler colonialism in the Western Cape, which regulated the town's civic development in the first place.

7. By no means do I mean to imply that SARU rugby was a world without pol-

itics. While some of my informants refused to concede that point, others confirmed Odendaal's (1995) observation that "Coloured" and "African" teams frequently clashed with each other. Furthermore, as Farred (2000) and others have noted, the "Coloured" community was itself constituted of multiple, in many cases conflicting, identities and forms of attachment and belonging. Rugby became a locus for such conflicts as well, with informants reporting that clashes were common between Christian and Muslim teams, especially in the Western Cape.

8. Consider, in contrast, an instance described by Gwen Ansell in her fascinating account of the "hidden histories" of black rugby and jazz in South Africa. When he was voted Castle Lager Jazz Musician of the Year in 1968, she writes, Winston Monwabisi Manunku Ngozi "was still forced by apartheid legislation to play behind a screen at the Green Point Arts Centre while a white musician mimed his notes," and "the programme named the tenorist 'Winston Mann'" (2010, 129).

9. C. L. R. James, a scholar renowned for his writings about cricket and colonialism, seems to have approved, on similar terms, of so-called rebel cricket tours to apartheid South Africa. Such tours were widely reviled for their apparent acquiescence to the apartheid state's desire for international sporting recognition, but James thought differently: "Think of [what a successful tour showcasing African abilities in cricket] will mean to the African masses, their pride, their joy, their contact with the world outside, and their anger at this first proof, before the whole world, of the shameful suppression to which they are subjected. Will this strengthen apartheid? To believe that is to substitute laws for human emotions. Instead, the South African government will live to curse that this project was ever put forward" (2005, 313). To James, the presence of anomalous bodies and the sentiments that spectators could attach to them threatened apartheid ideology far more than the sort of strict nonparticipation advocated by Alan Paton and others.

CHAPTER 6

1. The primary source documents used in this chapter—including press releases, letters, and the transcript of the Northern Transvaal Rugby Union *dinkskrum*—are drawn from the Northern Transvaal Rugby Union/Blue Bulls Rugby Union Archives, located in Pretoria South Africa, hereafter cited as "BBRU Archives."

2. That performative dimension has emerged in theories of nationalism in at least two key ways. First, following from the influential work of Benedict Anderson (2003) and Gellner (1983), performance has been understood in terms of horizontal and collective national performances. Not only did the content of regional and national newspapers make new forms of solidarity possible, but the act of reading those newspapers and the knowledge that others were performing the same activity facilitated those forms of solidarity. Ivor Chipkin's (2007) analysis of South Africa's post-apartheid national condition can be considered in those terms. Second, a group of scholars have paid particular attention to the relationship between nationalism and artistic perfor-

mances. Works by Kelly Askew and Bob White, both cited in the present chapter, are relevant here, as well as Handler's (1988) study of Québécois nationalism, McGovern's account of the politics of identity in Guinea (2013), Apter's (2005) analysis of the Second World African Festival of Arts and Culture (FESTAC, an oil-infused national spectacle in postcolonial Nigeria), and many other analyses. Thomas Turino has written extensively about nationalism and performance in terms of indexical signs. He argues, following Peirce, that if indexical signs appear self-evidently linked to that which they index, then nationalists who mobilize indexicality are in fact using the force of self-evidence as the means to lock conceptions of national belonging in place (cf. Turino 2008, 2000, 1999). That theory of self-evident significance, which bears a strong similarity to work on "realism" (Feldman 1994, Tagg 1988) and "planar semiotics" (Dumit 1999, Greimas and Courtes 1982), resonates in exciting ways with evidence found in the present project, particularly with respect to the "certain" interpretations generated of young male players that were discussed in chapter 4.

3. In the Transvaal during the Great Depression, Afrikaans-speaking members of the developing urban middle class (e.g., teachers, small business owners, and ministers of the Dutch Reformed Church) sat precariously above a growing population of poor, rural Afrikaners who were losing their land to large-scale capitalist farms and then moving to cities like Pretoria and Johannesburg for work. To briefly summarize O'Meara's (1983) argument, the middle class believed that the ruling political coalition, which had formed to serve the interests of all whites in a British-controlled South Africa following the Second Anglo-Boer War (1899–1902), was representing only British industrialists through its policies. As the Afrikaans-speaking middle class saw it, those industrialists were working to strengthen South Africa's fealty to Britain's economic and political needs, rather than breaking the bonds of imperialism and allowing (white) South Africa to pursue its own best interests. Developing an "indigenous" Afrikaner identity, then, would serve both the interests of rural Afrikaans speakers (by protecting them from predation from British capitalists) and the middle class that, for the most part, made its living by serving that rural population socially, religiously, and economically.

4. Critical theorists, in particular, have suggested that radio's reproduction and dispersal of the "voice" of authority made it a novel tool for regimes that sought to foster particular interests among their subject populations. Buck-Morss (2002, 140) credits radio for enabling mass identification with political leaders, and Adorno and Horkheimer (2002, 95–96) note wryly that it was not long before the interactive telephone became radio, effectively transforming a device capable of revolutionizing dialog into one designed primarily for listening.

5. Those features of radio were evident not just on the SABC but on the now-infamous Radio Bantu stations. While those stations tolerated a wider range of political perspectives and music than is often recognized (Coplan 2008, 250), they nevertheless contributed to the apartheid regime's policy of "separate development" (Meintjes 2003, 59–60). Not only did they target African groups with music that had been identified as belonging to their distinct tribal traditions, but Magaziner's work on the Black

Consciousness movement (2010, 30) demonstrates that Radio Bantu stations explicitly endorsed certain political positions.

6. As Krabill has noted, the absence of television in the country during apartheid was enforced as part of the National Party's attempt to control the limits of representation. The enforcement included restricting the circulation of both alternative or unfamiliar (and thus dangerous) conceptions of what it meant to be "African" or South African. South Africans were largely denied access to news of the international boycotts of their country, and state media depicted protests within the nation's borders in only the most sanitized ways.

7. In that respect, switching on the radio to listen to rugby during apartheid was not only a way to pass the time but also a way of establishing the "fact of whiteness" (Hartigan 1997), which naturalized whiteness as a position of social and economic privilege. To emphasize that point, Vaillant, writing about early American radio, offers the example of the propagation of whiteness in the incredibly segregated city of Chicago: "The hegemonic sound of whiteness that predominated on local radio in Chicago in the 1920s extended the racialized contours of structural inequality in the built urban environment into the air itself" (2002, 57).

8. MacAloon has made a similar claim about filmic representations of sporting spectacles relative to representations by other means: "The Olympic Games have inspired a wealth of written and spoken commentary, and symphonic, balletic, and plastic artworks. Often these are rich and provocative, but they are commentaries on the spectacle, interpretive glosses that cannot capture the visual ecstasies and terrors of the original. Only film effectively translates the spectacles into another medium, and only two films of the scores that have been made—Leni Riefenstahl's *Olympia* of 1936 and Kon Ichikawa's film of the 1964 Tokyo Games—have really succeeded in capturing the epic visual quality in the Games" (1984, 245).

9. That concern is consistent with an ideology of realism, which takes the photographic or filmic image as an unmediated encounter with lived reality (cf. Barthes 1981; Nead 2011; Sontag 1973) rather than as an active process of perceptual colonization that constructs and legitimizes a distant omniscient observer who has been detached from the scene of the shot (Feldman 1994, 90; Tagg 1988).

10. In his letter to Kellermann, Denton asked, "Do we want to have the public of South Africa, where the climate for sports participation and support is one of the best in the world, participating and supporting sports or that the public will spend Saturday afternoons at home, inactive in front of the television?" (Denton to Kellermann, November 26, 1976, BBRU Archives). As if to underline the possibility that the spectators might be to blame, the archive includes an editorial by J.C. Meyer, cut from the Afrikaans daily newspaper *Die Beeld* and apparently published during roughly the same period as the letter, headlined "TV-rugby: Ons mense is net lui" (TV-rugby: Our people are just lazy).

11. I am not arguing that newspapers did not seek to describe the excitement of rugby's performance or that they had no capacity to influence how rugby was produced

or perceived. Although little seems to have been written about the relationship between rugby and the South African press in the early 20th century, Michael Oriard's (1993) fantastic account of the influence of newspapers on American football is indicative of the potential that may lie in that line of research. Additionally, Robert Denton himself credited newspapers for rugby's popularity in a letter to HJ Human of the SABC. "Rugby and newspapers have come a long way together," Denton wrote. "They have made a huge contribution to making rugby a popular sport" (Denton to Human, October 31, 1977, BBRU Archives).

12. Fittingly, an Afrikaans word meaning "televise," *beeldsaai*, contains the word *beeld* as well.

13. Robert Denton, Secretary of the Northern Transvaal Rugby Union, seems to have recognized this quite early on (even if he did significantly underestimate the subsequent influence of television). In his letter to Kellerman, he argued that "Television cannot 'make' rugby—on the contrary, without rugby sport on television is nothing" (Denton to Kellermann, November 26, 1976, BBRU Archives).

14. The SABC's "Guidelines on the Televising of Sponsored Events and Related Advertising," circulated to the NTRU in 1983 with a letter complaining that many of the guidelines were being violated, outline what aspects of rugby matches and other televised sporting events mattered most to the SABC. The guidelines focus exclusively on issues of presentation—on reminding sponsors and sports organizations of the SABC's right to dictate the terms of broadcasts and on delineating its policies on advertising and branding, emblems and signage (BBRU Archives).

15. While the rugby establishment's relationship with television was taking shape in their letters, television was a new medium, with new expectations for the public dissemination of rugby. Newspapers and radio, which (to paraphrase the secretary of the NTRU) had traveled the long road with rugby, may have received special access to players, coaches, and administrators, but television was gaining control over the eyes and ears of casual spectators, and its interests could not be ignored. Television's novelty also gave it an unexpected audacity. If newspapermen and radio commentators had a cultivated rapport with rugby teams and players, such that they might be unlikely to stoop to a public condemnation of a winning style, television broadcasters had no such qualms.

16. The SABC's advertising use code of 1983, based solely on the needs of the SABC's cameras, lumped rugby together with the rest of the "outdoor sports."

17. Peter Alegi's account of football in South Africa suggests that the relationship between football teams and television in South Africa may have been less contentious than was rugby's relationship with the medium. "SABC-TV first showed football matches in 1977," he writes, "and then began to broadcast live games in October 1981. When the SABC added a second channel in 1982, its palimpsest featured a tape-delayed 'match of the day' on Saturday nights and a dozen live matches, the rights to which the PSL sold for R250 000. Companies relished the advertisement potential of soccer on television—a mass medium that allowed potential access to millions of black households" (2004, 142).

18. Ron Krabill's analysis of the significance of television in South Africa lends yet more depth to this argument. In his work, Krabill suggests that television's in-built intertextuality brought with it significant political implications for apartheid-era social relations. White South Africans, he argues, watched the channel intended for them, SABC 1, but also found themselves clicking through (and reflecting on) programs on SABC 2 and 3, which had been produced with black South Africans in mind (2010, 92). If this is the case, then white South African football fans would have found themselves entering into, and enjoying, less-familiar social worlds when they tuned in to watch the sport.

19. A useful parallel can here be drawn to Andrew Horn's (1997) analysis of popular theater under apartheid. Describing ideologically motivated theater, which targeted both domestic and international white audiences, Horn differentiates between "the theatre of manipulation" and "the theatre of exploitation." In the first case, radio dramas aimed at whites "never touched upon current affairs and rarely include black characters, except as grunting servants" (75). Largely determined by the Nationalist government's control over broadcast media, the world depicted was not only almost exclusively white but also isolated, safe, and protected. In contrast, Horn sees the "theatre of exploitation" as following two different formulas. Either those plays depicted a young rural African arriving to the city, becoming corrupted, and returning home to his "true" home, or they were spectacles of "traditional" African practices and lifeways in their proper, rural place. In both narratives, state-run theater was meant to show that "the apartheid 'Separate Development' and 'Bantustan' relocation policies" were "reasonable, humane and historically legitimate" (75).

Considering the spectacle of the Rugby World Cup in terms of Horn's "ideological theatre," apartheid-era rugby had been akin to a "theatre of manipulation": it was an exclusively white space, prepared for white "actors" and white "stories," which reproduced South Africa as a strong, white (and male) nation. The post-apartheid government complicated that depiction with what amounted to Horn's "theatre of exploitation." In effect, the Bantustans (and the stories that whites told themselves about separate development) entered the wrong play. Parading ethnically marked African bodies together, alongside equally dehistoricized depictions of white farmers (who would have been slave owners), demonstrated that rugby could be an idiom that might produce the timelessness of a South African nation as a whole. While undoubtedly problematic, then, the World Cup opening and closing ceremonies became opportunities for the ANC to explore rugby's utility as a post-apartheid nation-building device.

20. The South African Rugby Football Union was renamed the South African Rugby Union (SARU) in 2004.

21. Although the rugby administrators objected to the investigation on the grounds that it was beyond the scope of the state to investigate a private business, the Constitutional Court's ruling hinged not on the importance of rugby to South Africa's "national interest" (as suggested by then-president Nelson Mandela) but on the questionable criteria on which the previous judge ruled that the president had "abdicated his responsibility" to conduct such an investigation in the first place (President of the Republic

of South Africa and Others v. South African Rugby Football Union and Others [1999], CCT 16/98, South African Law Reports). The ruling left undecided the question of the responsibility of professional rugby teams to the post-apartheid nation.

22. Incidentally, a similar connection seemed to be in effect in the narrative I was told about Western Province's post-apartheid rebranding. "You'll notice now," an administrator told me slyly, "that the team is slowly abandoning black and going back to their original colors." If the Stormers almost murdered their brand, its *beeld* was still alive and kicking.

23. My research suggested that black, coloured, and African South Africans recognized that tendency. Once, for example, a black member of the Bulls staff remarked to me that another South African professional team seemed to play one particular black player only at the end of their games: "It's basically like, 'Hey Darkie, go do something. Step or something. Go *dance*.'" In a single moment of critical sporting commentary, that staff member signaled much that is relevant to this chapter and, indeed, this book as a whole. By marking the player as "Darkie" in the voice of the team and demanding that he "dance," he gestured to the team's tendency (in his estimation) to read all black players not just as an undifferentiated mass but also as a mass that was identifiable solely through the lens of racist and historically derived schema that conceptualized black persons in terms of the performative capacities of their bodies. Also discernable in the remark is the man's belief that the team apparently was unwilling to build its collective performative identity around the black player's abilities. That player mattered only when the team's usual strategies failed, and he was obligated to overcome the failings of the team by himself.

24. As students of South African rugby and readers of Albert Grundlingh's work might observe, Afrikaner spectators often use associations with animals, particularly in nicknames, to link rugby players to a rural identity. That tendency to naturalize players, particularly those of Afrikaner descent, is noteworthy, writes Grundlingh, because it "correlated with a dimension of Afrikaner nationalism which had as its representational theme the notion of Afrikaners as solid, pioneering men of the soil, subsumed under the honorary title 'boere'" (1994, 418). "The Beast," though, appears to be of an entirely different order than "'Jakkals' (jackal) Keevy, 'Hassie' (bunny) Versfeldt, 'Koei' (cow) Brink," and the other nicknames Grundlingh references. While those names link the male athletic body with a particular species or thing, Mtawarira's nickname presents him as a nonhuman Other that is amorphous, undifferentiated, and not yet defined. Not only does the name demonstrate that Mtawarira's body cannot be comfortably situated with a dominant symbolic order (as can those of his white Afrikaans-speaking peers), but it also transforms the player into a kind of point of articulation between human and animal, rationalized motion and unstructured force. As a beast but no beast in particular, he is regarded as available for physical labor but, as Perry Sherouse (2016, 111) has argued in relation to other animal-related nicknames, lacking the capacities of "mind" necessary for creative or critical thought. By framing Mtawarira's actions as those of an unthinking "beast," spectators are freed from the responsibility of linking his perfor-

mative style with that of his teammates and thus reckoning (however briefly) with the social and historical dynamics that have generated South Africa's dominant rugby style (cf. Sanger 2013, 63).

25. The theoretical premise of that position is elegantly summarized by Steven Mock in his consideration of Canadian television commercials about hockey during the 2010 Winter Olympics. In Mock's analysis, hockey matters in those commercials not because of any qualities of hockey—or qualities of Canadian hockey in particular—but because it is a vehicle of national sentiment: "Hockey . . . takes on the role of a national totem, which as such is void of any intrinsic content. It is an empty signifier akin to a national flag, an otherwise random assortment of shapes and colours whose only meaning lies in its status as an emblem of the group" (2012, 207). Though Mock may intend to emphasize the mere presentation of hockey in those commercials, the argument of the present book suggests that even that presentation cannot be separated from hockey's performance—the ways that hockey, as played (and perceived as played) positions spectators such that the activity becomes locally meaningful. Mock, in fact, acknowledges his own positioning by writing (at the beginning of the same analysis), "I have to confess to being a Canadian who doesn't like hockey."

CONCLUSION

1. That perspective was articulated explicitly by only one player in the *Road to Orlando* documentary, Bandise Maku, a player of African descent. "I think for me, myself," he said, "it was a great feeling obviously for South African rugby to go play in Soweto and for people in Soweto to embrace us as they did." "And it was very clear," Maku added, "in how Victor [Matfield, the captain of the team] approached it, in terms of that it was a team, there was no other option, and we had to take the option and embrace it to the best of the opportunity" (Willemse 2010, 1:27:39).

2. When one enters a sporting stadium, one often feels as though one is moving into a world of comprehensible symbols, characters, and narratives. Loftus Versfeld, the stadium that is home to the Blue Bulls, produces that kind of sentiment. Loftus, as it is generally called, or (more tellingly) "Fortress Loftus," does not merely sit in but seems to loom over the residential neighborhood of Clydesdale in Pretoria. When one enters the stadium on a game day, one meets dark, cavernous, and concrete hallways, the reverberations of music, and a public-address system that seems to coax the body inward, away from the city. One finds one's designated section, at which point one bursts out of the darkness and into the light of the sun or, if it is an evening game, the glow of the stadium's massive floodlights. Perched high above the action that unfolds at the center of the Loftus bowl, one finds a perhaps unexpected echo of an argument often made about museums: by its very design, Loftus appears to protect and validate the performances contained therein (cf. T. Bennett 1994; Marcuse 2007; Rancière 2009).

This book has shown that the connections between museum and stadium, art object and sporting performance, are deeper than one might initially expect. Bodies move in semi-coordinated ways on sporting fields across South Africa and around the world, and viewers of those bodies do not tend to acknowledge the real stakes (be they physical or political or economic) to which those bodies expose themselves, until the autonomous frame that structures and legitimizes those performances is called into question. Stadiums like Loftus underwrite that autonomy. Not only do they provide the scale necessary to turn a performance into a spectacle (cf. MacAloon 1984), but they contain elaborate behind-the-scenes mechanisms to make sure the performance runs as smoothly as possible.

3. Housing the team's *beeld* was no small undertaking, even in a familiar stadium. A stadium manager at Loftus Versfeld told me that preparations for a typical Saturday game begin on the Monday before. She and her colleagues must confirm security arrangements, medical resources, police support, and plans for cleaning and disaster management. Game days feature a choreographed minute-to-minute routine. She checks in with the opposing team to make sure its needs are met, confirms that the right sponsors and advertisements are in place for the announcer, and verifies that emergency electricians, plumbers, and elevator mechanics are present and prepared. Occasionally, she told me, problems arise. In an important match against an opponent from New Zealand, for example, the stadium completely lost power. The problem was solved within 20 minutes, and the game continued as scheduled. Such moments demonstrate how vital procedures are to the autonomous unfolding of a Bulls match. Not only do procedures make the match seem autonomous, by enabling fans to direct their attention inward toward the field and to watch the match without interruption, but they also artfully cover their own tracks. In their very insignificance, routineness, and invisibility, these procedures effectively conceal the processes by which the autonomous match is generated.

4. As students of South African history will know, Retief and a delegation of fellow Voortrekkers were captured and killed by Dingane, a Zulu king, after an 1838 meeting to discuss territorial boundaries. For the purposes of the present book, the precise details of that meeting and of Retief's death are less relevant than the overtones suggested in Barend van Graan's mention of his name. To cite Retief in the context of the Bulls' trip to Orlando was to allude not only to the whiteness of the Bulls' fan base and to the movement of that fan base en masse into a historically black area but also to white fears of a violent "ambush" in the township. As I show in the pages to come, some fans and players acknowledged those fears directly.

5. Vlok Cilliers, a kicking coach for the Bulls, notes the importance of rugby itself in *Road to Orlando*, albeit briefly. Over grainy footage of an Orlando Pirates match, Cilliers says, "To take rugby as the first union to Soweto and go and play there and expose rugby to that community which is like 100 percent soccer is just amazing" (cited in Willemse 2010, 1:18:07).

6. In *Touch, Pause, Engage*, McGregor notes another variant of the historical awareness described here. She writes that, after the semifinal match, "the first time an important rugby match had been played in Soweto and the first time thousands of white Afrikaners had visited this iconic site of anti-apartheid resistance," "an SMS [text mes-

sage] . . . did the rounds remarking that the last time there were so many Afrikaners in Soweto, they were in Casspirs [armored troop transport vehicles]" (2011, 161–62).

7. McGregor's *Touch, Pause, Engage* offers such a powerful and evocative description of this celebration of whiteness and Afrikaner identity that it is worth presenting it in full. She writes, "I follow the sound of boeremusiek [a style of South African folk music that is closely associated with Afrikaner cultural identity] and come to a quite extraordinary sight: hundreds of men and women in blue shirts and blue wigs and blue hats flashing blue lights, milling around in the sunshine, quaffing golden beer from huge plastic glasses. Mountains of beer cans everywhere. A giant TV screen is replaying [a recent Bulls match against their semi-final opponents]. Next to it is the source of the boeremusiek: a makeshift stage where two guys in blue cowboy hats are performing live. It's a hugely cheerful scene . . . Behind the stage runs a fence, outside which are several black men, jigging along to the music. Just beyond them is the road, and bus after bus from the Nasrec park 'n' ride pulls up, disgorging waves of more blue-hued Bulle, looking slightly bemused as they weave their way through the black bystanders, seeking out the narrow gate into the bull pen. Some stop to get their pictures taken with the locals, like tourists" (2011, 160).

8. To emphasize that the fantastical integration unfolded on terms established by the Bulls and their roughly 40,000 fans is not to suggest that residents of Soweto were rendered submissive at any stage of the process. A Bulls employee, for example, recalled being struck by the appearance of a taxi with the phrase "Go Bulls!" on the back, as well as coming across someone who had combined the Orlando Pirates and Bulls logos on a flag so that it read "Orlando Bulls." As those instances suggest, residents of Soweto perhaps regarded the matches as moments of playful, even strategic hybridization—as passing curiosities, more than anything necessarily transformative.

9. That experience was arguably at its most pronounced for spectators who watched the Bulls matches at home. Since the Bulls transported their *beeld* to Orlando, the matches appeared—at least superficially—to alter neither the presentation of the team's rugby nor its performance. Crowd shots did the work of aesthetic compensation (Roche 2000), by showing the "unreality" of the occasion. Broadcasts were full of ecstatic Bulls supporters blowing vuvuzelas to demonstrate their enthusiasm and mingling in the streets with Soweto residents, drinking in shabeens and shopping at makeshift stalls. Viewers were therefore able to feel included in the fantastical integration of Soweto without ever leaving the comfort of their own homes. As one of my informants observed, though, that positionality drained the matches of even the most superficial openness and political possibility. "We saw a blink of it afterwards on television," he said, "but all along it felt like we were part of this huge thing." For that man, the mediation of television cameras took the experience of the matches and reduced them to a blink.

10. In general, rugby fans seemed to use their vuvuzelas in a way that differed completely from their football counterparts. One of my informants, a follower of both rugby and football, observed that football fans in South Africa tend to use their horns collectively, producing undulating waves of noise to convey their disdain for opponents and

referees and to show support for their own players. Rugby fans used their vuvuzelas to great effect as well, making it hard for players and coaches to communicate. But the rugby fans appeared to view the vuvuzela as a novelty item more than a tool of collective communication. In the crowd shots captured in the recorded broadcast of the match, some fans blow their vuvuzelas while others wave them around. Some blow them upward, others outward toward the field, and still others directly into the ears of the fans sitting in adjacent seats and rows.

WORKS CITED

Abnet, Dustin A. 2020. *The American Robot: A Cultural History*. Chicago: Chicago University Press.

Adhikari, Mohamed. 2005. *Not White Enough, Not Black Enough: Racial Identity in the South African Coloured Community*. Athens: Ohio University Press.

Adorno, Theodor W. 1967. *Prisms*. Cambridge, MA: MIT Press.

Adorno, Theodor W. 1978. Minima Moralia: *Reflections from Damaged Life*. London: Verso.

Adorno, Theodor W. 1997. *Aesthetic Theory*. Minneapolis: University of Minnesota Press. Originally published 1970.

Adorno, Theodor W. 2005. *In Search of Wagner*. New York: Verso.

Adorno, Theodor W. 2007a. "Commitment." In *Aesthetics and Politics*, 177–95. New York: Verso.

Adorno, Theodor W. 2007b. "On the Fetish Character in Music and the Regression of Listening." In *The Culture Industry: Selected Essays on Mass Culture*, edited by J. M. Bernstein, 29–60. New York: Routledge.

Adorno, Theodor W. 2007c. "The Schema of Mass Culture." In *The Culture Industry*, edited by J. M. Bernstein, 61–97. New York: Routledge.

Adorno, Theodor W., and Max Horkheimer. 2002. *Dialectic of Enlightenment: Philosophical Fragments*. Stanford: Stanford University Press.

Albertyn, J. R., and M. E. Rothmann. 1932. *The Poor White Problem in South Africa: Report of the Carnegie Commission*. Vol. 5, *Sociological Report*. Stellenbosch: Carnegie Commission.

Alegi, Peter C. 2002. "Playing to the Gallery? Sport, Cultural Performance, and Social Identity in South Africa, 1920s–1945." *International Journal of African Historical Studies* 35 (1): 17–38.

Alegi, Peter C. 2004. *Laduma! Soccer, Politics and Society in South Africa*. Scottsville: University of KwaZulu-Natal Press.

Alegi, Peter. 2010. *African Soccerscapes: How a Continent Changed the World's Game*. Athens: Ohio University Press.

Allen, Dean. 2003. "Beating Them at Their Own Game: Rugby, the Anglo-Boer War and Afrikaner Nationalism, 1899–1948." *International Journal of the History of Sport* 20 (3): 37–57.

Alvarez, Natalie. 2016. "Foul Play: Soccer's 'Infamous Thespians' and the Cultural Politics of Diving." *The Drama Review* 60 (1): 10–24.

Anderson, Benedict. 2003. *Imagined Communities*. New York: Verso.

Ansell, Gwen. 2010. "The Bellowing Bull and the Thing That Is Not Round: Jazz and the Hidden History of Black Rugby." In *Sport versus Art: A South African Contest*, edited by Chris Thurman, 123–30. Johannesburg: Wits University Press.

Apter, Andrew. 2005. *The Pan-African Nation: Oil and the Spectacle of Culture in Nigeria*. Chicago: University of Chicago Press.

Archer, Robert, and Antoine Bouillon. 1982. *The South African Game: Sport and Racism*. London: Zed Press.

Armstrong, Gary. 2003. *Football Hooligans: Knowing the Score*. New York: Berg.

Asad, Talal. 2003. *Formations of the Secular: Christianity, Islam, Modernity*. Stanford: Stanford University Press.

Ashforth, Adam. 1990. *The Politics of Official Discourse in Twentieth-Century South Africa*. Oxford: Clarendon Press.

Ashforth, Adam. 2005. *Witchcraft, Violence, and Democracy in South Africa*. Chicago: University of Chicago Press.

Askew, Kelly. 2002. *Performing the Nation: Swahili Music and Cultural Politics in Tanzania*. Chicago: University of Chicago Press.

Bale, John. 2002. *Imagined Olympians: Body Culture and Colonial Representation in Rwanda*. Minneapolis: University of Minnesota Press.

Barad, Karen. 2007. *Meeting the Universe Halfway: Quantum Physics and the Entanglement of Matter and Meaning*. Durham: Duke University Press.

Barnard, Rita. 2004. "*Bitterkomix*: Notes from the Post-apartheid Underground." *South Atlantic Quarterly* 103 (4): 719–54.

Barthes, Roland. 1974. *Mythologies*. London: Jonathan Cape.

Barthes, Roland. 1981. *Camera Lucida: Reflections on Photography*. Translated by Richard Howard. New York: Hill and Wang.

Bateson, Gregory. 1972. *Steps to an Ecology of Mind*. Chicago: University of Chicago Press.

Bearak, Barry. 2010. "Rugby Fans Go Offside and Run into Racial Reconciliation in South Africa." *New York Times*, June 2.

Becker, Howard S. 1984. *Art Worlds*. Berkeley: University of California Press.

Belting, Hans. 2014. *An Anthropology of Images*. Translated by Thomas Dunlap. Princeton: Princeton University Press.

Benhabib, Seyla. 1986. *Critique, Norm, and Utopia*. New York: Columbia University Press.

Benhabib, Seyla. 1992. *Situating the Self: Gender, Community, and Postmodernism in Contemporary Ethics*. New York: Routledge.

Beningfield, Jennifer. 2006. *The Frightened Land: Land, Landscape and Politics in South Africa in the Twentieth Century*. London: Routledge.

Benjamin, Walter. 1968. "Theses on the Philosophy of History." In *Illuminations*, 253–64. New York: Schocken Books.

Benjamin, Walter. 1972. "Rastelli erzählt . . ." In *Gesammelte Schriften*, edited by Rolf Tiedemann and Hermann Schweppenhäuser, 777–80. Frankfurt: Suhrkamp.

Benjamin, Walter. 2005. "Doctrine of the Similar." In *Walter Benjamin: Selected Writings*, vol. 4, *1931–1934*, edited by Michael W. Jennings, Howard Eiland, and Gary Smith, 694–98. Cambridge, MA: Harvard University Press.

Benjamin, Walter. 2003. "The Work of Art in the Age of Its Technological Reproducibility: Third Version." In *Walter Benjamin: Selected Writings*, vol. 4, *1938–1940*, edited by Howard Eiland and Michael W. Jennings, 251–83. Cambridge, MA: Harvard University Press.

Bennett, Jane. 2010. *Vibrant Matter: A Political Ecology of Things*. Durham: Duke University Press.

Bennett, Tony. 1994. "The Exhibitionary Complex." In *Culture/Power/History: A Reader in Contemporary Social Theory*, edited by Nicholas B. Dirks, Geoff Eley, and Sherry B. Ortner, 123–54. Princeton: Princeton University Press.

Berger, John. 2008. *Ways of Seeing*. London: Penguin Books.

Bernstein, J. M. 2001. *Adorno: Disenchantment and Ethics*. Cambridge: Cambridge University Press.

Besnier, Niko. 2012. "The Athlete's Body and the Global Condition: Tongan Rugby Players in Japan." *American Ethnologist* 39 (3): 491–510.

Besnier, Niko, and Susan Brownell. 2012. "Sport, Modernity, and the Body." *Annual Review of Anthropology* 41: 443–59.

Besteman, Catherine Lowe. 2008. *Transforming Cape Town*. California Series in Public Anthropology Berkeley: University of California Press.

Biehl, João. 2001. "*Vita*: Life in a Zone of Social Abandonment." *Social Text* 19 (3): 131–49.

Bloch, Ernst. 1996. *The Principle of Hope*. Cambridge, MA: MIT Press.

Bloom, Lisa. 1993. "National Geographic Society and Magazine: Technologies of Nationalism, Race, and Gender." In *Gender on Ice: American Ideologies of Polar Expeditions*, 57–82. Minneapolis: University of Minnesota Press.

Boas, Franz. 2010. *Primitive Art*. New York: Dover.

Bolsmann, Chris. 2010. "White Football in South Africa: Empire, Apartheid and Change, 1892–1977." *Soccer and Society* 11 (1–2): 29–45.

Bolsmann, Chris. 2012. "Representation in the First African World Cup: 'World-Class,' Pan-Africanism, and Exclusion." *Soccer and Society* 13 (2): 156–72.

Booley, Abdurahman (Manie). 1998. *Forgotten Heroes: History of Black Rugby, 1882–1992*. Cape Town: Manie Booley Publications.

Booth, Douglas. 1998. *The Race Game: Sport and Politics in South Africa*. New York: Frank Cass.

Booth, Douglas. 1999. "The Antinomies of Multicultural Sporting Nationalism: A Case Study of Australia and South Africa." *International Sports Studies* 21 (2): 5–25.

Booth, Douglas. 2003. "Hitting Apartheid for Six? The Politics of the South African Sports Boycott." *Journal of Contemporary History* 38 (3): 477–493.

Borchardt, Simon. 2011. "Testing Times." *SA Rugby*, August.

Botes, Conrad, and Anton Kannemeyer, eds. 1998. *The Best of Bitterkomix.* Vol. 1. Cape Town: Bitterkomix Pulp CC.

Bourdieu, Pierre. 1984. *Distinction: A Social Critique of the Judgement of Taste.* Cambridge, MA: Harvard University Press.

Bourdieu, Pierre. 2007 *Outline of a Theory of Practice.* New York: Cambridge University Press.

Bozzoli, Belinda. 1998. "Public Ritual and Private Transition: The Truth Commission in Alexandra Township, South Africa 1996." *African Studies* 57 (2): 167–95.

Breckenridge, Keith. 2005. "Verwoerd's Bureau of Proof: Total Information in the Making of Apartheid." *History Workshop Journal* 59: 83–108.

Brook, Diane L. 1996. "From Exclusion to Inclusion: Racial Politics and South African Educational Reform." *Anthropology and Education Quarterly* 27 (2): 204–31.

Brownell, Susan. 1995. *Training the Body for China: Sports in the Moral Order of the People's Republic.* Chicago: University of Chicago Press.

Buck-Morss, Susan. 1977. *The Origin of Negative Dialectics: Theodor W. Adorno, Walter Benjamin, and the Frankfurt Institute.* New York: Free Press.

Buck-Morss, Susan. 1989. *The Dialectics of Seeing: Walter Benjamin and the Arcades Project.* Cambridge, MA: MIT Press.

Buck-Morss, Susan. 1992. "Aesthetics and Anaesthetics: Walter Benjamin's Artwork Essay Reconsidered." *October* 62: 3–41.

Buck-Morss, Susan. 1994. "The Cinema Screen as Prosthesis of Perception: A Historical Account." In *The Senses Still: Perception and Memory as Material Culture in Modernity*, edited by C. Nadia Seremetakis, 45–62. Chicago: University of Chicago Press.

Buck-Morss, Susan. 2002. *Dreamworld and Catastrophe.* Cambridge, MA: MIT Press.

Buck-Morss, Susan. 2009. *Hegel, Haiti, and Universal History.* Pittsburgh: University of Pittsburgh Press.

Bürger, Peter. 2002. *Theory of the Avant-Garde.* Translated by Michael Shaw. Minneapolis: University of Minnesota Press.

Burstyn, Varda. 1999. *The Rites of Men: Manhood, Politics, and the Culture of Sport.* Toronto: University of Toronto Press.

Butler, Judith. 2009. *Frames of War: When Is Life Grievable?* New York: Verso.

Carlin, John. 2008. *Playing the Enemy: Nelson Mandela and the Game That Made a Nation.* New York: Penguin Press.

Carrington, Ben. 2010. *Race, Sport and Politics: The Sporting Black Diaspora.* London: SAGE.

Carroll, Noël. 2008. "Art and Alienation." In *The Life and Death of Images*, edited by Diarmuid Costello and Dominic Willsdon, 89–109. Ithaca: Cornell University Press.

Carter, Thomas. 2008. *The Quality of Home Runs: The Passion, Politics, and Language of Cuban Baseball*. Durham: Duke University Press.

Cash, Corrine, and Larry Swatuk. 2011. "Integrated Development Planning in South Africa: Lessons from the Dwars River Valley." *Urban Forum* 22: 53–73.

Cassidy, Rebecca. 2002. *The Sport of Kings: Kinship, Class and Thoroughbred Breeding in Newmarket*. Cambridge: Cambridge University Press.

Chance, Kerry Ryan. 2015a. "Sacrifice after Mandela: Liberalism and Liberation among South Africa's First Post-apartheid Generation." *Anthropological Quarterly* 88 (4): 857–79.

Chance, Kerry Ryan. 2015b. "'Where There Is Fire, There Is Politics': Ungovernability and Material Life in Urban South Africa." *Cultural Anthropology* 30 (2): 394–423.

Chandler, Timothy, and John Nauright. 1999. *Making the Rugby World: Race, Gender, Commerce*. London: Frank Cass.

Chen, Mel Y. 2012. *Animacies: Biopolitics, Racial Mattering, and Queer Affect*. Durham: Duke University Press.

Chidester, David. 1996. *Savage Systems: Colonialism and Comparative Religion in Southern Africa*. Charlottesville: University of Virginia Press.

Chipkin, Ivor. 2007. *Do South Africans Exist? Nationalism, Democracy and the Identity of "The People."* Johannesburg: Wits University Press.

Chiweshe, Manase Kudzai. 2016. "Social Positionality and Xenophobia: The Case of Rugby Player Tendai Mtawarira in South Africa." *Africology: The Journal of Pan African Studies* 9 (7): 132–49.

Clarke, Alan. 1992. "Figuring a Brighter Future." In *Sport and Leisure in the Civilizing Process: Critique and Counter-critique*, edited by Eric Dunning and Chris Rojek, 201–20. London: Palgrave Macmillan.

Coakley, Jay. 2004. "Sports and Children: Are Organized Programs Worth the Effort?" In *Sports in Society: Issues and Controversies*, 126–57. Boston: McGraw Hill.

Cock, Jacklyn. 1991. *Colonels and Cadres: War and Gender in South Africa*. Cape Town: Oxford University Press.

Cock, Jacklyn. 1989. *Maids and Madams: Domestic Workers under Apartheid*. Rev. ed. London: Women's Press.

Cock, Jacklyn, and Laurie Nathan, eds. 1989. *War and Society: The Militarisation of South Africa*. Cape Town: David Philip.

Coetzee, J. M. 1988. "Playing Total(itarian) Rugby." *Die Suid-Afrikaan* 16 (August–September): 4–6.

Coetzee, J. M. 1995. "Retrospect: The World Cup of Rugby." *Southern African Review of Books* 38: n.p.

Collins, Tony. 1998. *Rugby's Great Split: Class, Culture and the Origins of Rugby League Football*. London: Frank Cass.

Comaroff, Jean, and John L. Comaroff. 1991. *Of Revelation and Revolution: Christianity, Colonialism, and Consciousness in South Africa*. Vol. 1. Chicago: University of Chicago Press.

Comaroff, Jean, and John L. Comaroff. 1997. *Of Revelation and Revolution: The Dialectics of Modernity on a South African Frontier.* Vol. 2. Chicago: University of Chicago Press.

Comaroff, Jean, and John L. Comaroff. 2005. "Naturing the Nation: Aliens, Apocalypse, and the Postcolonial State." In *Sovereign Bodies: Citizens, Migrants, and States in the Postcolonial World,* edited by Thomas Blom Hansen and Finn Stepputat, 120–47. Princeton: Princeton University Press.

Connell, B. 1985. "Masculinity, Violence and War." In *War/Masculinity,* edited by P. Patton and R. Poole, 4–10. Sydney: Intervention.

Consalvo, Mia. 2009. "There Is No Magic Circle." *Games and Culture* 4 (4): 408–17.

Coombes, Annie E. 2003. *Visual Culture and Public Memory in a Democratic South Africa.* Durham: Duke University Press.

Coplan, David B. 2008. *In Township Tonight!* Chicago: University of Chicago Press.

Craven, D.H. 1959. *Oubaas Mark.* Johannesburg: Afrikaanse Pers-Boekhandel.

Danto, Arthur C. 1964. "The Artworld." *Journal of Philosophy* 61 (19): 571–84.

Danto, Arthur C. 1973. "Artworks and Real Things." *Theoria* 39 (1–3): 1–17.

Danto, Arthur C. 1981. *The Transfiguration of the Commonplace: A Philosophy of Art.* Cambridge, MA: Harvard University Press.

Danto, Arthur C. 1988. *The Politics of Imagination: The Lindley Lecture, University of Kansas, October 29, 1987.* Lawrence: University of Kansas.

Danto, Arthur C. 1992. *Beyond the Brillo Box: The Visual Arts in Post-historical Perspective.* Berkeley: University of California Press.

Danto, Arthur C. 1997. *After the End of Art: Contemporary Art and the Pale of History,* The A. W. Mellon Lectures in the Fine Arts. Princeton: Princeton University Press.

Danto, Arthur C. 2005. *The Philosophical Disenfranchisement of Art.* New York: Columbia University Press.

Danto, Arthur C. 2013. *What Art Is.* New Haven: Yale University Press.

Davies, John. 1986. "Politics, Sport and Education." *African Affairs* 85 (340): 351–63.

Donnelly, Peter. 1997. "Child Labour, Sport Labour: Applying Child Labour Laws to Sport." *International Review for the Sociology of Sport* 32 (4): 389–406.

Downey, Greg. 2005. *Learning Capoeira: Lessons in Cunning from an Afro-Brazilian Art.* Oxford: Oxford University Press.

Downey, Greg. 2007. "Producing Pain: Techniques and Technologies in No-Holds-Barred Fighting." *Social Studies of Science* 37 (2): 201–26.

Downey, Greg. 2010. "'Practice without Theory': A Neuroanthropological Perspective on Embodied Learning." *Journal of the Royal Anthropological Institute* 16, "Making Knowledge": S22–40.

Dubow, Saul. 1995. *Scientific Racism in Modern South Africa.* Cambridge: Cambridge University Press.

Dumit, Joseph. 1999. "Objective Brains, Prejudicial Images." *Science in Context* 12 (1): 173–201.

Dunning, Eric. 1994. "The Social Roots of Football Hooliganism: A Reply to the Critics of the 'Leicester School.'" In *Football, Violence and Social Identity*, edited by Richard Giulianotti, Norman Bonney, and Mike Hepworth, 123–52. New York: Routledge.

Dunning, Eric, Patrick Murphy, and John Williams. 1988. *The Roots of Football Hooliganism: An Historical and Sociological Study*. London: Routledge and Kegan Paul.

Dunning, Eric, and Kenneth Sheard. 2005. *Barbarians, Gentlemen and Players: A Sociological Study of the Development of Rugby Football*. Oxford: Martin Robertson.

Dyck, Noel. 2012. *Fields of Play: An Ethnography of Children's Sports*. Toronto: University of Toronto Press.

Eagleton, Terry. 1990. *The Ideology of the Aesthetic*. Oxford: Basil Blackwell.

Eastwood, Clint, dir. 2009. *Invictus*. Hollywood: Warner Brothers.

Edgar, Andrew. 2013. "Sportworld." *Sport, Ethics and Philosophy* 7 (1): 30–54.

Elbourne, Elizabeth. 2002. *Blood Ground: Colonialism, Missions, and the Contest for Christianity in the Cape Colony and Britain, 1799–1853*. Montreal: McGill-Queen's University Press.

Eliade, Mircea. 1959. *The Sacred and the Profane: The Nature of Religion*. New York: Harcourt, Brace and World.

Ellis, Stephen. 1998. "The Historical Significance of South Africa's Third Force." *Journal of Southern African Studies* 24 (2): 261–99.

Epstein, Debbie. 1996. "Marked Men: Whiteness and Masculinity." *Agenda: Empowering Women for Gender Equity* 14 (37): 49–59.

Erasmus, Zimitri. 2001. "Introduction: Re-imagining Coloured Identities in Post-apartheid South Africa." In *Coloured by History, Shaped by Place: New Perspectives on Colored Identities in Cape Town*, edited by Zimitri Erasmus, 13–28. Cape Town: Kwela Book.

Evans, Gavin. 1989. "Classrooms of War: the Militarisation of White South African Schooling." In *War and Society: The Militarisation of South Africa*, edited by Jacklyn Cock and Laurie Nathan, 283–97. Cape Town: David Philip.

Evans-Pritchard, E. E. 1937. *Witchcraft, Oracles, and Magic among the Azande*. Oxford: Clarendon Press.

Fabian, Johannes. 1996. *Remembering the Present: Painting and Popular History in Zaire*. Berkeley: University of California Press.

Fabian, Johannes. 1998. *Moments of Freedom: Anthropology and Popular Culture*. Charlottesville: University of Virginia Press.

Fabian, Johannes. 2004. "On Recognizing Things: The 'Ethnic Artefact' and the 'Ethnographic Object.'" *L'Homme* 170 (April–June): 47–60.

Fair, Laura. 1997. "Kickin' It: Leisure, Politics and Football in Colonial Zanzibar, 1900s–1950s." *Africa: Journal of the International African Institute* 67 (2): 224–51.

Farley, Rebecca. 2000. "Game." *M/C: A Journal of Media and Culture* 3 (5). http://www.journal.media-culture.org.au/0010/game.php

Farred, Grant. 2000. *Midfielder's Moment: Coloured Literature and Culture in Contemporary South Africa*. Boulder: Westview Press.

Farred, Grant. 1997. "The Nation in White: Cricket in Post-apartheid South Africa." *Social Text* 50 (1): 9–32.

Fausto-Sterling, Anne. 1995. "Gender, Race, and Nation: The Comparative Anatomy of 'Hottentot' Women in Europe, 1815–1817." In *Deviant Bodies*, edited by Jacqueline Urla and Jennifer Terry, 19–49. Bloomington: Indiana University Press.

Feld, Steven. 1988. "Aesthetics as Iconicity of Style, or 'Lift-up-over Sounding': Getting into the Kaluli Groove." *Yearbook for Traditional Music* 20: 74–113.

Feldman, Allen. 1991. *Formations of Violence: The Narrative of the Body and Political Terror in Northern Ireland*. Chicago: University of Chicago Press.

Feldman, Allen. 1994. "From Desert Storm to Rodney King via Ex-Yugoslavia: On Cultural Anaesthesia." In *The Senses Still: Perception and Memory as Material Culture in Modernity*, edited by C. Nadia Seremetakis, 87–108. Chicago: University of Chicago Press.

Feldman, Allen. 1999. "Commodification and Commensality in Political Violence in South Africa and Northern Ireland." *Ethnographia* 3 (1): 113–29.

Feldman, Allen. 2002. "Strange Fruit: The South African Truth Commission and the Demonic Economies of Violence." *Social Analysis: The International Journal of Social and Cultural Practice* 46 (3): 234–65.

Foster, Hal. 1996. *The Return of the Real*. Cambridge, MA: MIT Press.

Foster, Robert J. 2006. "From Trobriand Cricket to Rugby Nation: The Mission of Sport in Papua New Guinea." *International Journal of the History of Sport* 23 (5): 739–58.

Foucault, Michel. 1998. "What Is an Author?" In *Aesthetics, Method, and Epistemology*, edited by James D. Faubion, 205–22. New York: New Press.

Fransch, Chet J. P. 2010. "Porosity of Locational and Racial Identities amongst the 'Coloured Communities' of Stellenbosch, c. 1890–1960s." *African Studies* 69 (3): 403–22.

Freedberg, David. 1977. "The Structure of Byzantine and European Iconoclasm." In *Iconoclasm: Papers Given at the Ninth Spring Symposium of Byzantine Studies, University of Birmingham*, 165–77. Birmingham: Centre for Byzantine Studies, University of Birmingham.

Gay, Peter. 2008. *Modernism: The Lure of Heresey*. New York: W. W. Norton.

Gedye, Lloyd. 2017. "Building the Business of Rugby." *Finweek*, May 4. http://www.fin24.com/Finweek/Featured/building-the-business-of-rugby-20170426

Gell, Alfred. 1992. "The Technology of Enchantment and the Enchantment of Technology." In *Anthropology, Art and Aesthetics*, edited by Jeremy Coote and Anthony Shelton, 40–63. Oxford: Clarendon Press.

Gellner, Ernest. 1983. *Nations and Nationalism*. Ithaca: Cornell University Press.

Gendler, Tamar Szabó. 2000. "The Puzzle of Imaginative Resistance." *Journal of Philosophy* 97 (2): 55–81.

Gendler, Tamar Szabó. 2006. "Imaginative Resistance Revisited." In *The Architecture of the Imagination*, edited by Shaun Nichols, 149–74. Oxford: Oxford University Press.

Gerber, Hennie. 1982. *Craven*. Kaapstad: Tafelberg.

"Gijima Billionaire Withdraws From Lions Deal." 2011. *Moneyweb*, July 1. https://www
.moneyweb.co.za/archive/gijima-billionaire-withdraws-from-lions-deal/

Gikandi, Simon. 2006. "Picasso, Africa, and the Schemata of Difference." In *Beautiful Ugly: African and Diaspora Aesthetics*, edited by Sarah Nuttall, 30–59. Durham: Duke University Press.

Giliomee, Herman, and Tommy Bedford. 1986. "Die Politiek van toe Rugby." *Die Suid-Afrikaan* 8 (Winter): 56.

Gilroy, Paul. 1993. *The Black Atlantic: Modernity and Double Consciousness*. Cambridge, MA: Harvard University Press.

Gmelch, George. 1978. "Baseball Magic." *Human Nature* 1 (8): 32–39.

Goehr, Lydia. 2008. *Elective Affinities: Musical Essays on the History of Aesthetic Theory*. Columbia Themes in Philosophy, Social Criticism, and the Arts. New York: Columbia University Press.

Goldberg, RoseLee. 2001. "Dada." In *Performance Art: From Futurism to the Present*, 50–75. London: Thames and Hudson.

Gould, Stephen Jay. 2003. "The Streak of Streaks." In *Triumph and Tragedy in Mudville: A Lifelong Passion for Baseball*, 173–88. New York: W. W. Norton.

Govender, Prega. 2011. "Steroid Scourge Rages in School Rugby." *Times of South Africa*, May 29. https://www.timeslive.co.za/sport/rugby/2011-05-29-steroid-scourge-rag es-in-school-rugby/

Guha, Ranajit. 1997. *Dominance without Hegemony: History and Power in Colonial India*. Cambridge, MA: Harvard University Press.

Gumbrecht, Hans Ulrich. 2006. *In Praise of Athletic Beauty*. Cambridge, MA: Belknap Press, an imprint of Harvard University Press.

Greimas, A.J., and J. Courtes. 1982. *Semiotics and Language: An Analytical Dictionary*. Bloomington: Indiana University Press.

Grundlingh, Albert. 1994. "Playing for Power? Rugby, Afrikaner Nationalism and Masculinity in South Africa, c. 1900–70." *International Journal of the History of Sport* 11 (3): 408–30.

Grundlingh, Albert. 2008. "Rands for Rugby: Ramifications of the Professionalisation of South African Rugby, 1995–2007." In *The Changing Face of Rugby: The Union Game and Professionalism since 1995*, edited by Greg Ryan, 63–81. Newcastle: Cambridge Scholars Publishing.

Grundlingh, Albert, and Siegfried Huigen. 2008. *Van Volksmoeder tot Fokofpolisiekar: Kritiese Opstelle oor Afrikaanse Herinneringsplekke*. Stellenbosch: SUN Press.

Grundlingh, Marizanne, and Albert Grundlingh. 2019. "Fractured Fandom and Paradoxical Passions: Explaining Support for New Zealand All Black Rugby Teams in South Africa, 1960–2018." *International Journal of the History of Sport* 36 (1): 67–82.

Guttmann, Allen. 1978. *From Ritual to Record: the Nature of Modern Sports*. New York: Columbia University Press.

Hacking, Ian. 1990. *The Taming of Chance*. Cambridge: Cambridge University Press.

Halsall, Francis. 2016. "Actor-Network Aesthetics: The Conceptual Rhymes of Bruno Latour and Contemporary Art." *New Literary History* 47 (2–3): 439–61.

Hamm, Charles. 1991. "'The Constant Companion of Man': Separate Development, Radio Bantu and Music." *Popular Music* 10 (2): 147–73.

Hammett, Daniel. 2010. "Ongoing Contestations: The Use of Racial Signifiers in Post-apartheid South Africa." *Social Identities* 16 (2): 247–60.

Handler, Richard. 1988. *Nationalism and the Politics of Culture in Quebec.* Madison: University of Wisconsin Press.

Haraway, Donna. 2004. "A Manifesto for Cyborgs: Science, Technology, and Socialist Feminism in the 1980s." In *The Haraway Reader*, edited by Donna Haraway, 7–46. New York: Routledge.

Hart, Gillian. 2002. *Disabling Globalization: Places of Power in Post-apartheid South Africa.* Berkeley: University of California Press.

Hartigan, John, Jr. 1997. "Establishing the Fact of Whiteness." *American Anthropologist* 99 (3): 495–505.

Hayles, N. Katherine. 1999. *How We Became Posthuman: Virtual Bodies in Cybernetics, Literature, and Informatics.* Chicago: University of Chicago Press.

Healey, Luke. 2017. "Drawing the Foul: Diving and Visuality in Contemporary English Football." In *Football and the Boundaries of History: Critical Studies in Soccer*, edited by Brenda Elsey and Stanislao G. Pugliese, 13–30. New York: Palgrave Macmillan.

Hickel, Jason. 2014. "'Xenophobia' in South Africa: Order, Chaos, and the Moral Economy of Witchcraft." *Cultural Anthropology* 29 (1): 103–27.

Hilmes, Michelle. 2012. "Radio and the Imagined Community." In *The Sound Studies Reader*, edited by Jonathan Sterne, 351–62. New York: Routledge.

Hofmeyr, Isabel. 1987. "Building a Nation from Words: Afrikaans Language, Literature and Ethnic Identity, 1902–1924." In *The Politics of Race, Class and Nationalism in Twentieth Century South Africa*, edited by Shula Marks and Stanley Trapido, 95–123. London: Longman Group.

Holdstock, T. L. 1990. "Violence in Schools: Discipline." In *People and Violence in South Africa*, edited by Brian McKendrick and Wilma Hoffmann, 341–72. Oxford: Oxford University Press.

Holt, Richard. 1989. *Sport and the British: A Modern History.* Oxford: Oxford University Press.

Horn, Andrew. 1997. "South African Theatre: Ideology and Rebellion." In *Readings in African Popular Culture*, edited by Karin Barber, 73–80. Bloomington: Indiana University Press.

Horowitz, Gad. 1977. *Repression: Basic and Surplus Repression in Psychoanalytic Theory; Freud, Reich, and Marcuse.* Toronto: University of Toronto Press.

Horton, Robin. 1993. *Patterns of Thought in Africa and the West: Essays on Magic, Religion, and Science.* Cambridge: Cambridge University Press.

Howe, P. David. 2001. "An Ethnography of Pain and Injury in Professional Rugby Union: The Case of Pontypridd RFC." *International Review for the Sociology of Sport* 36 (3): 289–303.

Huggins, Mike. 2006. "Prologue: Setting the Scene; Second-Class Citizens? English Middle-Class Culture and Sport, 1850–1910; A Reconsideration." In *A Sport-Loving Society: Victorian and Edwardian Middle-Class England at Play*, edited by J. A. Mangan, 11–42. London: Routledge.

Hughes, Robert, and Jay Coakley. 1991. "Positive Deviance among Athletes: The Implications of Overconformity to the Sport Ethic." *Sociology of Sport Journal* 8: 307–25.

Huizinga, Johan. 1980. *Homo Ludens*. New York: Routledge.

Ingold, Tim. 2010. "Bringing Things to Life: Creative Entanglements in a World of Materials." *ESRC National Centre for Research Methods*, 1–14.

Isaacs-Martin, Wendy, and Theodore Petrus. 2012. "The Multiple Meanings of Coloured Identity in South Africa." *Africa Insight* 42 (1): 87–102.

Jackson, Michael. 1998. Minima Ethnographica: *Intersubjectivity and the Anthropological Project*. Chicago: University of Chicago Press.

Jacobs, Sean. 2010. "'It Wasn't That I Did Not Like South African Football': Media, History and Biography." *Soccer and Society* 11 (1–2): 95–104.

James, C. L. R. 2005. *Beyond a Boundary*. London: Yellow Jersey Press.

Jameson, Fredric. 2007. *Late Marxism: Adorno or the Persistence of the Dialectic*. New York: Verso.

Jansen, Julian. 2011. "Seuns 'weggeraap' vir Blou Bul-rugby." *Rapport*, February 27, 2011.

Jay, Martin. 1996. *The Dialectical Imagination: A History of the Frankfurt School and the Institute of Social Research, 1923–1950*. Berkeley: University of California Press.

Jethro, Duane. 2014. "Vuvuzela Magic: The Production and Consumption of 'African' Cultural Heritage during the FIFA 2010 World Cup." *African Diaspora* 7:177–204.

Kapferer, Bruce. 1986. "Performance and the Structuring of Meaning and Experience." In *The Anthropology of Experience*, edited by Victor Turner and Edward Bruner, 188–203. Urbana: University of Illinois Press.

Karstens, Gerdie. 2011. "4 in Cravenweek positief getoets vir taboe middels." *Die Beeld*, April 8.

Keane, Webb. 2005. "Signs Are Not the Garb of Meaning: On the Social Analysis of Material Things." In *Materiality*, edited by Daniel Miller, 182–205. Durham: Duke University Press.

Keil, Charles. 1995. "The Theory of Participatory Discrepancies: A Progress Report." *Ethnomusicology* 39 (1): 1–19.

Kelly, John. 2005. "Integrating America: Jackie Robinson, Critical Events and Baseball Black and White." *International Journal of the History of Sport* 22 (6): 1011–35.

Kirksey, Eben, and Stefan Helmreich. 2010. "The Emergence of Multispecies Ethnography: A Special Guest-Edited Issue of Cultural Anthropology." *Cultural Anthropology* 25 (4): 545–76.

Kopytoff, Igor. 1986. "The Cultural Biography of Things: Commodization as Process." In *The Social Life of Things: Commodities in Cultural Perspective*, edited by Arjun Appadurai, 64–91. Cambridge: Cambridge University Press.

Kosek, Jake. 2010. "Ecologies of Empire: On the New Uses of the Honeybee." *Cultural Anthropology* 25 (4): 650–78.

Krabill, Ron. 2010. *Starring Mandela and Cosby: Media and the End(s) of Apartheid.* Chicago: University of Chicago Press.

Kuper, Leo. 1954. "The Control of Social Change: A South African Experiment." *Social Forces* 33 (1): 19–29.

Kynoch, Gary. 2016. "Apartheid's Afterlives: Violence, Policing and the South African State." *Journal of Southern African Studies* 42 (1): 65–78.

Lake, Robert J. 2009. "Real Tennis and the Civilising Process." *Sport in History* 29 (4): 553–76.

Lapchick, Richard E. 1979. "South Africa: Sport and Apartheid Politics." *Annals of the American Academy of Political and Social Science* 445: 155–65.

Levi, Heather. 2008. *The World of Lucha Libre: Secrets, Revelations, and Mexican National Identity.* Durham: Duke University Press.

Lévi-Strauss, Claude. 1966. *The Savage Mind.* Chicago: University of Chicago Press.

Lévi-Strauss, Claude. 1967. *Structural Anthropology.* Garden City: Anchor Books.

Light, Richard, and David Kirk. 2000. "High School Rugby, the Body and the Reproduction of Hegemonic Masculinity." *Sport, Education and Society* 5 (2): 163–76.

Limón, José E. 1994. *Dancing with the Devil.* Madison: Wisconsin University Press.

Livingston, Julie. 2012. *Improvising Medicine: An African Oncology Ward in an Emerging Cancer Epidemic.* Durham: Duke University Press.

Livingston, Julie, and Jasbir K. Puar. 2011. "Interspecies." *Social Text* 29 (1): 3–14.

Lucas, Gavin. 2006. *An Archaeology of Colonial Identity: Power and Material Culture in the Dwars Valley, South Africa.* New York: Springer Science and Business Media.

MacAloon, John J. 1984. *Rite, Drama, Festival, Spectacle: Rehearsals Towards a Theory of Cultural Performance.* Philadelphia: Institute for the Study of Human Issues.

Magazine, Roger. 2007. *Golden and Blue Like My Heart: Masculinity, Youth and Power among Soccer Fans in Mexico.* Tucson: University of Arizona Press.

Magaziner, Daniel R. 2010. *The Law and the Prophets: Black Consciousness in South Africa, 1968–1977.* Athens: Ohio University Press.

Mail and Guardian. 2008. "ANC Throws Weight behind Bok Emblem." October 10.

Mail and Guardian. 2009. "A Beastly Affair for SA Sport." November 20.

Maingard, J. 1997. "Imag(in)ing the South African Nation: Representations of Identity in the Rugby World Cup 1995." *Theatre Journal* 49 (1): 15–28.

Malcom, Nancy L. 2006. "'Shaking It Off' and 'Toughing It Out': Socialization to Pain and Injury in Girls' Softball." *Journal of Contemporary Ethnography* 35 (5): 495–525.

Mamdani, Mahmood. 1996. *Citizen and Subject.* Princeton: Princeton University Press.

Mamdani, Mahmood. 2002. "Amnesty or Impunity? A Preliminary Critique of the Report of the Truth and Reconciliation Commission of South Africa (TRC)." *Diacritics* 32 (3–4): 33–59.

Mangan, J. A. 1981. *Athleticism in the Victorian and Edwardian Public School: The Emergence and Consolidation of an Educational Ideology.* Cambridge: Cambridge University Press.

Mangan, J. A. 1996. "'Muscular, Militaristic and Manly': The British Middle-Class Hero as Moral Messenger." *International Journal of the History of Sport* 13 (1): 28–47.

Marcuse, Herbert. 2007. "The Affirmative Character of Culture." In *Art and Liberation: Collected Papers of Herbert Marcuse*, vol. 4, edited by Douglas Kellner, 82–112. New York: Routledge.

Marks, Shula. 2002. "An Epidemic Waiting to Happen? The Spread of HIV/AIDS in South Africa in Social and Historical Perspective." *African Studies* 61 (1): 13–26.

Markula, Prikko, and Richard Pringle. 2006. *Foucault, Sport and Exercise: Power, Knowledge and Transforming the Self*. New York: Routledge.

Massumi, Brian. 2014. *What Animals Teach Us about Politics*. Durham: Duke University Press.

Matravers, Derek. 2013. "Fictional Assent and the (So-Called) 'Puzzle of Imaginative Resistance.'" In *Imagination, Philosophy, and the Arts*, edited by Matthew Kieran and Dominic McIver Lopes, 90–105. New York: Routledge.

Mauss, Marcel. 1979. "Body Techniques." In *Sociology and Psychology: Essays*, 97–119. London: Routledge.

Mazer, Sharon. 2005. "'Real' Wrestling / 'Real' Life." In *Steel Chair to the Head: The Pleasure and Pain of Professional Wrestling*, edited by Nicholas Sammond, 67–87. Durham: Duke University Press.

Mbembe, Achille. 2003. "Necropolitics." *Public Culture* 15 (1): 11–40.

Mbembe, Achille. 2008a. "Aesthetics of Superfluity." In *Johannesburg: The Elusive Metropolis*, edited by Sarah Nuttall and Achille Mbembe, 37–67. Durham: Duke University Press.

Mbembe, Achille. 2008b. "The Politics of Racial Reconciliation in South Africa." *Public Culture* 20 (1): 5–18.

McClintock, Anne. 1991. "'No Longer in a Future Heaven': Women and Nationalism in South Africa." *Transition* 51: 104–23.

McClintock, Anne. 1995. *Imperial Leather: Race, Gender and Sexuality in the Colonial Contest*. New York: Routledge.

McDevitt, Patrick. 2004. *May the Best Man Win: Sport, Masculinity, and Nationalism in Great Britain and the Empire, 1880–1935*. New York: Palgrave Macmillan.

McGovern, Michael. 2013. *Unmasking the State: Making Guinea Modern*. Chicago: University of Chicago Press.

McGregor, Liz. 2011. *Touch, Pause, Engage! Exploring the Heart of South African Rugby*. Johannesburg: Jonathan Ball.

McGregor, Liz. 2010. "Blue Bulls: The Great Trek to Soweto." *The Leader*, May 13.

Mehlman, Jeffrey. 1993. *Walter Benjamin for Children: An Essay on His Radio Years*. Chicago: University of Chicago Press.

Mehta, Uday Singh. 1999. *Liberalism and Empire: A Study in Nineteenth-Century British Liberal Thought*. Chicago: University of Chicago Press.

Meintjes, Louise. 2003. *Sound of Africa! Making Music Zulu in a South African Studio*. Durham: Duke University Press.

Meintjes, Louise. 2017. *Dust of the Zulu: Ngoma Aesthetics after Apartheid*. Durham: Duke University Press.

Merrett, Christopher. 1995. *A Culture of Censorship*. Macon, GA: Mercer University Press.

Messner, Michael A. 1990. "When Bodies Are Weapons: Masculinity and Violence in Sport." *International Review for the Sociology of Sport* 25: 203–19.

Mitchell, Timothy. 1991. "The Limits of the State: Beyond Statist Approaches and Their Critics." *American Political Science Review* 85 (1): 77–96.

Mitchell, W. J. T. 1994. *Picture Theory: Essays on Verbal and Visual Representation*. Chicago: University of Chicago Press.

Mitchell, W. J. T. 1996. "What Do Pictures 'Really' Want?" *October* 77: 71–82.

Mitchell, W. J. T. 2005. *What Do Pictures Want? The Lives and Loves of Images*. Chicago: University of Chicago Press.

Mitchell, W. J. T. 2011. *Cloning Terror: The War of Images, 9/11 to the Present*. Chicago: University of Chicago Press.

Mock, Steven J. 2012. "'Whose Game They're Playing': Nation and Emotion in Canadian TV Advertising during the 2010 Winter Olympics." *Studies in Ethnicity and Nationalism* 12 (1): 206–26.

Moodie, T. Dunbar. 1975. *The Rise of Afrikanerdom: Power, Apartheid, and the Afrikaner Civil Religion*. Berkeley: University of California Press.

Morgan, John W., and Geoffrey Nicholson. 1959. *Report on Rugby*. London: Heinemann.

Morrell, Robert. 1994. "Boys, Gangs, and the Making of Masculinity in the White Secondary Schools of Natal, 1880–1930." *Masculinities* 2 (2): 56–82.

Morrell, Robert, ed. 2001a. *Changing Men in Southern Africa*. Pietermaritzburg: University of Natal Press.

Morrell, Robert. 2001b. "Corporal Punishment and Masculinity in South African Schools." *Men and Masculinities* 4 (2): 140–57.

Morrell, Robert. 2001c. "Corporal Punishment in South African Schools: A Neglected Explanation for Its Persistence." *South African Journal of Education* 21 (4): 292–99.

Narayan, Kirin. 1993. "How Native Is a 'Native' Anthropologist?" *American Anthropologist* 95 (3): 671–86.

Nattrass, Nicoli, and Jeremy Seekings. 2005. *Class, Race, and Inequality in South Africa*. New Haven: Yale University Press.

Nauright, John. 1996. "'A Besieged Tribe'? Nostalgia, White Cultural Identity and the Role of Rugby in a Changing South Africa." *International Review for the Sociology of Sport* 31 (1): 69–86.

Nauright, John. 1997. *Sport, Cultures and Identities in South Africa*. Edited by Stephen Wagg. Sport and Nation. London: Leicester University Press.

Nead, Lynda. 2011. "Stilling the Punch: Boxing, Violence and the Photographic Image." *Journal of Visual Culture* 10 (3): 305–23.

Nehamas, Alexander. 1999. *Virtues of Authenticity: Essays on Plato and Socrates*. Princeton: Princeton University Press.

Nel, Carryn-Ann. 2011. "Nek beseer in rugbystryd: Hy is skuldig." *Die Beeld*, April 5.

Nel, Zelim, and Junior Bester. 2015. "Saru's Black Player Plan No Quota System." *Cape Argus*, February 25.

Newman, James. 2013. *Videogames*. New York: Routledge.

Niehaus, Isak. 2014. "Warriors of the Rainbow Nation? South African Rugby after Apartheid." *Anthropology Southern Africa* 37 (1–2): 68–80.

Nixon, Rob. 1992. "Apartheid on the Run: The South African Sports Boycott." *Transition* 58: 68–88.

Nkomo, Mokubung, Zanele Mkwanazi-Twala, and Nazir Carrim. 1995. "The Long Shadow of Apartheid Ideology: The Case of Open Schools in South Africa." In *Racism and Anti-Racism in World Perspective*, edited by Benjamin Bowser, 261–84. Thousand Oaks: SAGE.

Nuttall, Sarah. 2009. *Entanglement: Literary and Cultural Reflections on Post-apartheid*. Johannesburg: Wits University Press.

Odendaal, André. 1995. "The Thing That Is Not Round: The Untold History of Black Rugby in South Africa." In *Beyond the Tryline: Rugby and South African Society*, edited by Albert Grundlingh and André Odendaal, 24–63. Johannesburg: Ravan Press.

O'Meara, Dan. 1983. *Volkskapitalisme: Class, Capital and Ideology in the Development of Afrikaner Nationalism, 1934–1948*. Cambridge: Cambridge University Press.

One of Many Who Love "The Making of English Men." 1897. Letter to the editor. *Times*, September 25.

Oriard, Michael. 1981. "Professional Football as Cultural Myth." *Journal of American Culture* 4 (3): 27–41.

Oriard, Michael. 1993. *Reading Football: How the Popular Press Created an American Spectacle*. Chapel Hill: University of North Carolina Press.

Overman, Steven J. 2010. *Living Out of Bounds: The Male Athlete's Everyday Life*. Lincoln: University of Nebraska Press.

Parsons, Timothy. 2004. *Race, Resistance, and the Boy Scout Movement in British Colonial Africa*. Athens: Ohio University Press.

Peffer, John. 2005. "Censorship and Iconoclasm: Unsettling Monuments." *RES: Anthropology and Aesthetics* 48: 45–60.

Peffer, John. 2009. *Art and the End of Apartheid*. Minneapolis: University of Minnesota Press.

Pinney, Christopher. 2005. "Things Happen: Or, From Which Moment Does That Object Come?" In *Materiality*, edited by Daniel Miller, 256–72. Durham: Duke University Press.

Pope, S. W. 1996. "Amateurism and American Sports Culture: The Invention of an Athletic Tradition in the United States, 1870–1900." *International Journal of the History of Sport* 13 (3): 290–309.

Posel, Deborah. 2001. "Race as Common Sense: Racial Classification in Twentieth-Century South Africa." *African Studies Review* 44 (2): 87–113.

Potgieter, Carl. 2008. "Unleash the 'Beast.'" *Finding Touch: Transformation and Development in SA Rugby* 20: 30–32.

Price, Sally. 2001. *Primitive Art in Civilized Places*. Chicago: University of Chicago Press.

Pringle, Richard. 2009. "Defamiliarizing Heavy-Contact Sports: A Critical Examination of Rugby, Discipline, and Pleasure." *Sociology of Sport Journal* 26: 211–34.

Pronger, Brian. 1999. "Outta my Endzone: Sport and the Territorial Anus." *Journal of Sport and Social Issues* 23 (4): 373–89.

Pronger, Brian. 2000. "Homosexuality and Sport: Who's Winning?" In *Masculinities, Gender Relations, and Sport*, edited by J. McKay, M. Messner, and D. Sabo, 222–44. London: SAGE.

Pronger, Brian. 2002. *Body Fascism: Salvation in the Technology of Physical Fitness.* Toronto: University of Toronto Press.

Rademeyer, Cobus. 2014. "Entrenching Apartheid in South African Sport, 1948 to 1980: The Shaping of a Sporting Society during the Strijdom-, Verwoerd- and Vorster Administrations." *Journal for Contemporary History* 39 (2): 119–37.

Ranciére, Jacques. 2009. "Contemporary Art and the Politics of Aesthetics." In *Communities of Sense: Rethinking Aesthetics and Politics*, edited by Beth Hinderliter, Williams Kaizen, Vered Maimon, Jaleh Mansoor, and Seth McCormick, 31–50. Durham: Duke University Press.

Randle, Tracey. 2014. "The Inheritance of Loss." In *Winelands, Wealth and Work: Transformations in the Dwars River Valley, Stellenbosch*, edited by Kees van der Waal, 27–54. Pietermaritzburg: University of KwaZulu-Natal Press.

Ray, Gene. 2005. *Terror and the Sublime in Art and Critical Theory.* New York: Palgrave Macmillan.

Reid, Graeme, and Liz Walker, eds. 2005. *Men Behaving Differently: South African Men since 1994.* Cape Town: Double Storey Books.

Robins, Steven L. 2008. *From Revolution to Rights in South Africa: Social Movements, NGOs and Popular Politics after Apartheid.* Pietermaritzburg: University of KwaZulu-Natal Press.

Roche, Maurice. 2000. *Mega-Events and Modernity: Olympics and Expos in the Growth of Global Culture.* New York: Routledge.

Roderick, Martin, Ivan Waddington, and Graham Parker. 2000. "Playing Hurt: Managing Injuries in English Professional Football." *International Review for the Sociology of Sport* 35 (2): 165–80.

Ruberg, Bonnie. 2019. *Video Games Have Always Been Queer.* New York: New York University Press.

Ryan, Greg, ed. 2008. *The Changing Face of Rugby: The Union Game and Professionalism since 1995.* Newcastle: Cambridge Scholars Publishing.

Ryan, Joan. 2000. *Little Girls in Pretty Boxes: The Making and Breaking of Elite Gymnasts and Figure Skaters.* New York: Warner Books.

Sahlins, Marshall. 1981. *Historical Metaphors and Mythical Realities: Structure in the Early History of the Sandwich Islands Kingdom.* ASAO Special Publications. Ann Arbor: University of Michigan Press.

Samudra, Jaida Kim. 2008. "Memory in Our Body: Thick Participation and the Translation of Kinesthetic Experience." *American Ethnologist* 35 (4): 665–81.

Sanger, Nadia. 2013. "Imagining Possibilities: Feminist Cultural Production, Non-violent Identities, and Embracing the Other in Post-colonial South Africa." *African Identities* 11 (1): 61–78.

Schieffelin, Edward L. 1985. "Performance and the Cultural Construction of Reality." *American Ethnologist* 12 (4): 707–24.

Schneewind, J. B. 1998. *The Invention of Autonomy: A History of Modern Moral Philosophy*. Cambridge: Cambridge University Press.

Schneider, Rebecca. 2011. *Performance Remains*. New York: Routledge.

Seekings, Jeremy. 2008. "The Continuing Salience of Race: Discrimination and Diversity in South Africa." *Journal of Contemporary African Studies* 26 (1): 1–25.

Seel, Martin. 2005. *Aesthetics of Appearing*. Translated by John Farrell. Stanford: Stanford University Press.

Seremetakis, C. Nadia, ed. 1994. *The Senses Still: Perception and Memory as Material Culture in Modernity*. Chicago: University of Chicago Press.

Seremetakis, C. Nadia. 2019. *Sensing the Everyday: Dialogues from Austerity Greece*. New York: Routledge.

Serres, Michel. 2007. *The Parasite*. Minneapolis: University of Minnesota Press.

Sharp, John. 1998. "'Non-Racialism' and Its Discontents: A Post-apartheid Paradox." *International Social Science Journal* 50 (156): 243–52.

Sherouse, Perry. 2016. "Skill and Masculinity in Olympic Weightlifting: Training Cues and Cultivated Craziness in Georgia." *American Ethnologist* 43 (1): 103–15.

Shore, Bradd. 1994. "Marginal Play: Sport at the Borderlands of Time and Space." *International Review for the Sociology of Sport* 29 (4): 349–65.

Smith, Nicholas Rush. 2017. "The Rule of Rights: Comparative Lessons from Twenty Years of South African Democracy." *Comparative Politics* 50 (1): 123–41.

Sontag, Susan. 1973. *On Photography*. New York: Farrar, Straus and Giroux.

Sourgen, Gavin. 2010. "Artless Sport and Sportless Art: Democracy's Dilemmas of Representation." In *Sport versus Art: A South African Contest*, edited by Chris Thurman, 112–22. Johannesburg: Wits University Press.

Starn, Orin. 2011. *The Passion of Tiger Woods: An Anthropologist Reports on Golf, Race, and Celebrity Scandal*. Durham: Duke University Press.

Steenveld, Lynette, and Larry Strelitz. 1998. "The 1995 Rugby World Cup and the Politics of Nation-Building in South Africa." *Media, Culture and Society* 20: 609–29.

Stewart, Kathleen. 2007. *Ordinary Affects*. Durham: Duke University Press.

Stoddart, Brian. 1988. "Sport, Cultural Imperialism, and Colonial Response in the British Empire." *Comparative Studies in Society and History* 30 (4): 649–73.

Stoler, Ann L. 1995. *Race and the Education of Desire: Foucault's "History of Sexuality" and the Colonial Order of Things*. Durham: Duke University Press.

Stoler, Ann L. 2001. "Tense and Tender Ties: The Politics of Comparison in North American History and (Post) Colonial Studies." *Journal of American History* 88 (3): 829–65.

Tagg, John. 1988. *The Burden of Representation: Essays on Photographies and Histories*. Amherst: University of Massachusetts Press.

Taussig, Michael T. 1980. *The Devil and Commodity Fetishism in South America*. Chapel Hill: University of North Carolina Press.

Taussig, Michael T. 1992. *The Nervous System*. New York: Routledge.

Taussig, Michael T. 1993. *Mimesis and Alterity: A Particular History of the Senses*. New York: Routledge.

Trimbur, Lucia. 2013. *Come Out Swinging: The Changing World of Boxing in Gleason's Gym*. Princeton: Princeton University Press.

Trouillot, Michel-Rolph. 1995. *Silencing the Past: Power and the Production of History*. Boston: Beacon Press.

Turino, Thomas. 1999. "Signs of Imagination, Identity, and Experience: A Peircian Semiotic Theory for Music." *Ethnomusicology* 43 (2): 221–55.

Turino, Thomas. 2000. *Nationalists, Cosmopolitans, and Popular Music in Zimbabwe*. Chicago: University of Chicago Press.

Turino, Thomas. 2008. *Music as Social Life: The Politics of Participation*. Chicago: University of Chicago Press.

Vaillant, Derek W. 2002. "Sounds of Whiteness: Local Radio, Racial Formation, and Public Culture in Chicago, 1921." *American Quarterly* 54 (1): 25–66.

van der Berg, René-Jean, and Hanri Wondergem. 2011. "Derde van skoolseuns gebruik steroïde; hoofde tjoepstil." *Rapport*, June 4, 2011.

van der Heijden, Ingrid. 2014. "Women as 'Dorp Supporters': New Opportunities for Female Entrepreneurship." In *Winelands, Wealth and Work: Transformations in the Dwars River Valley, Stellenbosch*, edited by Kees van der Waal, 155–75. Pietermaritzburg: University of KwaZulu-Natal Press.

van der Riet, Jane. 1995. "Triumph of the Rainbow Warriors: Gender, Nationalism and the Rugby World Cup." *Agenda: Empowering Women for Gender Equity* 11 (27): 98–110.

van der Waal, Kees. 2014. "Researching the Social Experience of Transformation in the Dwars River Valley." In *Winelands, Wealth and Work: Transformations in the Dwars River Valley, Stellenbosch*, edited by Kees van der Waal, 3–26. Pietermaritzburg: University of KwaZulu-Natal Press.

Viviers, Gerhard. 1971. *Rugby Agter Doringdraad: Agter die Skerms Saam Met die 1969/70-Springbokke in England*. Pretoria: J. P. van der Walt en Seun (Edms) Bpk.

von Schnitzler, Antina. 2013. "Traveling Technologies: Infrastructure, Ethical Regimes, and the Materiality of Politics in South Africa." *Cultural Anthropology* 28 (4): 670–93.

Vossen, Emma. 2018. "The Magic Circle and Consent in Gaming Practices." In *Feminism in Play*, edited by Kishonna L. Gray, Gerald Voorhees, and Emma Vossen, 205–20. Cham, Switzerland: Palgrave Macmillan.

Wacquant, Loïc. 1995. "The Pugilistic Point of View: How Boxers Think and Feel about Their Trade." *Theory and Society* 24 (4): 489–535.

Wacquant, Loïc. 2004. *Body and Soul: Notebooks of an Apprentice Boxer*. New York: Oxford University Press.

Wacquant, Loïc. 2007. "The Social Logic of Sparring: On the Body as Practical Strate-gist." In *Physical Culture, Power, and the Body*, edited by Jennifer Hargreaves and Patricia Vertinsky, 142–57. New York.

Waddington, Ivan. 2004. "Sport and Health: A Sociological Perspective." In *Handbook of Sports Studies*, edited by Jay Coakley and Eric Dunning, 408–21. London: SAGE.

Walker, Harry. 2013. "State of Play: The Political Ontology of Sport in Amazonian Peru." *American Ethnologist* 40 (2): 382–98.

Walsh, Adrian, and Richard Giulianotti. 2001. "This Sporting Mammon: A Normative Critique of the Commodification of Sport." *Journal of the Philosophy of Sport* 28 (1): 53–77.

Walsh, Adrian, and Richard Giulianotti. 2007. *Ethics, Money and Sport: This Sporting Mammon*. London: Routledge.

Walton, Kendall L. 2006. "On the (So-called) Puzzle of Imaginative Resistance." In *The Architecture of the Imagination*, edited by Shaun Nichols, 137–48. Oxford: Oxford University Press.

White, Bob W. 2008. *Rumba Rules: The Politics of Dance Music in Mobutu's Zaire*. Durham: Duke University Press.

Willemse, Braam. 2010. *Road to Orlando*. Pretoria. FMD. DVD NuMetro.

Williams, Elizabeth. 1988. "Art and Artifact at the Trocadero: *Ars Americana* and the Primitivist Revolution." In *Objects and Others: Essays on Museums and Material Culture*, edited by George W. Stocking, 146–66. Madison: University of Wisconsin Press.

Williams, John, and Stephen Wagg. 1991. *British Football and Social Change: Getting into Europe*. Leicester: Leicester University Press.

Williams, Quentin E., and Christopher Stroud. 2014. "Battling the Race: Stylizing Lan-guage and Coproducing Whiteness and Colouredness in a Freestyle Rap Perfor-mance." *Journal of Linguistic Anthropology* 24 (3): 277–93.

Williams, Raymond. 1977. *Marxism and Literature*. Oxford: Oxford University Press.

Williams, Raymond. 2003. *Television: Technology and Cultural Form*. New York: Routledge.

Wilson, Richard Ashby. 2000. "Reconciliation and Revenge in Post-apartheid South Africa." *Current Anthropology* 41 (1): 75–98.

Wolpe, Harold. 1988. *Race, Class and the Apartheid State*. Trenton: Africa World Press.

Worby, Eric. 2009. "The Play of Race in a Field of Urban Desire: Soccer and Spontaneity in Post-apartheid Johannesburg." *Critique of Anthropology* 29 (105): 105–23.

Worby, Eric, and Shireen Ally. 2013. "The Disappointment of Nostalgia: Conceptualis-ing Cultures of Memory in Contemporary South Africa." *Social Dynamics* 39 (3): 457–80.

Young, Christopher. 2008. "Kantian Kin(a)esthetics: Premises, Problems and Possibil-ities of Hans Ulrich Gumbrecht's *In Praise of Athletic Beauty*." *Sport in History* 28 (1): 5–25.

Young, James E. 1992. "The Counter-monument: Memory against Itself in Germany Today." *Critical Inquiry* 18 (2): 267–96.

Young, Kevin. 1993. "Violence, Risk, and Liability in Male Sports Culture." *Sociology of Sport Journal* 10: 373–96.

INDEX

Note: Page numbers in italics refer to figures.

Printed and bound by CPI Group (UK) Ltd, Croydon, CR0 4YY

09/06/2025

14686133-0001